Singing the Lord's Song
in a Strange Land

RELIGION AND AMERICAN CULTURE

Series Editors
David Edwin Harrell Jr.
Wayne Flynt
Edith L. Blumhofer

Singing the Lord's Song in a Strange Land

Hymnody in the History of North American Protestantism

EDITED BY
Edith L. Blumhofer and Mark A. Noll

THE UNIVERSITY OF ALABAMA PRESS
Tuscaloosa

For Marie Louise van Dyke

Copyright © 2004
The University of Alabama Press
Tuscaloosa, Alabama 35487-0380
Manufactured in the United States of America

Typeface: Galliard

∞

The paper on which this book is printed meets the minimum requirements of
American National Standard for Information Science–Permanence of Paper for
Printed Library Materials, ANSI Z39.48-1984.

Library of Congress Cataloging-in-Publication Data

Singing the Lord's song in a strange land : hymnody in the history of North
American Protestantism / edited by Edith L. Blumhofer and Mark A. Noll.
    p.   cm. — (Religion and American culture)
  Includes bibliographical references and index.
  ISBN 0-8173-1396-6 (cloth : alk. paper)
  1. Hymns—North America—History and criticism. 2. Protestant
churches—North America—History. 3. North America—Church history.
I. Blumhofer, Edith Waldvogel. II. Noll, Mark A., 1946– III. Religion and
American culture (Tuscaloosa, Ala.)
  BV310.S66 2004
  264′.23′0973—dc22

                                                        2004000764

Initial versions of the following essays have appeared in earlier publications:

Darryl G. Hart's essay "In the Shadow of Calvin and Watts: Twentieth-
Century American Presbyterians and Their Hymnals" appeared in Darryl G.
Hart's book *Recovering Mother Kirk*, Baker Academic, Baker Book House
Company, © 2003. Used by permission.

Kay Norton's essay "Reading between the Lines: Slaves, Women, and Native
Americans Reflected in an Important Southern Hymnal of 1810" appeared in
Kay Norton's book *Baptist Offspring, Southern Midwife—Jesse Mercer's Cluster
of Spiritual Songs (1810): A Study in American Hymnody*, Detroit Monographs
in Musicology/Studies in Music, No. 34, Harmonie Park Press, Michigan, ©
2002. Used by permission.

Contents

Introduction

In the fall of 1908, Chicago newspapers advertised a revival with a difference. The brainchild of Amzi Clarence Dixon, a Southern Baptist who braved the ire of his Baptist cohorts by accepting the pastorate of the independent Moody Memorial Church, the Gospel Song Evangelistic Movement seemed novel, even to jaded Chicago reporters. For as long as anyone could recall, evangelists had used music to supplement preaching. Now Dixon proposed a months-long format in which the songs, not speakers, would take center stage. He knew that hymns of all kinds stirred deep chords in Protestant souls. Chicago teemed with immigrants, and for Protestants among them, hymns helped bridge the gap between their old and new lives. Hymns evoked memories, touched emotions, carried theology, elaborated on religious experiences, and effectively popularized Christian faith and patriotic convictions. Dixon's 1908 focus on hymns encouraged public awareness of the power of texts and tunes that derived from many places, but belonged to everyone. It summoned hymns out of the churches and into public space. It concluded on New Year's Eve with the largest hymn festival the city had ever seen. Thousands jammed the city's largest auditorium, the Chicago Stadium, while thousands more huddled in the cold outside. The occasion was a marathon hymn festival that filled the last five hours of 1908 and ushered in the new year.

Dixon acted on a widely shared assumption: hymns played a central—if somewhat hazy—role in Protestant cultural memory as well as in contemporary practice. They offered markers of sorts, evoking moments, people, decisions, and places. The polyglot mix that was Chicago in 1908 was intent on defining itself in space contested among immigrants and Anglos, Protestants and Catholics, abject and rich. This book explores how Protestants among such people used hymns to clarify identity and relate to America and American Christianity. It considers how hymns helped immigrants in different times and parts of the country negotiate a new identity as Americans and contribute as well to the emergence of a richly textured body of American worship resources. How did hymns help immigrants become Americans? Did they nurture ethnic identity? Ease transitions? How did ethnic traditions of religious song mingle, and what results followed? The authors of this collection look at the role of hymns in shaping personal and corporate life and reflect on the value of hymns for studying those spheres. Hymnody forged wider American awareness of the cadence of Christianity elsewhere and enabled Americans to participate in songs of other peoples. But American hymnody also helped transform the religious practices of immigrant groups. It often sprang from sources unfamiliar to recent immigrants, and it sustained religious practices beyond their familiarity. As established and immigrant communities rubbed shoulders, religious music posed problems that often seemed more compelling than its promise. These chapters examine the influence of such new proximities on American religious life. Translations of American and British hymns made their ways around the world. Immigrants brought their hymns to America, providing translations that expanded the corpus of English song. Conditions of life—slavery, death, unionism, temperance—as well as visions for America animated American Christian song.

This book's distinguishing features are (1) the study of hymns in particular denominations and movements with attention to the ability of such hymns to reveal, as they were altered and adapted, shifts in American religious life; (2) considerations of hymns and acculturation in particular religious groups; and (3) a focus on the roles hymns played in changing attitudes about race, class, gender, business, politics, and society.

These chapters are meant to be suggestive rather than comprehensive. The subject of American hymnody is so vast that any pretension to addressing the whole was quickly tempered by a more modest ambition to probe at various points and see what one might learn. The research presented here is part of a three-year project on the history of American hymnody sponsored by the Institute for the Study of American Evangelicals (ISAE) at Wheaton College and funded by the Lilly Endowment.

The ISAE hymnody project involved several years of preparation. The project's planners knew that hymns played a vital role in the history of American evangelicalism, but exploring that role with attention to the larger world of American religious life presented a daunting challenge. How might one construct a coherent project with an attainable, if modest, objective? The goal was simple: to suggest some of the uses to which the study of hymns might be put within the framework of the historiography of American Christianity. Thousands of hymnals and millions of hymns constituted a range of primary sources that demanded organization before historians could undertake an exploration of their potential with reference to the project's specific purpose.

Fortunately, ISAE staff discovered that our interests coincided with those of Wellesley College professor Stephen Marini. His grappling with the methodological question led him to approach the history of evangelical hymnody by asking specific questions about the publication histories of hymns. Although this approach admittedly has its limits, it offered a promising organizational mechanism. Marini created a database into which he entered the first lines of hymns from the indexes of more than 200 evangelical hymnals published in the United States, beginning with John Wesley's 1737 *Collection of Hymns* and concluding with the Assemblies of God's 1969 *Hymns of Glorious Praise*.

In chapter 1, Marini presents his database, gives his rationale, and reflects on the portrait of evangelicalism it discloses. Other authors had access to his database and used it primarily as a way of giving coherence to the project's research. The database is still under construction. It is available in Archives and Special Collections at Wheaton College Library as well as from Professor Marini at Wellesley College.

At the ISAE, we recognize that there are other databases to assist those who want to study American hymnody, and we do not intend to compete with them or to make ambitious claims for the one we opted to use. Each database has its own particular parameters and purpose. Especially noteworthy is the vast database built by the Hymn Society of America and housed at Oberlin College. Under the supervision of Mary Louise van Dyke, this rich resource greatly enhanced our work. However, it is much more ambitious and comprehensive than we needed in order to accomplish our goal. Marini constructed his database to pursue specific historical questions about evangelicalism. Although our larger project was not limited by his work, we chose to allow his findings to suggest boundaries for our inquiries.

A brief description of the way in which this book uses the word *evangelical* may be helpful. Most simply, evangelicals are people who focus on the evangel—the good news, or the gospel. During the Reformation, the word distinguished Protestants from Catholics. German Lutherans were evangelicals; Catholics were not. Since the eighteenth century, the word *evangelical* has come to describe the ethos and essence of large clusters of Protestants whose polity and practice vary dramatically. There are self-styled evangelical movements, denominations, and congregations, but there are also evangelicals and evangelical impulses within contexts not identified as evangelical. British scholar David Bebbington offers useful general categories that underscore evangelicalism's essence. In a groundbreaking study of British evangelicalism (*Evangelicalism in Modern Britain*), Bebbington identifies four features that cross cultural and theological boundaries to unite a diverse constituency: Biblicism, a particular regard for the authority of the Bible; conversionism, the insistence that each individual must come to a life-changing moment of faith; activism, the belief that this saving faith manifests itself in good works; crucicentrism, a focus on the redemptive work of Christ on the cross. Combinations of these emphases have historically animated wide varieties of religious activity, and they have consistently sustained enthusiastic Christian song. The following chapters focus especially on song in different times and places as a revealer of the evangelical ethos.

Marini's opening chapter charts how using hymns to think historically about American evangelicalism clarifies the changing culture of a popular religious movement. The chapters that follow his focus particularly on how time and place affected American religious song. The collection's title, *Singing the Lord's Song in a Strange Land,* is taken from Psalm 137:4, a meditation on the dilemma of faithfulness to God in unfamiliar—even alien—surroundings. For Americans, finding a pitch for the Lord's song in a new environment was more likely a matter of choice than of the duress that prompted the Psalmist's query. Did their new setting require fresh harmonies and revised texts? Could proximity to new neighbors be permitted to alter one's song without diminishing one's heritage? How would old-world identities and quarrels play out in new-world settings? Would ethnic minority status in a new country push people together or simply guarantee space for a stubborn clinging to old differences? Did old music make sense in a new religious environment? How fundamentally was religious identity tied to hymns? What about Christian music in the alien land of modern media? Such questions and many more prompted the following inquiries.

In chapter 2, Kay Norton uses an important southern hymnal, *Mercer's Cluster* (1810), to listen to nonprivileged voices of women, slaves, and Native Americans and to ponder how Jesse Mercer navigated the troubled waters of race, class, and gender in the South in the Early Republic. For Norton's subjects, the "strange land" was one of spiritual freedom and equality complicated by the paradox of second-class worldly status.

Two chapters on Presbyterians follow. Barbara Murison views the question through a Canadian lens. Her principal subjects represent the varied shades of Scottish Presbyterianism transplanted to Canada. In Murison's capable hands, the story of the process of hymnal creation becomes a revealing moment in the larger narrative of Presbyterians removed in space and time from their denomination's origins. Collective memory powerfully influences the hammering out of the compromises that issued in a Canadian Presbyterian hymnal. Darryl G. Hart considers the practice and sources of twentieth-century American Presbyterian song. In the "strange land" of American modernity, Hart proposes that Presbyterian hymnody is most deeply influenced by two stalwarts of long ago—John Calvin and Isaac Watts.

The "strange land" with which Scott Erickson wrestles is America itself. His subjects are Swedish immigrants, especially those who later formed the Evangelical Covenant Church. He traces how changes in Sweden's Lutheran state church impacted the choices of Swedish immigrants, examines the content and place of singing among evangelical Swedish immigrants, and reflects on the impact of American hymn traditions in this immigrant community.

In the nineteenth century, no group of immigrants was more important to the story of American Protestant hymnody than were German settlers—Lutheran, Reformed, Baptist, and Mennonite. David Rempel Smucker offers an insightful look at the German hymn tradition by focusing on one group—Mennonites—and one theme—the transition from German to English. His story is particularly suggestive because each immigrant group at some time faces this challenge and the alteration of identity that it posits. How one community opted to understand its historic musical tradition while adapting to its new surroundings suggests how acculturation proceeds.

John and Charles Wesley loom large in the writing of English hymns and in the practice of singing. In the United States, the Wesleyan holiness movement and the camp-meeting tradition with which it was identified erupted in songs old and new. Devotees of the holiness movement sang lustily the standard Protestant favorites and a myriad of texts that promoted their particular idiom of Christian life. Chris Armstrong uses the lens of hymnody to clarify and explore the emotions and themes that animated the holiness movement.

The rapid growth of Pentecostalism in Latin America generates a growing scholarly corpus. Latin American Pentecostalism has its counterpart in the United States, where it both influences and is influenced by the Latin American surge of charismatic fervor. Daniel Ramírez writes with facility about the hymnody of Latino Pentecostalism—or, more broadly, about popular Protestant musical practice in the American-Mexican borderlands. He explores how Latinos use hymnody to enhance identity and solidarity. His interdisciplinary approach is richly suggestive for several historiographies, especially that of Latino Pentecostalism.

The book concludes with a sustained look at a twentieth-century Protestant phenomenon: the startling popularity of a radio broadcast known as "The Old Fashioned Revival Hour." The authors explore the appeal of Protestant hymnody in the "strange land" of radio. Charles and Grace Fuller, pioneers of evangelical broadcasting, built their program around careful use of particular music. The musical idiom they promoted set the standards for a generation of evangelical endeavors.

The chapters of this book do not pretend to offer a comprehensive account. Each author approaches the task differently and demonstrates possibilities and limitations of certain lines of inquiry. From an exploration into the process of creating a hymnal to inquiries about emotion, empowerment, Americanization, acculturation, and media, these chapters suggest how hymn texts and the hymnals that collect those texts can be used to deepen and finesse historians' generalizations about American religion. Because evangelicalism is a movement that crosses denominations and molds countless voluntary associations and agencies, scholars wrestle with problems of definition. This book proposes that hymn texts and hymnals are essential to the definition of evangelicalism. In a very real sense—as historian Mark Noll has noted—evangelicalism is at its best when seen through its hymns.

Several people and agencies especially facilitated the preparation of these chapters. The Lilly Endowment funded research. ISAE research assistants Blake Killingsworth and Jeremy Cunningham provided invaluable assistance in tracking down details. Monica Sawyer prepared the indexes. ISAE Resources and Research Assistant Katri Delac devoted her technical expertise to the project. Without her capable efforts, there would be no book. Mary Louise van Dyke graciously offered the resources of the Hymn Society of America's hymns database. We are grateful to all the above.

The ISAE dedicates this book to Mary Louise who has been for us and for all who study hymns a "one-woman army" at Oberlin College. Her enthusiasm for hymns has no rival, and her passion for making hymns accessible bodes well for the current interest among historians of American religion for understanding the role of hymnody in the shaping of American Christianity.

Singing the Lord's Song
in a Strange Land

I

From Classical to Modern

Hymnody and the Development of American Evangelicalism, 1737–1970

Stephen Marini

From its origin in the Great Awakening to its most recent efflorescence in the late twentieth century, American Evangelicalism has been a popular religious movement.[1] Interdenominational from the outset, the evangelical movement has persistently challenged the Reformation traditions from which it emerged. In America, evangelicalism has been especially polyvalent. It has supported both Calvinist and Arminian doctrinal systems, thrived in episcopal polities as well as congregational and presbyterial church institutions, and supported both conservative and liberal political causes and cultural styles. At its sectarian margin, American Evangelicalism has spawned new religious communities with radical forms of institutional organization, belief, ritual, and spirituality. Driven by frequent mass revivals, the popular energy of the movement has consistently outstripped the capacity of received ecclesial traditions to contain it.

What has held together this protean and enduring religious movement? What are its distinguishing marks as a religious culture? How has American Evangelicalism changed over time? These questions have challenged interpreters since the Great Awakening and continue to spark spirited debate today. Hymnody offers a unique body of evidence through which to consider these fundamental historical inquiries.

Since the mid-eighteenth century evangelicals have published an enormous outpouring of hymns and hymnals. Every aspect of evangelical culture, from worship, preaching, and revivals to Christian education and mission, has been saturated by the presence of hymns sung, recited, and prayed.

This ubiquitous medium of religious expression has attracted a distinguished legacy of scholarship, and the field of hymn studies is enjoying a renaissance at the turn of the twenty-first century. This chapter suggests the extraordinary promise of hymns as a resource for understanding the evangelical movement in America, but hymn studies have been deeply constrained by the absence of any reliable empirical account of the historical publication and availability of hymns upon which to base judgments about their religious significance. This chapter reports one effort to supply such evidence and makes a preliminary assessment of what it suggests about the historical development of American Evangelicalism.

Studying Hymns

Nineteenth-century British hymnologists began the critical study of Christian hymn texts, producing a vast literature on authorship, publication, and textual variation that John Julian summarized in his massive 1892 *Dictionary of Hymnology.* Succeeding generations contributed critical historical and theological studies of English language hymns, of which Louis F. Benson's *The English Hymn: Its Use and Development,* Horton Davies's *Worship and Theology in England,* and Erik Routley's studies of both texts and tunes have proved the most important.[2] Since the 1970s English language hymn texts in their British context have received a broad range of cultural interpretation including the literary criticism of Donald Davie and J. R. Watson, the social analyses of Susan Tamke and Ian Bradley, the denominational inquiries of Madeleine Forell Marshall and Janet Todd, and the genre studies of Richard Arnold.[3]

Major works devoted specifically to American Evangelical hymnody have been rarer. Over sixty years after publication, Henry Wilder Foote's *Three Centuries of American Hymnody* remains the preeminent study in the field. Since the rise of postmodernism in the 1970s, however, hymnody has attracted attention from scholars exploring the importance of popular American religious culture. Landmarks of this growing interest include Dickson Bruce's anthropological study of the antebellum camp meeting, Sandra Sizer's rhetorical analysis of postbellum gospel hymns, the reconstruction of African American sacred song by Albert Raboteau and Jon Michael Spencer, Nathan Hatch's identification of hymnody as a central element in "the democratization of American Christianity," and Jane Hadden Hobbs's interpretation of "the feminization of American hymnody" between 1870 and 1920.[4]

Despite the strength of this textual scholarship, however, music historians have done the most to secure a place for hymnody in the American cultural canon.

George Pullen Jackson pioneered the study of early American hymn tunes during the 1930s and 1940s. It was the publication of Irving Lowens's *Music and Musicians in Early America,* in 1964, however, that has inspired the two most recent generations of music historians to edit, document, and interpret the sacred music of American singing schools in the revolutionary and early national periods. In 1972 H. Wiley Hitchcock began producing facsimile editions of historic tune books in the *Earlier American Music* series. Seven years later Nicholas Temperley published *The Music of the English Parish Church,* the definitive study of the musical tradition upon which early American singing school compositions were modeled. Richard Crawford made a crucial contribution with the 1984 publication of *The Core Repertory of Early American Psalmody,* a compilation and critical edition of the 101 most frequently published hymn settings between 1698 and 1810, along with the hymn texts most often associated with them, and over the past two decades complete critical editions have appeared of the music of Williams Billings, Daniel Read, Stephen Jenks, and Timothy Swan, four of the greatest New England singing school masters.[5]

The recovery of American singing school music is a scholarly achievement of first importance, and one of its most significant aspects has been the extraordinary level of documentation that it has provided for the circulation of hymn texts and musical settings in early America. In 1990 Crawford completed the work of Lowens and Allen Britton in *American Sacred Music Imprints, 1698–1810,* an exhaustive census and bibliography of 545 works. Karl Kroeger's 1994 *American Fuging-Tunes, 1770–1820* identified the hymn texts originally published with 1,298 musical settings containing "fugues," a repeated refrain with serial, imitative entrances for each choral part that was the most characteristic feature of the singing school style.[6] In 1998 Temperley, assisted by Charles Manns and Joseph Herl, achieved a quantum leap beyond these already impressive compilations with the publication of *The Hymn Tune Index,* a massive four-volume study that reports every tune setting of every English language hymn published between 1535 and 1820. The *Hymn Tune Index* identifies nearly fifteen thousand hymn tunes by name, key, time signature, and musical first line or "incipit," each presented with a complete listing of its publications including the first line of hymn text. Fully cross-indexed, the *Hymn Tune Index* represents the state of the art for recovering the structure of hymn text use by composers.[7]

Through these critical editions, compilations, indexes, and a growing body of interpretive literature, the musical dimension of hymnody has become a staple element in the cultural interpretation of colonial and early America. Similar studies of postbellum and twentieth-century American hymn tunes have not yet appeared, but the musicological study of American hymnody has established a decisive lead over textual scholarship. That advantage exists in large measure because there are no comparable studies of hymn text publication in America to match those of hymn tunes. Music historians have measured the universe of Americans hymn tune publication within which individual works and composers can be interpreted. Textual scholars, by contrast, continue to work without knowing the basic dimensions of American hymn text publication and therefore lack basic data for assessing their historical availability, popularity, and religious significance. An approach to hymn texts based in the history of the book, an important new interdisciplinary field of research, offers the best remedy.[8]

The Formation of an American Evangelical Hymn Canon

The earliest praise books used by evangelicals in colonial America were Psalters, translations of the biblical Book of Psalms prepared by Anglican, Congregational, and Presbyterian authorities for uniform worship in their churches.[9] During the Great Awakening, hymn collections by English evangelical poets became popular. Most of these were also collections of uniform authorship, most notably Isaac Watts's *Hymns and Spiritual Songs* (1707) and *The Psalms of David Imitated* (1719). Early New England singing school books, beginning with William Billings's *New England Psalm Singer* (1770), also relied very heavily on Watts's hymns and metrical psalms.

The Methodists were the first to diversify evangelical hymnody across theological and denominational lines. John Wesley's first hymnal, *A Collection of Psalms and Hymns,* originally published in 1737 in Charleston, South Carolina, contained seventy hymns, twenty-five of them by Watts and thirty-three by members of Wesley's family, along with a dozen of his own translations and paraphrases. George White-field's *Hymns for Social Worship,* a larger collection published in London in 1753 and reprinted at Newburyport, Massachusetts, in 1767, followed a similarly eclectic strategy.[10]

English Evangelical Calvinists published mixed hymn collections of Congregationalist, Baptist, Methodist, and Moravian texts beginning in the 1750s, culminating in Baptist John Rippon's massive 588-hymn collection *A Selection of Hymns from the Best Authors, intended to be an Appendix to Dr. Watts's Psalms and Hymns* (1787).[11] In America, by contrast, Watts reigned supreme among New England Calvinists until after 1800, whereas the Methodists, after they organized an autonomous American church in 1784, rejected the principle of hymnodic diversity and used *The Methodist Pocket Hymn-Book* (1790, 1802) edited by Francis Asbury and William McKendree.[12]

A decisive change in this American hymnodic insularity took place during the early nineteenth century, driven by the extraordinary energy of the Second Great Awakening (1798–1844). Nathan Hatch has provided the most important recent study of the Second Great Awakening in his 1989 book *The Democratization of American Christianity,* an interpretation that points directly to hymns and hymnals as important vehicles of religious change. Hatch argues that the Second Great Awakening's popular religious movements reversed the pattern of religious and cultural authority entrenched in the colonial Episcopal, Congregational, and Presbyterian churches. A crucial element in that reversal was a leveling strategy of sectarian writing and publication that appealed directly to personal judgment and attacked all forms of received religious authority. The result was a categorical rejection of clerical and institutional influence and the creation of "the sovereign audience" as the arbiters and creators of their own religious culture.[13]

Hatch assigned a principal role in this democratization process to hymnal and tune book compiling and publishing. Like Wesley and Whitefield before them, many founders of the new American Evangelical sects, including Elias Smith, Alexander Campbell, Lorenzo Dow, and Joshua Hines, edited hymn collections designed for "the sovereign audience" of actual and potential converts. The new sects, however, were not often blessed with great hymnists and their hymnal editors routinely supplemented in-house hymns with those by Watts, Wesley, and their eighteenth-century English evangelical successors. Editors of the new sectarian hymnals therefore published many of the same hymns despite competing with one another for the ear of "the sovereign audience," and their colleagues in the older evangelical communions soon joined them in constructing a broadly shared hymn corpus. Baptist hymnals such as *The Psalmist* (1843) included numerous lyrics by Methodists, Moravians, and Anglican Evangelicals, whereas *A Collection of Hymns for the Use of the Methodist Episcopal Church* (1820, 1832) featured many texts by Evangelical Calvinists such as Watts, Doddridge, Steele, Stennett, and Kelly.[14]

Hatch's interpretation of these hymn collections emphasized texts that voiced the "democratizing" anticlerical sentiments and sectarian identities of the new religious movements. He did not, however, address the crucial role played by the rest of this hymn corpus. In the relentless give-and-take of sectarian competition and laicization, a deep structure of American Evangelical consensus on belief and practice gradually emerged through the continuous republication and performance of shared hymn texts. This developing core of shared hymn texts was perhaps the quintessential product of the democratization of American Christianity. The "sovereign audience" of American Evangelicalism found its collective voice not through any single leader, but through the hymns it sang day and night, in season and out, everywhere and always.

The process of hymn canon formation continued after 1860. The gospel hymn, introduced in the revivals of Dwight L. Moody and Ira D. Sankey during the 1870s and 1880s, exposed American Evangelical audiences to the English Victorian lyrics of Charlotte Elliott and Henry F. Lyte and made the blind Methodist poet Fanny J. Crosby America's most popular hymn writer of the postbellum period. In addition, advances in printing technology made it possible to produce hymn tune scores with complete text underlay, as opposed to the old singing school tune books, which could supply only a single verse or two under the music. With new gospel hymns, improved technology, and mass marketing techniques, hymnal publishing became big business, dominated by denominational publishing houses and independent companies such as Biglow and Main and Hope Publishing Company. Their products were specifically targeted to niche markets and were edited increasingly by committee rather than by individuals. These changes in hymnal production rationalized the postbellum hymn market and in the process expanded the evangelical hymn canon to include the new gospel hymns as well as the enduring favorites of the First and Second Great Awakenings.

To a significant degree, American Evangelicalism created itself through this democratically constructed canon of hymn texts. To recover that hymn canon is therefore to gain a new understanding of what "democratized American Christianity" has meant to its followers. It is possible to gain a surprisingly precise description of American Evangelicalism's popular beliefs, practices, and piety through the hymns that it held most in common. Recall John Wesley's definition of the hymnal as "a complete body of practical and experimental divinity."[15] In that phrase is embedded hymnody's greatest potential for reconstructing the religious life of the people. American Evangelical hymnal editors have followed that admonition with singular fidelity. Their hymnals are comprehensive statements of Evangelical beliefs, rituals, institutions, and spirituality. No other single source provides this kind of information. Hymns also have the advantage of being relatively fixed texts whose circulation can be tracked by publication records. Editorial bias and denominational interest inevitably distort somewhat the picture of popular evangelicalism that emerges from its hymn collections, but the most widely published, interdenominationally popular hymns provide unexcelled textual access to the living religious beliefs and practices of American Evangelical Protestants.[16]

The American Protestant Hymns Database

The American Protestant Hymns Database has been compiled to assist this hymnodic reconstruction of popular religion in America, especially popular evangelicalism. The database is comprised of three interactive databanks. The first contains individual records for each hymn published in 211 historic American hymnals, songsters, tune books, and gospel hymn collections, of which 200 are Evangelical texts beginning with John Wesley's 1737 *Collection of Psalms and Hymns* and extending to the Assembly of God's 1969 *Hymns of Glorious Praise*. More than 100,000 hymn texts in Databank I are identified by first line, hymnal, and page/hymn number and will eventually include data fields for primary and secondary subject, author, date, and original source bibliographic information. The second databank is devoted to bibliographic records for each hymnal, tune book, songster, and gospel hymn collection in the database. The individual hymn records in Databank I are cross-referenced to the bibliographic record of their sources in Databank II. A third databank is envisioned that will contain records for each tune printed with the database hymn texts and will be similarly cross-referenced to the Databank II bibliographic records.

The database has been designed to reflect the historical development of American Protestantism in general and American Evangelicalism in particular. Statistical surveys, church records, and hymnological scholarship have been used to identify the most significant hymn collections. I began with hymnals officially published or authorized by forty major evangelical denominations or interdenominational organizations from 1737 through 1970. Some of these communities published many hymnals, others few. In some denominations a burst of hymn publishing was followed by decades of hymnodic neglect, whereas other communions produced a slow but steady stream of hymn collections. Despite such variations, this group of authorized hymnals creates a reliable base line for a representative sample of American Protestant hymnody.

To this group of denominational collections I have added a substantial number of privately published hymnals and musical collections. In many evangelical denominational families before 1845, notably Congregationalists, Baptists, and Disciples, widely used hymnals were published privately by well-known denominational leaders rather than by ecclesiastical publishing houses. At the opposite end of the publishing spectrum, singing schools and camp meetings spawned popular nondenominational evangelical tune books and songsters such as William Walker's *Southern Harmony* and Leonard Myers's *Zion's Songster*. After 1900, Pentecostals and Fundamentalists promoted a nondenominational gospel hymn collection, and the inclusion of this collection is a major innovative feature of the database. By overlaying authorized denominational hymnals with a representative selection of such privately published and nondenominational hymn collections, I have sought to provide a reliable index to historic evangelical hymn availability and use.

Table 1.1
The American Protestant Hymns Database: Evangelical Hymnals by
Denominational Family, N = 200

Name	Number of Books
Baptist	48
Baptist to 1844	17
Northern Baptist/American Baptist	8
Southern Baptist	9
Freewill Baptist	6
Primitive Baptist	4
Seventh Day Baptist	1
Regular Baptist	1
Six-Principle Baptist	1
American Baptist Association	1
National Baptist Convention	2
Methodist	43
Methodist to 1843	11
Northern Methodist	7
Southern Methodist	6
Free Methodist	1
Methodist Protestant	2
Wesleyan Methodist	3
African Methodist	5
African Methodist Zion	1
Christian Methodist	1
United Brethren	4
United Evangelical Brethren	1
Moravian	1
Reformed/Restorationist	41
Congregational	12
Disciples/Churches of Christ	16
Presbyterian to 1837	6
New School Presbyterian	4
Old School Presbyterian	1
Cumberland Presbyterian	1

Continued on the next page

Table 1.1
Continued

Name	Number of Books
Holiness/Pentecostal/Fundamentalist	28
Seventh Day Adventist	1
Christian/Missionary Alliance	2
Advent Christian	1
Holiness	2
Nazarene	6
Church of Christ Holiness	1
Assemblies of God	4
Foursquare Gospel	3
Church of God Cleveland	2
Church of God of Prophecy	1
Pentecostal	6
Tune Books/Songsters/Gospel Hymns	40
Tune Books	10
Gospel Hymns	19
Songsters	6
Youth	5

Hymns of Classical Evangelicalism

A study of theological content and literary form is the best approach to understanding the transformation of American Evangelical hymnody and through it the changing nature of the movement itself. A major problem with such an approach is the extraordinary density of hymn texts. Though they were often originally published with titles and scripture mottos, it is difficult to reduce the subject of such texts to a single category. After 1800, however, hymnal editors performed precisely that reduction by grouping hymns under theological categories listed in the table of contents; after 1840 they supplied even more specific subject indexes. Using categorical labels to characterize complex hymn texts, then, is a time-honored if necessarily cursory method of shorthand interpretation, and I have employed it here.

For this study the two hundred evangelical books in the American

Table 1.2
Classical Evangelical Hymnody: Most Printed American Evangelical
Hymns, 1737–1860, N = 86

Rank	First Line	Printings/Overall Rank/ Author/Subject
1	Jesus my all to heaven is gone	58/15/Cennick/Witness
2	Come thou fount of every blessing	57/7/Robinson/Sanctification
3	Come we that love the Lord	55/3/Watts/Praise
4	Am I a soldier of the cross	51/6/Watts/Perseverance
	Blow ye the trumpet blow	51/18/Wesley/Praise
	How firm a foundation	51/4/ "K"Rippon/Scripture
	When I can read my title clear	51/14/Watts/Perseverance
5	On Jordan's stormy banks	46/9/S.Stennett/Heaven
6	All hail the power	45/1/Peronnet/Praise
	Children of the heavenly king	45/21/Cennick/Praise
	He dies the friend of sinners	45/27/Watts/Atonement
7	Jerusalem my happy home	44/18/Anon/Heaven
8	There is a land of pure delight	42/18/Watts/Heaven
9	Alas and did my savior bleed	41/5/Watts/Atonement
10	Hark from the tombs	39/49/Watts/Death
	O for a closer walk with God	39/19/Cowper/Sanctification
11	Jesus lover of my soul	38/2/Wesley/Faith
	Salvation o the joyful sound	38/27/Watts/Salvation
12	Come humble sinners	37/37/E.Jones/Invitation
	God moves in a mysterious way	37/24/Cowper/Providence
	Jesus and shall it ever be	37/21/J.Grigg/Witness

Protestant Hymns Database were analyzed to create short lists of the
most published hymns for 1737–1860 and 1861–1970. The 1737–1860 list
was compiled from eighty-six books and more than 32,000 hymns;
the 1861–1970 list used 114 books and more than 70,000 hymns. The
difference in size between the samples reflects the increasing pace of
hymnal publication after 1860 as well as the growing denominational
diversity of the evangelical movement during the last century.

The most published classical evangelical hymns focused on the
economy of grace, the morphology of conversion, and the saint's life.
These foci reflect the early movement's preoccupation with systematic
approaches to belief and practice. Classical evangelicals joined together
two traditional Protestant Christian doctrinal schemas, the economy

of grace, which provided a macroscopic, cosmological explanation of how God saved fallen humanity from eternal death through the sacrifice of Jesus Christ, and the morphology of conversion, which gave a microscopic, psychological account of the stages through which individuals experience saving grace and spiritual purification. From these cosmological and psychological schemes, woven together around the leading themes of Christ's atonement and the Christian's sanctifying transformation, evangelicals derived a compelling moral theology for the Christian life grounded in prayer, praise, devotion, witness, perseverance, and providence.

The classical hymns reflect these features of early evangelical belief and practice. Nine of the twenty-one most published hymns between 1737 and 1860 address themes from the economy of grace, beginning with "How Firm a Foundation," the anonymous meditation on the word of God and summary of the gospel from John Rippon's 1787 *Selection of Hymns*. Classical evangelical hymnody placed special emphasis, however, on two crucial elements in the economy of grace: the atoning sacrifice of Christ on the cross whereby salvation comes and the vision of heaven in which that salvation is finally confirmed and eternally celebrated by the saints. Two of Isaac Watts's greatest and most popular poems, "He Dies, The Friend of Sinners Dies" and "Alas! And Did My Savior Bleed?" present emotionally heightened depictions of the atonement from different narrative perspectives, the former as a poetic depiction of scriptural fact and the latter as the saint's grieved and amazed reflection on Christ's sacrifice. "Alas! And Did My Savior Bleed?" the poet asks,

> And did my sovereign die?
> Did he devote his sacred head
> For such a worm as I?
>
> 2
> Was it for crimes that I have done
> He groaned upon the tree?
> Amazing pity, grace unknown,
> And love beyond degree!

Three of the most published hymns of the classical period express the evangelical vision of heaven, whereas another treats the allied theme of death. Watts's "Hark, From the Tombs a Doleful Sound" delivers a stark confrontation with the inevitability of death:

Hark! from the tombs a doleful sound!
Mine ears attend the cry,
"Ye living men, come view the ground
Where you must shortly lie.

2
"Princes, this clay must be your bed
In spite of all your tow'rs;
The tall, the wise, the reverend head
Must lie as low as ours."

Of the heaven hymns, Watts's "There Is a Land of Pure Delight" and Samuel Stennett's "On Jordan's Stormy Banks I Stand" share a pastoral symbology of heaven and an insistence that those Arcadian realms stand far off "over Jordan" and cannot be entered here on earth.[17]

The morphology of conversion also receives considerable attention among the most published classical hymns. Evangelicals generally followed the English Puritan formulation of this series of inward transformations from repentance and invitation to regeneration and sanctification. Four morphological hymns appear on the early list. The first in theological order is Edward Jones's invitation hymn "Come, Humble Sinner in Whose Breast," which depicts humiliation before a just God as a necessary preparatory stage to receiving the divine invitation to saving grace. Isaac Watts's celebration of regeneration "Salvation, O the Joyful Sound" is followed by two sanctification hymns, Robert Robinson's "Come Thou Fount of Every Blessing" and William Cowper's "O for a Closer Walk with God." Cowper's eloquent lyric follows a characteristic sensibility in classical evangelical hymnody by pleading for sanctifying grace rather than celebrating it:

O for a closer walk with God!
A calm and heavenly frame!
A light to shine upon the road
That leads me to the Lamb!

3
The dearest idol I have known,
Whate'er that idol be,
Help me to tear it from thy throne,
And worship only thee.

Based on this admittedly small sample of the most published hymns, salvation and sanctification seem to have been the primary morphological concerns of classical evangelicalism. Such an interpretation gains credibility when combined with the emphasis on atonement and heaven in early lyrics about the economy of grace.

The final group of hymns on the short list addresses the Christian life, cast in narrative form as a Bunyanesque pilgrimage from prayer, praise, and faith to witness, perseverance, and providence. To these moral obligations evangelicals added the duties of worship and praise. Classical Evangelical hymnody is suffused with themes from this understanding of the Christian life. Although prayer is surprisingly absent from the short list and faith is represented by just one hymn, Charles Wesley's "Jesus, Lover of My Soul," the moral imperatives of witness and perseverance riveted the classical evangelical poetic imagination. Two hymns of witness bracket the short list, John Cennick's "Jesus, My All, To Heaven Is Gone," the most published hymn of the classical period, and Joseph Grigg's "Jesus, And Shall It Ever Be." Cennick's lyric gives straightforward voice to the imperative of witness to "see" and "follow" the costly "narrow way" until joining Jesus in heaven:

Jesus, my all, to heaven is gone;
He, whom I fix my hopes upon!
His track I see, and I'll pursue
The narrow way till him I view.

2
The way the holy prophets went,
The road that leads to banishment;
The King's highway of holiness,
I'll go; for all his paths are peace.

Grigg's poem, on the other hand, offers repeated challenges to the believer to accept the duty of witness and never be "ashamed of Jesus."

The theological consequence of witness was perseverance, the belief that grievous trials necessarily accompany a life of Christian witness but that God's grace will enable the saint to face and finally overcome them. Isaac Watts wrote the two most popular classical perseverance hymns, "Am I a Soldier of the Cross?" and "When I Can Read My Title Clear." Both of these lyrics begin with a characteristic note of doubt, a questioning and provisional attitude toward the saint's own salvation. In both poems Watts asks first whether the believer is in fact willing to pay the price of Christian life before moving on to militant proclamations of perseverant triumph. "Sure I Must Fight If I Would Reign," Watts announces in "Am I a Soldier":

Increase my courage, Lord;
I'll bear the toil, endure the pain,
Supported by thy word.

A similar confidence infuses the climax of "When I Can Read":

Should earth against my soul engage,
And hellish darts be hurl'd,
Then I can smile at Satan's rage,
And face a frowning world.

Finally, classical evangelical hymns place great stress on praise as both a private exercise of faith and a public duty of the regenerate community. Four hymns on the short list articulate this theme, all of them extremely popular during the early period: Watts's "Come We That Love the Lord," Wesley's "Blow Ye the Trumpet Blow," Edward Peronnet's "All Hail the Power of Jesus's Name," and John Cennick's "Children of the Heavenly King." Peronnet's brilliant hymn of cosmic praise to Christ the king, the most published sacred lyric in American history, and Wesley's hymn for New Year's Day link the duty of praise to the apocalyptic imagery of the Last Judgment. The other two hymns, however, associate praise with the moral imperatives of witness and perseverance. Watts's "Come We That Love the Lord"

begins on a millennial note but moves quickly to interpose the saint's
pilgrimage up "the hill of Zion" and "through Emmanuel's ground":

9
The hill of Zion yields
A thousand sacred sweets,
Before we reach the heavenly fields,
Or walk the golden streets.

10
Then let our songs abound,
And every tear be dry;
We're marching through Immanuel's ground
To fairer worlds on high.

This theme of pilgrim praise is most pronounced in Moravian John
Cennick's "Children of the Heavenly King," in which the saint's persevering journey through the world is defined by the act of praise:

1
Children of the heavenly king,
As ye journey, sweetly sing;
Sing your savior's worthy praise,
Glorious in his works and ways.

2
Ye are trav'ling home to God,
In the way the fathers trod;
They are happy now, and ye
Soon their happiness shall see.

Classical evangelical hymns articulate these themes of atonement,
sanctification, witness, perseverance, and heaven through what might
be a literary hermeneutic of popular religion comprised of three principal elements: an apostolic narrative, an objectified spirituality, and a
distanced subjectivity. The first of these elements refers to the lyrical
voice's location inside the New Testament narrative, an imagined position of participation in the history and experience of the archetypal

Christian community. The second characteristic of the early hymns is their extraordinarily concrete metaphors of spiritual experience drawn from the traditional diurnal culture of Anglo-American rural society. The last aspect is a subjective attitude that acknowledges and expresses an ontological distance between the human and the divine, even in the regenerate experience of the believer. If such a complex set of forms, metaphors, and voices can be reduced to a single quality, it would be the otherness of the sacred.[18]

Such a literary hermeneutic of divine transcendence seems at first to be incongruent with a religious movement whose distinguishing tenet was the direct experience of the sacred through spiritual rebirth and sanctification. But the hymns emphasize the persistence of human finitude despite the presence of divine grace and observe an imperative to measure the experiential and metaphysical distance between the sacred and the profane. Classical evangelical hymns reach across time and space to participate in the sacred narrative that alone can interpret their religious reality as recipients of Christ's atoning grace and pilgrims persevering through a fallen world on their way to heaven. They use homely metaphors and vividly depictive language to articulate an ineffable spirituality that finally lies beyond the capacity of words to express. Their very lyrical voice registers amazement at the sanctification wrought by God in the believer, never losing the note of profound humility that only the redeemed can genuinely apprehend. In combining the theological themes of sacrifice, transformation, and hope with the literary hermeneutic of apostolic narrative, objective spirituality, and distanced subjectivity, the most widely circulated classical evangelical hymns provided a potent and pointed articulation of popular evangelicalism during its first century.

Hymns of Modern Evangelicalism

Evangelical hymns of the modern period have a quite different doctrinal and literary character. The aggregate short list of them seems to be an eclectic and rather inchoate combination of classical and Victorian lyrics. It comes as something of a shock, for example, to learn that no less than fourteen of the twenty most published hymns of the postbellum era are classical lyrics from the eighteenth century. A number of reasons might be cited for this surprising pattern, but the most

Table 1.3
Modern Evangelical Hymnody I: Most Frequently Published
Evangelical Hymns, 1861–1970, N = 114

Rank	Title	Printings	Overall Rank
1	Jesus lover of my soul	102	2
2	Just as I am without one plea	89	11
3	Alas and did my savior bleed	88	5
	Nearer my God to thee	88	17
4	All hail the power	86	1
5	Rock of ages	85	8
6	My faith looks up to thee	79	18
	There is a fountain	79	8
7	How firm a foundation	76	4
8	Come we that love the lord	75	3
9	Guide me o thou great Jehovah	71	12
	O happy day	71	20
10	Abide with me	70	26
	Am I a soldier of the cross	70	6
	Blest be the tie	70	11
11	O for a thousand tongues	67	14
	Stand up stand up for Jesus	67	31
	When I survey	67	11
12	Must Jesus bear the cross	66	37
	Sweet hour of prayer	66	38

important influence seems to be the continuing force of tradition. American Evangelicals have proven to be quite conservative about their hymn texts, retaining much of the classical canon through the late nineteenth and into the twentieth centuries. Perennial favorites such as Watts's "Alas! And Did My Savior Bleed?" and Charles Wesley's "Jesus, Lover of My Soul" in fact were even more popular after 1860 than before.

But American Evangelicalism is a restless movement, no less in hymnody than in its better-known theological and political proclivities. It is not surprising, therefore, that the list of most printed hymns from 1861 to 1970 also differs decisively from its predecessor. Some huge favorites of the antebellum period virtually dropped out of sight after 1860, including three of the top five hymns from the earlier era,

Watts's "Jesus My All to Heaven Is Gone," Wesley's "Blow Ye the Trumpet, Blow," and Watts's "When I Can Read My Title Clear." Conversely, some relatively neglected eighteenth-century hymns enjoyed sharply increased popularity in postbellum and twentieth-century decades, including Augustus Toplady's "Rock of Ages, Cleft for Me," Doddridge's "O Happy Day That Fixed My Choice," and Thomas Shepherd's "Must Jesus Bear the Cross Alone."

The most important change in modern evangelical hymnody, however, was the addition of Victorian hymns from England and new American gospel hymns, especially those of women hymnists such as Fanny J. Crosby, Katherine Hankey, and Annie S. Hawks. These hymns are suffused with different theological and literary qualities, but the continuing popularity of the classical canon after 1860 tends to obscure their impact in any aggregate listing. The American Protestant Hymns Database, however, permits further refinement in order to sharpen the contrast between the two periods. By removing the eighteenth-century poems it is possible to isolate the most popular newer hymns and through them to identify the most distinctive themes of modern evangelicalism.

These texts are the subject of two important recent studies of postbellum American hymnody. In her pioneering 1978 book *Gospel Hymns and Social Religion,* Sandra Sizer argued that the rhetoric of gospel hymns reflected a shift in evangelical sensibility from individual salvation and public witness to "social religion," a passive, vulnerable realm of "ordered passion" and communal religiousness embodied in the revival meeting, the congregation, and above all in the female domestic circle. Nearly twenty years later Jane Hadden Hobbs extended Sizer's argument into a fully delineated postmodern feminist interpretation of postbellum hymnody. In her 1997 book *"I Sing for I Cannot Be Silent": The Feminization of American Hymnody, 1870–1920,* Hobbs read hymn texts written by American women through a hermeneutic of gendered power and religious authority, arguing that hymn writing gave women power over language denied them by patriarchal evangelical culture and that hymns written by women expressed a female spirituality grounded in charismatic inspiration and the erotic experience of the divine.

Both of these views have undeniable merit. Taken as a whole, the most popular modern hymns of the Christian life certainly convey a

Table 1.4

Modern Evangelical Hymnody II: Most Printed Victorian and Gospel Hymns in America, 1861-1970, N = 114

Rank	First Line	Printings/Overall Rank/ Author/Subject
2	Just as I am	89/11/Elliott/Invitation
3	Nearer my God to thee	88/17/Adams/Devotion
6	My faith looks up to thee	79/18/Palmer/Devotion
10	Abide with me	70/26/Lyte/Providence
11	Stand up stand up for Jesus	67/31/Duffield/Mission
12	Sweet hour of prayer	66/38/Walford/Prayer
16	Onward Christian soldiers	60/37/Baring-Gould/Mission
19	What a friend we have in Jesus	57/45/Scriven/Prayer
20	I love to tell the story	56/46/Hankey/Witness
	My hope is built on nothing less	56/48/Mote/Providence
	Work for the night is coming	56/49/Coghill/Mission
21	We praise thee O God for the son	55/42/MacKay/Revival
	Pass me not O gentle savior	55/54/Crosby/Repentance
	I can hear my savior calling	55/55/Blandy/Witness
22	My Jesus I love thee	54/50/Featherston/Devotion
23	Jesus savior pilot me	53/48/Hopper/Providence
24	Blessed assurance Jesus is mine	52/57/Crosby/Salvation
	Where he leads me I will follow	52/54/Blandy/Providence
25	He leadeth me O blessed thought	51/46/Gilmore/Providence
	I need thee every hour	51/45/Hawks/Devotion
	Jesus keep me near the cross	51/54/Crosby/Devotion

new sense of vulnerability and domestic reference. Likewise there is no doubting the salience of women's poems in evangelical hymnody since the Civil War. Women wrote seven of the twenty most printed hymns of the postbellum century, including the two most popular, "Just As I Am" by Charlotte Elliott and "Nearer, My God, to Thee" by Sarah Flower Adams. Whether or not the full range of Sizer's rhetorical analysis or Hobbs's feminist interpretation can be sustained, however, neither of them supplies a sufficient perspective for understanding the changing character of evangelical hymnody as a whole. A fuller picture of postbellum hymnody and its implications for understanding the development of the evangelical movement can be gained by examining both doctrinal content and literary strategy, then comparing them with those of the classical period.

Modern evangelical hymns place special emphasis on the preliminary stages of the morphology of conversion. Fanny J. Crosby's "Pass Me Not, O Gentle Savior" is a powerful hymn of humiliation and repentance that reaches out to Christ for grace and salvation:

> Pass me not, O gentle savior,
> Hear my humble cry;
> While on others Thou art calling,
> Do not pass me by.
>
> 2
> Let me at thy throne of mercy
> Find a sweet relief;
> Kneeling there in deep contrition,
> Help my unbelief.

Closely related in tone is Charlotte Elliott's "Just As I Am," the most frequently published hymn of the modern period, which depicts the moment when the repentant soul responds to Christ's offer of salvation "without one plea." Often used as an invitation hymn, "Just As I Am" is liturgically and thematically related to revivalism, evangelicalism's distinctive ritual practice that is explicitly addressed in the modern period by William P. Mackay's "We Praise Thee, O God," better known as "Revive Us Again." Mackay begins with three verses of Trinitarian praise to Christ's atonement and the Spirit's indwelling, then concludes with an exhortation to spiritual revival:

> Revive us again;
> Fill each heart with thy love;
> May each soul be rekindled
> With fire from above.
> Hallelujah! Thine the glory.
> Hallelujah! Amen.
> Hallelujah! Thine the glory.
> Revive us again.

Hymns of the Christian life, however, thoroughly dominate the short list of twenty modern hymns, including two on mission, two on prayer, five on devotion, and five on providence. The first two, George Duffield's "Stand Up, Stand Up for Jesus" and Sabine Baring-Gould's "Onward, Christian Soldiers," offer an aggressive array of images from the *milites Christianum* tradition to produce a millennial vision of the missionary enterprise at the zenith of its influence in the evangelical movement. These lyrical exhortations urging the "soldiers of the cross . . . from victory unto victory," as Duffield put it, lie quite outside the dominant theological, moral, and rhetorical vocabularies of the modern hymns as a whole. Even the period's leading witness hymn, Katherine Hankey's "I Love to Tell the Story," which might be expected to mirror some of this missionary militancy, does not do so. Hankey's idea of witness is not the John Cennick's "narrow way" of obedience but the verbal practice of sharing "the old, old story of Jesus and his love . . . because I know it's true; it satisfies my longing as nothing else can do." The presence of militant mission hymns on the short list indicates the importance of mission in postbellum evangelicalism, but their textual dissonance suggests that the missionary enterprise was a contested element in a religious movement that was losing cultural coherence during the period.[19]

By contrast, the short list hymns about prayer and devotion seem to articulate the very heart of postbellum evangelicalism. They certainly contributed some of the movement's most striking poetic language. W. W. Walford's "Sweet Hour of Prayer" depicts meditation as a therapeutic exercise that brings "relief" from "a world of care" and "escape" from temptation:

> Sweet hour of prayer! Sweet hour of prayer!
> That calls me from a world of care,
> And bids me at my Father's throne
> Make all my wants and wishes known;
> In seasons of distress and grief,
> My soul has often found relief,
> And oft escaped the tempter's snare
> By thy return, sweet hour of prayer.

In a similar vein Canadian Joseph Scriven described prayer as an intimate conversation with a special friend:

What a friend we have in Jesus,
All our sins and griefs to bear,
What a privilege to carry,
Everything to God in prayer!
O what peace we often forfeit,
O what needless pain we bear,
All because we do not carry
Everything to God in prayer!

This spiritual intimacy found its most emotionally charged expression in postbellum hymns of devotion. Five poems of this type appear on the short list, led by English Unitarian Sarah Flower Adams's enormously popular "Nearer, My God, to Thee," her poetic rendering of Jacob's dream in Genesis 28:11–12. The other four hymns, however, were written by Americans, suggesting that devotionalism has been an especially important part of modern evangelicalism in the United States. The first of these American lyrics is Congregationalist Ray Palmer's "My Faith Looks Up to Thee," the most printed American hymn of the period. Palmer begins with a verse strongly reminiscent of Watts's "When I Survey the Wondrous Cross":

My faith looks up to thee,
Thou lamb of Calvary, Savior divine!
Now hear me while I pray,
Take all my sins away,
O let me from this day
Be wholly thine!

Mixing themes of prayer, providence, and heaven, Palmer, like Sarah Flower Adams, conveys a devotional sense of physical as well as spiritual closeness to Christ:

3
While life's dark maze I tread,
And griefs around me spread,
Be thou my guide;
Bid darkness turn to day,
Wipe sorrow's tears away,

Nor let me ever stray
From thee aside.

In the postbellum century Canadian William R. Featherston's hymn
"My Jesus I Love Thee" enjoyed popularity equal to or greater than
any of Fanny Crosby's lyrics. Featherston's poem presents the believer's loving adoration of Christ the redeemer in life and in death:

My Jesus, I love thee, I know thou art mine;
For thee, all the follies of sin I resign;
My gracious redeemer, my savior art thou;
If ever I loved thee, my Jesus, 'tis now.

3
I'll love thee in life, I will love thee in death,
And praise thee as long as thou givest me breath
And say, when the death dew lies cold on my brow;
If ever I loved thee, my Jesus, 'tis now.

It was Methodist poet Fanny J. Crosby's remarkable output of hymns,
however, that gave definitive voice to postbellum American Evangelicalism. Her devotional lyric "Jesus keep me near the cross" weaves
together a compendium of images from classical evangelical hymnody—
the fountain, the stream, Calvary's "mountain," the morning star, the
river—in a bravura statement of "nearness" to Christ's atoning death:

Jesus, keep me near the cross,
There a precious fountain,
Free to all, a healing stream,
Flows from Calv'ry's mountain,
In the cross, in the cross
Be my glory ever,
Till my ransomed soul shall find
Rest beyond the river.

The final devotional hymn on the short list, Annie Hawks's "I Need
Thee Every Hour," is arguably the most characteristic expression of
the urgency and emotional intensity of postbellum devotionalism. The

lyrical voice confesses its "need" for the "tender voice" of Christ "nearby" and gives itself utterly in prayer to the "most gracious Lord":

I need thee ev'ry hour,
Most gracious Lord,
No tender voice like thine
Can peace afford.

2
I need thee ev'ry hour,
Stay thou close by;
Temptations lose their pow'r
When thou art nigh.

3
I need thee every hour,
In joy or pain;
Come quickly and abide,
Or life is vain.

Refrain:
I need thee, O I need thee;
Ev'ry hour I need thee!
O bless me now my savior,
I come to thee.

Lyrics about providence complete the short list of modern hymns about the Christian life. Two of these texts, Henry Francis Lyte's "Abide with Me, Fast Falls the Eventide" and Edward Mote's "My Hope Is Built on Nothing Less," popularly known as "The Solid Rock," were written by English Victorians. Lyte's enormously popular hymn gives quintessential voice to the saint's absolute dependence on Christ "in life, in death":

Abide with me: fast falls the eventide;
The darkness deepens; Lord, with me abide:
When other helpers fail, and comforts flee,
Help of the helpless, O abide with me.

Mote's lyric covers similar ground, but draws on the parable of the two houses in Matthew 7 and Luke 6 to supply a more celebratory and confident focus on Christ's providential aid to believers:

I
My hope is built on nothing less
Than Jesus' blood and righteousness;
I dare not trust the sweetest frame,
But wholly lean on Jesus' name.

3
His oath, his covenant, his blood
Support me in the whelming flood;
When all around my soul gives way,
He then is all my hope and stay.

Refrain:
On Christ, the solid rock, I stand;
All other ground is sinking sand.

The other three providence hymns were written by Americans: Edward Hopper's "Jesus, Savior, Pilot Me," E. W. Blandy's "Where He Leads Me," and Joseph Henry Gilmore's "He Leadeth Me, O Blessed Thought." These American lyrics employ more active metaphors of divine guidance than the English poems' stress on being or standing with God or Christ through troubles. Yet all five maintain a clear sense of dependency on God for direct, detailed guidance in every aspect of life. Hopper's hymn employs familiar nautical imagery of life's perilous voyage in a plea for Christ's guidance and protection:

Jesus, Savior, pilot me
Over life's tempestuous sea:
Unknown waves before me roll,
Hiding rocks and treacherous shoal;
Chart and compass come from thee,
Jesus, Savior, pilot me.

It is Blandy and Gilmore, however, who offer the most explicit hymnodic account of the saint being lead directly by Christ's providence. Blandy's hymn begins as a perseverance hymn—"I can hear my savior calling, / 'Take thy cross and follow, follow me'"—but its overriding image is one of providential travel, "going with" an ever-present Jesus "thro' the garden" and "thro' the judgment." Gilmore's "He Leadeth Me" turns "following" and "going with" Jesus into a full-throated song of providential confidence in Christ's guiding hand:

He leadeth me! O blessed tho't!
O words with heavenly comforts fraught!
Whate'er I do, where'er I be,
Still 'tis God's hand that leadeth me.
He leadeth me, he leadeth me,
By his own hand he leadeth me:
His faithful follower I would be,
For by his hand he leadeth me.

Modern evangelical hymnody also employed a literary hermeneutic that, like its doctrinal emphasis, differed significantly from the classical hymn corpus. Translated into the categories of narrative, spirituality, and subjectivity that I have used for the classical hymns, these modern evangelical lyrics seem to construct an autobiographical narrative rather than a biblically based apostolic one, concentrate on emotional rather than objective spirituality, and articulate an intimate subjectivity toward the divine rather than a distanced one. If modern evangelical hymns can be reduced to a narrow term, it would be nearness to Christ rather than the otherness of the sacred.

Giving up the earlier evangelical hymnodic focus on the transcendent distance between the sacred and the profane, modern hymns strive to close that gap with an autobiographical account of the believer's spiritual and emotional intimacy with Christ. The modern hymns speak within the perimeter of the believer's experience of the divine, referencing the biblical narrative and the world alike as attenuated iconic symbols whose meaning derives not from their objective reality but from the saint's personal appropriation. The spirituality of these texts similarly exchanges classical hymnody's concrete everyday metaphors of divine grace for intensely emotional symbols expressing the immediate experience of the sacred, especially through a personal encounter with Christ. Above all, the lyrical voice of modern evangelical hymns no longer speaks from the knowledge of ontological estrangement from the divine. Instead it asserts, even assumes, an intimacy with Christ that knows no bounds, physical or metaphysical. After the Civil War American Evangelicals spoke a dramatically altered hymnodic language to voice their similarly changed understanding of the movement's faith.

From Classical to Modern: A Preliminary Assessment

This chapter has argued that many important differences exist between classical and modern evangelical hymnody. The major comparisons and contrasts may be represented schematically as follows.

What inferences can the historian draw about the development of American Evangelicalism from these two bodies of hymnody? The best approach, I think, is to regard their doctrinal content and literary form as rough outlines of the most salient aspects of popular American Evangelicalism during each period. By comparing these hymnodic outlines, some new perspectives emerge on the movement's changing religious identity and the forces that shaped it.

The classical list presents early evangelicalism as a conversionistic form of Protestantism grounded in Calvinist and Arminian Reformed theological traditions, a religion of both the head and the heart. Classical evangelical hymns balanced a juridical formulation of the economy of grace that located the salvific process squarely in Christ's atonement with a distinctive morphology of conversion that stressed divine initiative in enabling the fallen human soul to receive regeneration and sanctification. These evangelical teachings about transcendent reality and spiritual transformation issued a doxological vision of the Christian life as a praise-filled pilgrimage through a darkening world of temptation and trial, with hope of heaven at last. Classical hymns express this epic sacred vision in language saturated with references to the biblical narrative and the world of diurnal experience, uttered by the voice of the believer who is humbled and awed to take part in God's redemptive plan.

Table 1.5
Characteristics of Classical and Modern Evangelical Hymnody

Hymn Subject	Classical	Modern
Economy of Grace	Atonement, Heaven	————
Morphology of Conversion	Invitation	Repentance
	Salvation	Invitation
	Sanctification	Revival
Christian Life	Praise	Prayer
	Witness	Devotion
	Perseverance	Providence
		Mission
Literary Hermeneutic		
Narrative	Apostolic	Autobiographical
Spirituality	Objective	Emotional
Subjectivity	Distanced	Intimate

This hymnodic version of early American Evangelicalism possesses a conceptual, experiential, and literary coherence that marks it as a product of a historically mature religious movement. The evidence from the classical hymns suggests that despite decades of endemic sectarian conflict, the "sovereign audience" had established this stable core of principal sacred beliefs, religious practices, and moral imperatives by the end of the Second Great Awakening. Even the militant antebellum public campaigns for moral reform did not seem to disrupt the emergent evangelical consensus. As the hymns tell it, antebellum moral reform remained rooted in the necessity of individual regeneration; only from that sanctifying source could authentic public witness spring. That evangelicalism could maintain such a coherent popular religious culture under the pressures of escalating sectarian conflict during the Second Great Awakening and mounting political and economic instability after the Panic of 1837 is testimony both to the movement's continuing appeal and to the power of hymns to articulate the essence of its faith.

Modern evangelical hymns present a set of dramatic contrasts to the classical corpus. The first important difference is the almost complete eclipse of the economy of grace as a subject of popular hymnody.

Many postbellum lyrics are sprinkled with references to creation, human sin, incarnation, and atonement, but not a single one of the twenty hymns on the short list is primarily about the economy of grace. What can this pattern mean? It could be, of course, that classical hymns continued to carry the primary doctrinal burden in the later period. The ongoing popularity of two classical atonement hymns, Watts's "Alas! And Did My Savior Bleed?" and Toplady's "Rock of Ages, Cleft for Me," after 1860 lend some credence to this view.

The question remains, however, why none of the most widely circulated new Victorian and gospel hymns referred to the economy of grace. One explanation of this hymnodic abandon lies in the devastating impact of the Civil War on evangelical doctrine. Recent scholarship has shown an ever-widening evangelical rift during the 1870s and 1880s between advocates of the Lost Cause in the South and triumphalist liberals in the North. Much has been made of the polarizing regional and cultural impact of these two important trends, but their greatest significance, as suggested by the hymns, may have been their inability to come to grips with the tragic implications of the war for Evangelical Calvinist and Arminian beliefs. It is not too much to suggest that war's wounding rendered the evangelical mind numb and its hymnodic voice dumb. The mutual ravaging of a people who believed itself regenerate and sanctified was a devastation so great that even a belief system based on Christ's own sacrificial death could not adequately explain it.

Whether or not evangelicals endured this kind of theological shock after the war, they soon enough renewed doctrinal polemic in vast disputes over the Social Gospel, Fundamentalism, and Pentecostalism. For a half-century after 1880 these disputatious rivals shattered the evangelical denominations, and through the entire postbellum century they continued to undermine evangelical doctrinal consensus. Small wonder then that the economy of grace, the most abstract and theologically sophisticated aspect of evangelical tradition, slipped away as a focus of popular religion and as a subject for hymnody. Nonetheless this eclipse of the Reformed theological heritage constituted an unprecedented shift in the movement's identity that is nowhere more clearly marked than in the doctrinal silence of its modern hymnody.[20]

Hymns of the more recent period retain the evangelical emphasis on the morphology of conversion, but here too a major change occurred. The modern hymns restrict their morphological range to repentance, invitation, and revival, leaving behind the classical emphasis on salvation and sanctification. The professionalization of revivalism after the Civil War by Dwight L. Moody and Ira D. Sankey certainly had something to do with this change, but the modern period's relative neglect of hymns celebrating salvation and sanctification demands further explanation especially in light of the emergence of the Holiness and Pentecostal movements during the postbellum period.[21] One clue comes from classical sanctification hymns such as Cowper's "O For a Closer Walk with God," which express the believer's ongoing hope for sanctifying grace. The Holiness and Pentecostal movements, by contrast, premised the believer's conscious possession of sanctification. Their confident hymns of "the victorious life," however, like the sectarian lyrics of the Second Great Awakening, failed to gain interdenominational acceptance from a doctrinally and culturally embattled evangelical majority. For those believers, a categorical experiential claim to sanctifying power did not disclose sufficient religious meaning in a suddenly changed world.

If modern hymns attenuated the classical focus on the economy of grace and the morphology of conversion, they provided a fresh articulation of popular evangelicalism by relocating the center of its hymnody in the Christian life, especially in the themes of prayer, devotion, and providence. These texts are the hymnodic key to understanding modern evangelicalism. The postmodern and feminist critics Sandra Sizer and Jane Hadden Hobbs have questioned any approach to them based in doctrinal categories, arguing that evangelical doctrinal systems were inherently elitist, an oppressive intellectual order imposed especially upon women by male ecclesial institutions. They argue instead that these poems, many of them written by women, articulate a religiousness of "ordered passion" grounded in the communal experience of family and the eroticized physicality of female experience that are such prominent features of nineteenth-century domestic literature.

In this reading, it is necessary to remove the patina of doctrine from these feminized hymns of the Christian life in order to discover their real subject, women's religious experience, through the metaphorical figures and literary techniques they borrowed from popular women's fiction of the period. The problem with this approach is not its findings, but how those findings have been generalized as the primary if not exclusive meaning of postbellum evangelical lyrics. Granting these postmodernist and feminist constructions, one is left asking what is evangelical about gospel hymns and why evangelical men in particular would sing them, let alone write them. To regard postbellum hymns as "the cultural property of women," as Hobbs does, is in effect to exclude them as expressions of evangelicalism, thereby to limit the range of their religious meaning unnecessarily.[22]

Much of that religious meaning can be reclaimed, however, by restoring the theological subject matter of modern Christian life hymns. In fact, such a doctrinal restoration actually complements postmodern and feminist literary interpretations. Sizer and Hobbs found that after the Civil War gospel hymns expressed a new rhetoric of vulnerability, communality, and intimacy focused on the private, domestic circle rather than the realm of public affairs. The explicit theological content of Christian life hymns follows much the same pattern when compared to the classical evangelical hymn corpus. The earlier imperative of public praise, for example, shifts to the private practice of prayer. While Charles Wesley invokes "a thousand tongues to sing / my great redeemer's praise" to a listening cosmos, Charles Scriven addresses a suffering remnant of believers, reminding "us" of "what a friend we have in Jesus."

It is the dimensions of devotion and providence, however, that most directly tie together doctrinal content with the "feminized" literary style of the modern hymns. Devotional texts like Featherston's "My Jesus I Love Thee," Crosby's "Jesus Keep Me Near the Cross," and Hawks's "I Need Thee Every Hour" amply demonstrate a rhetoric of spiritual and physical intimacy, but they also disclose an emotional dependency on the person of Christ so absolute as to virtually eliminate autonomous action. In this sense modern devotional hymns express a rejection of the classical evangelical imperative of Christian witness as expressed in Cennick's "Jesus My All to Heaven Is Gone" or Grigg's "Jesus, And Shall It Ever Be." Regarded in this way, devotional gospel hymns continue to embody Sizer's "social religion" and Hobbs's feminized domesticity, but now it is possible to make evangelical sense of them as a shift from witness in the fallen world to testimony among the redeemed remnant. Witness becomes, in Katherine Hankey's words, "telling the story" not to the world, but "to those who know it best."

The final contrast between classical and modern hymns, the transition from perseverance to providence, offers the most subtle yet most theologically substantive indicator of the changing nature of popular evangelicalism since the Civil War. As rendered by Watts's "Am I a Soldier of the Cross" and "When I Can Read My Title Clear," classical evangelical perseverance was the Christian's militant yet joyful struggle against "Satan's rage" in "a frowning world." The regenerate soul embraced the world both as a duty to God and as a free act of faith, believing that no trial would prove too great and certain that sin would ultimately be overcome. Classical providence, on the other hand, was a mysterious promise to the faithful, the full meaning of which was known only in the mind of God. "God moves in a mysterious way, / His wonders to perform," William Cowper wrote in the most printed classical providence hymn. "He sets his footsteps in the sea, / And rides above the storm."

Perseverance disappears altogether on the short list of modern evangelical hymns, replaced by a new understanding of providence less mysterious and more concrete than its predecessor. Modern providence hymns such as Hopper's "Jesus, Savior, Pilot Me," Blandy's "Where He Leads Me I Will Follow," and Gilmore's "He Leadeth Me, O Blessed Thought" feature an immediate sense of Christ's providential guidance in every circumstance of life. There is no distance, and no mystery, between Christ who leads and the believer who follows: "His faithful follower I will be," Gilmore wrote, "For by his hand he leadeth me." The believer's relationship to Christ is worked out not as a pursuit of transcendence along "the narrow way" but as a journey through life hand in hand with the Savior. Even more importantly, modern providence hymns reposition the primary action of the believer from the struggling, suffering present of classical perseverance lyrics to a predetermined, protected future. This move gives up the embrace of the world for Christ's sake in order to gain the embrace of Christ for the believer's sake. The saint is now safe, secure, and separated from the world not by a difficult discipline of faithful action in it but by a Savior who shelters his own from it.

This is "social religion" and feminized domesticity, indeed, but now with profound doctrinal and moral significance. Modern providential hymn language entails not only a new emphasis on nearness to Christ but also a concomitant flight from the world. Such a reorientation does not easily square with the postbellum evangelical public reform like prohibition, but from the hymnodic evidence there seems to have been much tension between private spirituality and public witness as hymnody lost both a transcendent doctrinal horizon and a moral theology of perseverance in the world. It may not be coincidental that in the postbellum decades evangelicals moved from voluntary to coercive strategies of public reform, especially regarding alcohol. Certainly the failure of prohibition during the 1920s, the simultaneous collapse of the Fundamentalist effort to dominate the denominations, and the subsequent self-imposed cultural isolation of many evangelicals until midcentury contributed much to this pervasive need for providential guidance and protection.[23]

Whatever one makes of modern evangelicalism's public postures, its most popular and characteristic hymns speak of a religious movement that has turned inward, disengaged from the world, and lost its internal cohesion. The cosmological, morphological, and moral trajectories of the modern hymns all exhibit a pronounced tendency to abandon the everyday world and even the biblical narrative as explicit reference points for hymnodic expression and to replace them with a radically infrapsychic horizon of religious experience. It is the search for spiritual nearness to Christ, a haven in a heartless world, that compels modern evangelical hymnody.

Postmodernists and feminists have with good reason claimed that search as a manifestation of evangelical women's religious culture, but the very popularity of these lyrics indicates that they have a wider significance. Women's religious culture was just one strand of postbellum evangelicalism, albeit a crucially important one. Revivalism, foreign missions, the Social Gospel controversy, the prohibition crusade, Fundamentalism, and Pentecostalism also played critical roles in defining the movement in the century after the Civil War. A reading of popular modern hymns against this background, however, suggests that despite and perhaps because of the enormous energy consumed by these many ministries, postbellum evangelicalism was a disintegrating movement. The plangent tone and emotive subjectivity of the hymns speak ultimately not of a world to conquer but of a cause that has been lost. Whether it resulted from the spiritual and physical wounds of fratricidal conflict, alienation from the new cultural forces abroad in postbellum America, countervailing forces within evangelicalism itself, or the failure of its public agenda, the modern hymns bespeak the fragmentation of the movement's traditional doctrinal and moral core and a spiritual retreat to the one remaining place of certainty and solace: safe in the arms of Jesus.

These reflections on American Evangelical hymnody have highlighted the contrasts between the classical and modern periods in order to suggest the potential of hymns as a resource for broader historical and cultural inquiry. The American Protestant Hymns Database provides a new kind of information about hymns, and the effort in this preliminary chapter has been to press the interpretive boundary as far as a limited but highly suggestive body of new data permits. A more nuanced and possibly rather different result might come from analysis of, say, the one hundred most frequently printed hymns, or from hymnody counts of shorter time periods. Hymn texts also require a much fuller consideration of their ritual contexts and of the larger cultural situation and internal dynamics of American Evangelicalism than it has been possible to provide here. The results of such inquiries can scarcely be predicted, but the outline of a new approach to hymnody can be discerned, grounded in the claims that hymns are a unique and foundational resource for understanding American Evangelicalism, that empirical analysis of their publication and popularity yields new formulations of evangelical beliefs, practice, and spirituality, and that those formulations can open surprising vistas and unexpected inquiries about the head, the heart, and the history of America's most important religious movement.

Notes

1. An earlier version of this paper was read on May 17, 2000, as the keynote address for "American Protestant Hymnody," a conference sponsored by the Institute for the Study of American Evangelicals at Wheaton College, Wheaton, Illinois.

2. John Julian, *A Dictionary of Hymnology* (London: John Murray, 1892); Louis F. Benson, *The English Hymn: Its Development and Use* (1915; reprint, John Knox Press, 1962); Horton Davies, *Worship and Theology in England*, 5 vols. (Princeton: Princeton University Press, 1961–75; reprint, Eerdmans, 1996); Erik Routley, *The Church and Music: An Inquiry into the History, the*

Nature, and the Scope of Christian Judgment on Music (London: Duckworth, 1950); *I'll Praise My Maker: A Study of the Hymns of Certain Authors Who Stand in or near the Tradition of English Calvinism* (London: Independent Press, 1951), *The Music of Christian Hymnody: A Study of the Development of the Hymn Tune since the Reformation* (London: Independent Press, 1957), *Words, Music, and the Church* (Nashville: Abingdon, 1968), and *Christian Hymns Observed: When in Our Singing God Is Glorified* (Princeton: Prestige Publications, 1982).

3. Donald Davie, *A Gathered Church: The Literature of the English Dissenting Interest* (New York: Oxford University Press, 1978), *The New Oxford Book of Religious Verse* (New York: Oxford University Press, 1981), *Dissentient Voice: The Ward-Philips Lectures for 1980 with Some Related Pieces* (Notre Dame: University of Notre Dame Press, 1982), and *The Eighteenth Century Hymn in England* (New York: Cambridge University Press, 1993); J. R. Watson, *The English Hymn: A Critical and Historical Study* (New York: Oxford University Press, 1997); Susan Tamke, *Make a Joyful Noise unto the Lord: Hymns as a Reflection of Victorian Social Attitudes* (Athens: Ohio University Press, 1978); Madeleine Forell Marshall and Janet Todd, *English Congregational Hymns of the Eighteenth Century* (Lexington: University Press of Kentucky, 1982); Lionel Adey, *Class and Idol in the English Hymn* (Vancouver: University of British Columbia Press, 1988); Ian Bradley, *Abide with Me: The World of Victorian Hymns* (London: SCM Press, 1997); Richard Arnold, *The English Hymn: Studies in a Genre* (New York: Peter Lang, 1995).

4. Henry Wilder Foote, *Three Centuries of American Hymnody* (Cambridge: Harvard University Press, 1940); Dickson R. Bruce, *And They All Sang Hallelujah: Plain-Folk Camp-Meeting Religion in the South, 1800–1845* (Knoxville: University of Tennessee Press, 1974); Sandra L. Sizer, *Gospel Hymns and Social Religion: The Rhetoric of Nineteenth-Century Revivalism* (Philadelphia: Temple University Press, 1978); Albert Raboteau, *Slave Religion: The "Invisible Institution" in the Antebellum South* (New York: Oxford University Press, 1978); Jon Michael Spencer, *Protest and Praise: Sacred Music of Black Religion* (Minneapolis: Augsburg Fortress, 1990), and *Black Hymnody: A Hymnological History of the African-American Church* (Knoxville: University of Tennessee Press, 1992); Jane Hadden Hobbs, *"I Sing for I Cannot Be Silent": The Feminization of American Hymnody, 1870–1920* (Pittsburgh: University of Pittsburgh Press, 1997).

5. George Pullen Jackson, *White Spirituals in the Southern Uplands* (Chapel Hill: University of North Carolina Press, 1933), *Spiritual Folk-Songs of Early America* (New York: J. J. Augustin, 1937), and *Down-East Spirituals and Others* (New York: J. J. Augustin, 1943); Irving Lowens, *Music and Musicians in Early America* (New York: Norton, 1964); H. Wiley Hitchcock, *Ear-*

lier American Music, 27 vols. (New York: Da Capo, 1972–80); Nicholas Temperley, *Music of the English Parish Church,* 2 vols. (New York: Cambridge University Press, 1979); Richard Crawford, *The Core Repertory of Early American Psalmody* (Madison, Wis.: A-R Editions, 1984); Karl Kroeger, ed., *The Complete Works of William Billings* (Boston: American Musicological Society/ Colonial Society of Massachusetts, 1981–90), and *Daniel Read: Collected Works* (Madison, Wis.: A-R Editions, 1995); Daniel Warren Steel, ed., *Stephen Jenks: Complete Works* (Madison, Wis.: A-R Editions, 1995); and Nym Cooke, ed., *Timothy Swan: Psalmody and Secular Songs* (Madison, Wis.: A-R Editions, 1997).

6. Irving Lowens, *A Bibliography of Songsters Printed in America before 1821* (Worcester: American Antiquarian Society, 1976); Richard Crawford, Allen Perdue Britton, and Irving Lowens, eds., *American Sacred Music Imprints, 1698–1820: A Bibliography* (Worcester: American Antiquarian Society, 1990); Karl Kroeger, *American Fuging-Tunes, 1770–1820: A Descriptive Catalogue* (Westport: Greenwood, 1994).

7. Nicholas Temperley, *The Hymn Tune Index: A Census of English-Language Hymn Tunes in Printed Sources from 1535 to 1820; Assisted by Charles G. Manns and Joseph Herl,* 4 vols. (New York: Oxford University Press, 1998).

8. See David D. Hall and John B. Hench, eds., *Needs and Opportunities in the History of the Book* (Worcester: American Antiquarian Society, 1987); Michael Warner, *The Letters of the Republic: Publication and the Public Sphere in Eighteenth Century America* (Cambridge: Harvard University Press, 1990); David D. Hall, *Cultures of Print: Essays in the History of the Book* (Amherst: University of Massachusetts Press, 1996); and Hugh Amory and David D. Hall, eds., *The Colonial Book in the Atlantic World* (Worcester: American Antiquarian Society, 2000).

9. Congregationalists sang from *The Bay Psalm Book* (1640), Anglicans employed *A New Version of the Psalms of David* (1698) by Nahum Tate and Nicholas Brady, and Presbyterians used either *The Psalms of David in English* by Francis Rous (1646) or *The Psalms of David in Meter* (The Scottish Psalter of 1650). Julian, *Dictionary,* 119, 799–802, 1023.

10. Julian, *Dictionary,* 332; John Wesley, *A Collection of Psalms and Hymns* (Charleston: Lewis Timothy, 1737), E; George Whitefield, *Hymns for Social Worship* (London: H. Cock, 1767) E.

11. John Rippon, *A Selection of Hymns from the Best Authors* (London: Thomas Wilkins, 1787).

12. Foote, *Three Centuries,* 147.

13. Nathan Hatch, *The Democratization of American Christianity* (New Haven: Yale University Press, 1989), 125–54.

14. Baron Stow and Samuel F. Smith, *The Psalmist* (New York: American

Baptist Publication Society, 1843); Methodist General Conference, *A Collection of Hymns for the Use of the Methodist Episcopal Church,* revised and corrected (New York: Waugh and Mason, 1832).

15. John Wesley, *A Collection of Hymns for the People Called Methodists* (London, 1780), ix.

16. See David D. Hall, *Lived Religion in America: Towards a History of Practice* (Princeton: Princeton University Press, 1997), vii-xiii, 133–59.

17. The third heaven hymn "Jerusalem, My Happy Home" is surprisingly enough an English Reformation hymn based on a passage from Augustine's *Liber Meditationem;* Julian, *Dictionary,* 580–83. The classical evangelical hymn corpus is lightly studded with such unlikely items, of which Anglican Non-Juror Bishop Thomas Ken's hymns for morning and evening prayer, "Awake, My Soul, And with the Sun" and "Glory to Thee My God This Night," are the most notable.

18. See Stephen Marini, "Hymnody as History: Early Evangelical Hymns and the Recovery of American Popular Religion," *Church History: Studies in Christianity and Culture,* 71 (June 2002): 273–306.

19. Sizer, *Gospel Hymns,* 40–44; Hobbs, "*I Sing,*" 97–101, 131–39, 171–72.

20. Mark Noll, *The Scandal of the Evangelical Mind* (Grand Rapids: Eerdmans, 1994), 109–48.

21. See Edith W. Blumhofer, *Restoring the Faith: The Assemblies of God, Pentecostalism, and American Culture* (Urbana: University of Illinois Press, 1993); Grant Wacker, *Heaven Below: Early Pentecostalism and American Culture* (Cambridge: Harvard University Press, 2001).

22. Hobbs, "*I Sing,*" 34–69.

23. See George M. Marsden, *Fundamentalism and American Culture: The Shaping of Twentieth-Century Evangelicalism, 1870–1925* (New York: Oxford University Press, 1980); Joel A. Carpenter, *Revive Us Again: The Reawakening of American Fundamentalism* (New York: Oxford University Press, 1997).

2

Reading between the Lines

Slaves, Women, and Native Americans Reflected in a Southern Hymnal of 1810

Kay Norton

Jesse Mercer's *Cluster of Spiritual Songs* illuminates an emerging young American culture seeking to define itself.[1] Spanning nine editions and encompassing 677 hymns in the final edition of 1835, its texts are a study in the humanities. Hymns derived from diverse cultures—British, Gaelic, African, German, Appalachian—and formed a tradition beloved by males and females, slaves and free people, wealthy and "plain folk," blacks, whites, and Native Americans. Mercer's earliest surviving edition of 1810, comprising 199 texts and hardbound for the first time, represents the birth of an icon in Southern sacred music. Free of denominational imperatives such as the Methodist insistence on Wesleyan hymns, Mercer exercised great ecumenism in his selection of hymns for the 1810 edition. "Limited atonement" and "free grace" enjoy equal footing. Although he personally eschewed the "corrupting influence" of the camp meeting, he included several of its products in his collection. His near lifelong association with Phillips Mill Baptist Church, a leader in the recognition and support of black Baptists, gives his choices special significance. In addition, Mercer's advocacy of Christian missions among Georgia's Creek and Cherokee Nations attests a belief, albeit limited, that Native Americans could share in God's kingdom. A wealth of correspondence and published theological opinion addresses females, in his mind, valued members of home, church, and community. No player in the daily life of Jesse Mercer (1769–1841) escaped the burning question of salvation, a fact illustrated in his letters and sermons and often punctuated with a hymn text from the *Cluster*. Analyzing the textual repertory shared by this diverse population contributes a crucial view of the environment that fostered the South's perpetual relationship with sacred music.

Slaves in Jesse Mercer's World

In common perception, the antebellum South was a patch-work of massive plantations and white Southerners, shameless roman-tics who created luxury for themselves at the expense of an entire race of humans. At the core of this exaggeration is the fact that, prior to the Civil War, the South's nineteenth-century economy did revolve around the exported products of plantation agriculture. Especially in the coastal areas of Georgia, a single plantation might be home to 700 or more slaves who cultivated rice in an otherwise uninhabitable swamp. In those settings, institutionalized abuse was considered a "necessary evil" to a prospering enterprise. During this era, Georgia's wealthy planters joined those of her neighboring states to construct a devastating confluence of politics, economy, and prejudice; this story of the Southern elite is the one most often told. The 1790 census, however, shows that the country's 700,000 slaves, living mostly in the Deep South, were owned by only 25 percent of white Southerners. Fewer than 15 percent of slave masters held more than twenty slaves.[2] Roughly 36 percent of Georgia's 1790 population of 82,548 was black; its 25 percent of the white population who were slaveholders averaged twelve slaves each. When the Civil War began more than seven decades later, slaves were owned by only 25 percent of Southern white house-holds.

Jesse Mercer's circle did include state leaders and wealthy planters, but most of his daily contacts were the forgotten 75 percent of white Georgians, the plain folk of the Old South whose "lives have remained of secondary importance to historians."[3] The economy at large may have been geared to plantation agriculture, but most Southerners were subsistence farmers who lived and died without making any notice-able impact in the world.[4] Controversies over plantation slavery and abolition swirled about the plain folk, but they would remain on the periphery until "state's rights" was coined as the South's unifying cause.[5] Unlike their wealthy planter neighbors who were insulated from blacks by layers of administrative foremen and drivers, plain-folk knowledge of African Americans came from the firsthand experience of working side by side and, in many cases, worshipping in the same church.

As white settlers learned to coexist with neighbors running the gamut from German to Portuguese, the acculturation of black immigrants was complicated by an equally diverse mixture of dark-skinned people. They came to Georgia from the African coastal regions of Sierra Leone and Liberia and southward to the lower Guinea coast and were augmented by natives from far in the interior, captured in African warfare or slave raids.[6] Other African-descended peoples arrived via the West Indies, where their forebears had been brought by Spaniards, the British, and the French.[7] Even if a slave found a compatriot in this foreign land, however, socialization was strictly limited.

Devalued as they were within the slavery system, black Baptists were often treated as important players in Georgia's Baptist records. From the time of the First Great Awakening (ca. 1730s–1740s), blacks had been attracted to the intense emotionalism and relative equality of the camp meeting. In these settings, they were welcomed by Presbyterians, Methodists, and Baptists alike. Many slaves and free blacks preferred the nonelitist call of Methodism that eschewed Calvinist predestination, a tenet held by many Baptists. Others, however, were lured by a Baptist faith in which response was easy and baptism by river immersion resembled African tribal customs.[8] From their disparate social levels, whites and blacks found promise in revivalist religion— evidence that society was "on the verge of a major transformation that would hasten their liberation [from poverty or slavery]."[9] Not all who were lured by the Great Awakening would become church members, however. Especially for slaves, outward acceptance of Christianity conflicted with age-old and ingrained beliefs. Pagan ancestry might be "overgrown by . . . Christian teachings but deep in [the African] mind [it was] still active."[10] This collision of African and European religion proved a fertile complement for emotion-based American revivalism.

Mercer and African Americans

Although Mercer's fortune was never tied to the institution of slavery, his lifelong interactions with African Americans reflected the paternalistic models of the middle class. Three indentured children were listed in his father's household as early as 1773, and he eventually became owner of about twenty working slaves after his second marriage in 1827. Clergymen of Georgia's upper region promoted a benevolent treatment of slaves—Phillips Mill Church, shepherded by

Mercer's minister father, had black members as early as 1785—and Mercer perpetuated this tradition. Birth dates of slave children were recorded in Mercer's family Bible after 1827, and other slaves received special mention in the minister's writings. On October 20, 1839, the household absorbed the death of a favorite servant girl named Mary Ann, age fourteen. Having lost his only two daughters, one in infancy and the other at age nine, Mercer's grief was perhaps even more keenly felt. More important to the aging Mercer, however, was the status of Mary Ann's salvation. He wrote, "[Her death] falls with considerable weight on us, as it not only deprives us of a great benefit, but of the most dear inmate of our house. Our little house girl, Mary, is now a corpse in our house. . . . She was so intimately connected with us and our happiness, that we feel it almost as the loss of a daughter. But the thought of our loss is nothing to the fear of the loss of her soul."[11]

Mercer's last will and testament also showed the era's curious humanitarian values within the abomination of slavery: "All my servants [are] to be sold in mercy, that is, to give them time to find masters—such masters as may be desirable to them."[12] He also emphasized the care that he wished to be taken by adding, "(This [process] will be very lengthy)." Reportedly, Mercer was well loved by his slaves; after his death his constant companion, "old Manual," was heard to exclaim, "What shall I do now? Old master (and here he faltered) is no more!"[13]

A year before his death in 1841, Mercer made his views on the abolition controversy known in a letter to the Triennial Convention, a national organization supporting Christian missions at home and abroad. Having reached the age of seventy-one, Mercer often attempted to use his waning influence to stabilize a world he believed to be increasingly out of balance. Responding to a meeting of the national missionary organization he had championed for decades, he wrote:

> The address of the Anti-Slavery Convention held in New York last spring . . . [has] acted as [a] fire brand through all our parts. Our abolition brethren are exceedingly mistaken in the case they have undertaken to remedy; and therefore, their measures can only operate a *bad influence;* and the tendency will inevitably be

to break up all our united operations, and, I seriously fear, our civil union also. They ought to consider that the institution of slavery is a *civil* and not an *ecclesiastical* one; and that it is not one of our (the present owners') making; that we, as a slave-holding people, are mostly the inheritors of them from our forefathers—that they came into possession under the prejudice of early education. We have been taught from our cradles that they were *our money,* that we had a right or title to them. . . . Now be this right or wrong, it ought to be kept in mind that this prejudice is not to be removed by any immediate cause, nor by hard words, or by arbitrary condemnation.[14]

Here, Mercer begs the question of justice in his efforts to explain the reason that slavery was so ingrained in the South. That slaves could have rights equal to those of whites was not a conceptual possibility for many slave owners. Just as certainly, Mercer knew that most Northern Baptists he addressed would have no context for understanding how the slave-based economy had rescued Georgia, which had struggled on the brink of collapse for decades after its founding. Compared to his more zealous proslavery neighbors, Mercer's position was surprisingly rational, even though its premise is contemptible from the modern perspective.

Slaves and the 1810 *Cluster*

The first compilation of hymns especially intended for the use of African Americans in this country was Richard Allen's *A Collection of Hymns and Spiritual Songs of Various Authors* (Philadelphia, 1801), which was printed twice in its first year. Allen had founded the African Methodist Episcopal Church in 1794 and drew from Watts, the Wesleys, and Baptist favorites for his collection. During most of Allen's life, Philadelphia was a promised land on Earth for blacks nationwide. Yet Allen himself was imprisoned by those who doubted his free status; persecution from white Methodist brethren led him to break all ties with white religious bodies in 1816. Already a seasoned traveler by the age of twenty-one, Mercer made his first tour of the northern states in 1798. Not until 1814 was his first trip to Philadelphia documented, but when he compiled the 1810 edition of the *Cluster of Spiritual Songs,* he chose seventeen hymns that also had appeared among Allen's sixty-four texts. The authors include English and American contributors to high church and camp-meeting traditions.

Mercer could have extracted most of the intersecting hymns from other sources, but Henry Alline's "As Near to Calvary I Pass" had no other printing prior to 1810. It is also interesting that Richard Allen placed "The Voice of Free Grace" by Richard Burdsall first in his collection, whereas Mercer made it second only after John Newton's popular invocation hymn "Now May the Lord Reveal His Face."[15] Times were changing in Georgia, however. As the abolition debate gained momentum in the North, Southerners became more convinced of their "state's right" to self-government, which included slavery. Reflecting this narrowing cultural view, Mercer had discarded "The Voice of Free Grace" by the time of the 1823 *Cluster.* Still, his duplication of the Allen hymns in the 1810 edition is a reminder of the biracial complexion of Mercer's congregations.

Another historic publication, *Slave Songs of The United States* (comprising tunes and texts), resulted directly from Abraham Lincoln's 1861 blockade of the Confederate coast from Virginia to Texas, which persisted throughout the Civil War.[16] A resultant Union stronghold in coastal South Carolina between Charleston and Savannah became the site of "a grand [Northern] experiment to demonstrate that slaves could work and learn as free men."[17] Each of the future editors of *Slave Songs of the United States* came to Port Royal, South Carolina, as workers in the relief effort—Charles P. Ware and Lucy McKim in 1862, joined by Ware's cousin William Francis Allen in 1863. In praise meetings at the close of each working day, these Northerners notated songs of black plantation workers. Although the Sea Islands, embracing the South Carolina and Georgia coasts, were too isolated to duplicate inland activity in the adjoining Confederate states, the body of 144 spirituals eventually published in 1867 became a valuable starting point for the documented history of black singing in America.

What association could these songs have with Jesse Mercer's upland environs of Wilkes County, Georgia? Allen assured the reader that "there was constant intercourse between neighboring plantations, also between different states, by the sale of slaves from one to another."[18] Indeed, a direct connection exists between *Slave Songs* and Augusta,

Georgia, where Mercer's 1810 *Cluster* was published. Six songs were sung to Allen by blacks in that city: "Who Is on the Lord's Side," "Hold Out to the End," "Come Go with Me," "Every Hour in the Day," "In the Mansions Above," and "Shout On, Children."[19] The fifty-seven years that separate Mercer's 1810 edition and *Slave Songs* is less of a barrier than it might seem. Music recorded from oral tradition often represents tremendous longevity in practice. The idea that former slaves in Augusta began singing these songs only toward the end of the Civil War is less plausible than the possibility of others in the region singing them as early as 1810.

Work done by George Pullen Jackson (1874–1953) in the 1940s completes the link between *Slave Songs* and Mercer's 1810 *Cluster*. In *White and Negro Spirituals,* Jackson presented valid data on shared tune tendencies in his "Tune Comparative List," "116 melodies of white people paired with the same number of Negro-sung variants."[20] Although discovering similarities between white and black spirituals led Jackson to assert that the black counterparts were always derivative of white forebears, no such claim of white primacy is perpetuated in this study. Jackson pointed out that Mercer's hymn number 60, John Leland's "O When Shall I See Jesus," had been paired with the tune "Ecstasy" in *The Sacred Harp* (1844). That tune shares its musical genealogy with two *Slave Songs,* "O Daniel" and "Every hour in the day." The latter was one of the six tunes that had been sung in Augusta, Georgia, for William Francis Allen.

Females in Mercer's World

Even in a post-Revolutionary culture that remained overwhelmingly patriarchal, Georgia women were active players in the state's diverse society. In the private world of the plantation, disparate classes were often woven together by a complex web of sexuality in which women played many roles. The sexual license of many male slave owners—"begetting in a manner not unlike that of biblical patriarchs"[21]—was an accepted fact among Georgia's upper crust, still a minority in society as a whole. Abusive slave owners viewed slave women as unintelligent heathens with no conscience or soul and thereby rationalized a sexual violence against them that would otherwise have been unthinkable in polite society. Turning abuse into opportunity, some female slaves found sex with the master or his sons a resource for improving their own lives or those of their children. More frequently, female slaves paid dearly for a beauty that doomed them to levels of submission and violence not experienced by their male counterparts.

White females in planter society applied their sexual power more subtly than their husbands and sons did. Bertram Wyatt-Brown pointed out that Southern men feared women for their *potential* misconduct: "Women *were* dangerous, they could present a husband, father, or brother with an illegitimate child and thereby cast doubt on the legitimacy of the line and desecrate the inmost temple of male self-regard."[22] Furthermore, the wife of a promiscuous slave owner often had total control of the household, which included his illegitimate, biracial children. In this twisted society, female slaves therefore suffered double indemnity for their sexuality, because the cruel, unreasonable mistress was known to punish the female slaves who were objects of her husband's affection. Ironically, slave girls were almost always allowed to marry for love, whereas daughters of slave owners often were forced into marriages that were economically advantageous to the father.[23] Still, the black advantage was tenuous; most intimate slave relationships were subject to disruption at any time because of the slave trade: either member of a couple could be sold to another plantation at any time.

For all white women, the private trump cards of sexuality and domesticity were fortified in the public sphere by 1755, when widows became the first Georgia women allowed to own land. Previously, the absence of a male heir after the death of a husband meant forfeiture of family acreage. Between 1755 and 1775, a total of 248 land grants were made to 164 individual women for an approximate total of 67,000 acres.[24] This new provision ensured women the opportunity to achieve limited equity, financial independence, and simultaneous entree into civic and social matters previously closed to them.[25] Ironically, landowners of both sexes benefited by slave ownership, because any dependent—slave or free—entitled the owner to fifty additional acres of land in post-Revolutionary lotteries. Thus as upper-class women left the ranks of the economically oppressed, many also assumed a more active role in a society of racial oppressors.

At Church

Inhabiting both public and private spheres of influence, religion has always provided women with avenues of self-expression, education, and relative equity unmatched elsewhere in society, but female role definition in American Protestantism has never been straightforward. Debates on "women's place" naturally had accompanied the waves of revivalism that characterized eighteenth-century American life, as sinners were "harvested" regardless of race, class, or gender.[26] Tensions between egalitarian revivalism and the more universal Western tendency to sex-biased stratification intensified, however, as "dissenter" denominations such as the Baptists and Methodists grew in numbers toward the end of the century. Once women accepted the "free grace" offered at Southern revivals and camp meetings, male church leaders faced a shared validity of thought, feeling, and experience unprecedented in the secular world. How could women continue to be submissive to males in all areas of life and simultaneously remain equal to men before God? Women's roles in post-Revolutionary Southern churches were necessarily complex as they balanced these limitations with the free evangelical tradition firmly ensconced in the South by 1800.

In practice, the average Georgia woman touched by religion was expected to extend her home roles of nurturer, educator, and guardian of morality. Giving public thanks to God for pious mothers was indispensable in the rhetoric of males converted to Christianity.[27] Marriage was viewed as the lesser of two evils by the apostle Paul, whose New Testament writings formed the basis for much evangelical theology.[28] Wayward young males sought godly brides partially to hold sin in abatement and inspire repentance. Expectations of female conduct were predictably conservative, and preachers such as Jesse Mercer openly chastised ungodly behavior: "Whence is it that there are among your women, *bare* elbows—*naked* arms—*exposed* breasts—*shorn* heads—*ruffled,* or shamefully *tight* dresses, connected with a light, airy deportment, and vain, carnal conversation?"[29]

In 1990, Connie Garmon studied female activities in Georgia Baptist life beginning in 1733 and extending almost to Mercer's death.[30] When a female church member required permission to transfer membership to a distant church, the request could be made either by the woman herself or her male representative.[31] Matters of church discipline involved females as often as males. All were bound to explain long absences from monthly business meetings of the church and, if the explanation was not acceptable, excommunication was the penalty.[32] While Mercer was pastor at Phillips Mill, "Elizabeth D. was charged with 'prophane [sic] swearing, drinking too much, sending her husband's property away without his leave and for leaving him without a cause'"; a female slave was expelled in 1799 for harboring runaway slaves and receiving stolen goods.[33] Mercer did, however, adopt a reasonable attitude toward married slaves whose permanent separation resulted from the slave trade. Under his leadership, the Georgia Association of Baptist Churches ruled in 1833 that separated slave members could marry again if there was no chance of being reunited.[34]

Female participation in church was clouded by dominant Biblical metaphors that described the "church," or universal body of believers, as the bride of Christ.[35] Hymn 34 in Mercer's 1810 *Cluster,* "Let Christ the Glorious Lover," revolves around imagery common in the evangelical language of the day.[36] Even the most devout male believer would be hard-pressed to identify with the sinner labeled "she" thirty-nine times in this text. No less challenging is the sinner, in a stereotype of feminine behavior, stubbornly resisting an amorous Christ as the suitor. The irony of a congregation's singing these lines is intensified by the typical church seating arrangement: "According to custom, the women, girls, and little children sat together on one side of the church, the men and boys on the other, the slaves at the rear and preachers at the front."[37] Even if sexual segregation ensured the triumph of piety, it is no small wonder that Mercer permanently deleted "Let Christ the Glorious Lover" from the *Cluster* after 1810.

As in the secular world, female experience in Western culture has revolved around subtlety, the weapon of those denied a more direct route to power. Mercer's churches adhered to this paradigm, and within its strictures, his female worshippers influenced all aspects of worship and church life, including music. In discussing roots of Old Baptist singing practices, Beverly Bush Patterson observed, "singing appears to be linked in some important way to gender because it is the one place in which women consistently have a voice in the worship service."[38] The female vocal attributes of lyricism and flexibility, enlivened by natural invention and expressiveness, shaped the evolving genre of religious song as surely as did the male voice at the head of the congregation. Printed hymn collections had long indicated sectional singing, which gave women their moment in the limelight during worship.

In special revivals as well as regular Sunday worship services, believers of both sexes freely expressed their religious experiences. This freedom, however, created a conundrum, for although giving testimony and requesting, singing, and improvising revival songs were essential to religious experience, the apostle Paul had warned that women should not speak in church.[39] Notable exceptions to this rule included Martha Marshall, whose husband, Daniel (1706–84), was pastor of the first continuing Baptist church in Georgia. Prior to the Revolution, Daniel Marshall was arrested for preaching without governmental sanction, and at his hearing Martha "quoted several texts of Scripture with so much force as to confound the opposers and [convert] several persons."[40] Another contemporary account described her as "a lady of good sense, singular piety, and surprising elocution, [who] has, in countless instances, melted a whole concourse into tears by her prayers and exhortations!"[41]

The Marshalls were contemporaries with Silas Mercer and worked in the same region; Martha Marshall's reputation could not have been unknown to Jesse Mercer in the succeeding generation. Seeing his theological mission as the faithful explication of the Scriptures, Mercer thus faced a dilemma. His position on females in church relied on Pauline doctrines but left the distinction between various forms of female participation vague.

> There is a sense in which women are not permitted to speak in the churches; and yet there is a sense in which they may speak. Now in what may they not speak? In teaching and governing. . . . But in what may they speak? In praying and prophesying . . . but this prophesying, when used by women, must not be teaching, but only for edifying. For it is not permitted for women to teach. . . . Women are . . . debarred the right of voting in the

churches in all matters of government, because they cannot use this right without being on a par with men, and in many instances taking the ascendancy . . . which is at variance with what is required of them.[42]

Mercer therefore allowed girls and women to express their spiritual insights, but their words were decorative only, stripped of direct influence. Female prophesying, wrote Mercer, was permissible, but would not be readily accepted.[43]

This outward marginalization satisfied Pauline dictates but simultaneously gave "airtime" to the powerful religious experiences of the oppressed sex. In his study of the camp meeting, Dickson Bruce further observed social implications of female religious activity that can be applied to Mercer's world.

The conversion services began with participants arranged in a way that conformed to the manner in which Southern society was itself arranged, especially in terms of the distinctiveness of sex and religious roles and in racial segregation. Then, at the height of conversion activities, this structuring of the setting was completely broken down as mourners, saints, and preachers entered the pen [place reserved for conversions] together. More, the original structure was actually turned upside down, for not only did everyone enter the pen, but people who were ordinarily assigned a subordinate place in Southern life, the women and children, actually assumed leadership of the activities in their roles as counselors and, in the case of new converts, as exhorters. . . . To the extent that one draws much of his orientation to himself and to other people from the kind of social structure in which he participates, the negation of structure in the conversion period must have had the effect of invalidating the secular images of self and society which most plain folk had. . . . The whole thrust of the frontier credo—which urged every person to attempt to get the better of every other person—was effectively blunted by the equalizing ceremony of the glory pen where brother embraced brother in a common joy. This spirit of community was emphasized even more strongly in the closing exercises culminating in a march around the encampment with all the saints joining hands and singing.[44]

As authors of hymns by 1810, female contributions to the hymn tradition defined by the likes of Isaac Watts, George Whitefield, and Charles Wesley were well documented. Mercer's 1823 collection contained nineteen texts by British hymn writer Anne Steele (1716–78),[45] two by Mrs. Vokes (ca. 1799), one by Elizabeth Shirley Scott (ca. 1708–76), and one by Sarah Slinn (eighteenth century).[46] None of these hymns had appeared in the 1810 version. Despite the Pauline injunction against feminine teaching, female hymn writing was sanctioned by Mercer in every extant edition of the *Cluster*. One female contributor to the 1810 edition is Anna Beeman, a Baptist from Warren, Vermont, whose hymn "What Think You My Friends of the Preaching of John?" is Mercer's number 151.[47] Beeman's hymns were first published separately in 1792, and according to James Cecil Downey, they were at times "somewhat rough":

Behold this sodom here below
I leave it all to you;
Hinder me not for I must Go,
My Jesus to pursue.

And at others, sensual:

If I'm a Saint I long to rest
Dear Jesus on thy holy breast;
Yes, lay enfolded in thy arms
To view thy beauty and thy charms.[48]

Beeman's contribution to the *Cluster* also displays a relatively primitive poetic style, not unlike Mercer's own, in lilting fiddle-tune meter. This hymn is the first entry under Mercer's rubric "Believers' Baptism," its inclusion clearly due to the advocacy of baptism by immersion in stanza fourteen.

How could a female literally place her words in the mouths of male worshippers without assuming the forbidden role of teacher? One an-

swer lies in the self-effacing language adopted by early hymn writers
and compilers of both sexes that typically diverted attention from the
author's identity. In the hands of a female, the prefatory remarks could
be an effective tool for legitimizing one's poetic gifts and the more
questionable desire to see her hymns published. A rural Baptist from
Windsor, Vermont, Lucy Allen thus contextualized her own products
to make them more acceptable to males.

> The author, being illiterate, or her education such that she is in-
> capable of writing, or even of reading writing, and professes not
> to be endowed with any natural poetic genius; but, being a pro-
> fessor of religion, of the Baptismal order, she was frequently,
> and almost constantly, meditating on divine and eternal things;
> and having certain impressions made on her mind, by acci-
> dents, and other occurrences, taking place during her Christian
> travel, from the year of our Lord, 1784–88.[49]

In this way, Allen distanced herself from the poetic depictions of her
Christian experience sufficiently to deny blame for any impropriety
their publication might cause. Although Mercer never reproduced any
verses of this resourceful author, her apologetic preface effectively
would have removed any theological barriers to his doing so. These
words were of the Lord's making, after all, and not her own.

"Reforming Nations": Jesse Mercer and Native Americans

The century of interaction between Anglo-Saxons and Native
Americans on Georgia soil that ended with the Trail of Tears (1838–39)
rivals and surpasses the ignominy even of black-white relations in the
state. Because they inhabited the lands and traveled the waterways
near the mouth of the Savannah River, the Creek Indians had first
contact with whites. Theirs was also the first nation forced to leave;
the Creek exodus was complete by 1827. Living in the Appalachian
highlands of Georgia and neighboring states, the Cherokees saw their
lands similarly invaded until the federal government created the treaty
that sealed their fate in 1835. Anglo-Saxon lust for land and hatred for
people of color, hastened by the discovery of gold in North Georgia,

ensured the demise of Georgia's remaining Native Americans. Between 1790 and 1830, the white population in the state increased six-fold; by 1840, only scattered remnants of the two aboriginal nations remained.

Most whites believed that Native Americans occupied a slightly higher position on the cultural ladder than blacks, a difference explained by the complex cultures that greeted the eighteenth-century European settlers. On the one hand, Africans had been forcibly removed from their established systems and thrown together in the New World with no recognition of the disparate regions and cultures they represented. In marked contrast, whites encountered Native Americans in their chosen environments and even visited and admired their prehistoric monuments. William Bartram wrote about one cultural marvel, the Indian Mounds at Etowah in North Georgia, in 1775: "It is altogether unknown to us what could have induced the Indians to raise such a heap of earth in this place. . . . It is reasonable to suppose, however, that they were to serve some important purpose in those days, as they were public works, and would have required the united labour and attention of a whole nation."[50] European immigrants to the New World also witnessed Native American systems of self-government and knew too well their capacity to execute well-organized raids and town burnings. Because their communal autonomy was at first undisturbed by white invasion, Native Americans therefore gained a dubious respect from the whites. Still, whites considered these people, who had occupied Georgia for centuries, as "heathens" in the way of the necessary progress of the newcomers. Native American perception of the invaders is symbolized by the Cherokee alphabet's title, chosen by Sequoyah, its inventor. In the numerous treaties that were initiated and subsequently ignored by whites, written words carried no more weight than "Talking Leaves."

Mission Work

The most benign white approach to Native Americans in this hostile century accompanied efforts by Moravians, Methodists, Presbyterians, and Baptists to Christianize them.[51] Because the U.S. government maintained an interest in the movements of Native Americans in Georgia, missionary efforts in education often received federal funding. Jesse Mercer's passion for the salvation of sinners and his activity in national missionary efforts place him squarely in the midst of Native American contact with whites. According to his first biographer, Mercer was inspired early in life by John Rippon's accounts of English Baptist missionary activity in India. Mercer remained a champion of missions to his death, even when the issue threatened his cherished Baptist unity.[52] Ever a believer in the literal interpretation of the Bible as he read it, Mercer's favorite Biblical command to missions was Acts 13:47, "For thus the Lord has commanded us, 'I have placed you as a light for the Gentiles, That you should bring salvation to the end of the earth.'"[53] As early as 1801 Mercer was involved in discussions about Indian missions, as his minutes from the October meeting of the Georgia Baptist Association indicate: "A letter was addressed to the Body this year from the meeting at Powelton . . . which called the attention of the Association to the propriety and expediency of forming a Missionary Society in this State, for the purpose of sending the gospel amongst the Indians, bordering on our frontiers, which was unanimously and cordially approbated."[54] Nevertheless, more than a decade would pass before Mercer again documented his interest in ministering to the Creeks. The 1814 minutes of the Georgia Association relate that "Brother Mercer presented and read the Circular and Constitution of the 'Savannah Baptist Society for Foreign Missions' and then moved for the approbation of the Association."[55] Mallary named Mercer as one of the "most liberal and efficient supporters" of the mission to the Creeks.[56]

At the 1817 meeting in Philadelphia of the Triennial Convention, Mercer represented Georgia's Baptists interested in missionary activities to the Cherokees.[57] Mercer's national visibility contributed to the project's success, and the Convention appointed three ministers to the Cherokees as a result.[58] Thereafter, Mercer maintained an active supervisory role. His only documented sermon to the Cherokees occurred during a Convention-requested visit to North Carolina's Valley Town Mission Station in 1823. There is no indication that he personally visited Georgia's missions himself; instead, Mercer was apprised of mission activity by the Convention's appointed teacher to the Cherokees, Duncan O'Bryant, and Mercer's colleague who superintended the mission, Littleton Meeks.

In 1821, Tinsawattee School was established among the Cherokees in present-day Dawson County. In 1825 it was moved to a more favorable location in the same region and was known as Bread Town School. There it remained active until 1829. Duncan O'Bryant taught the Cherokee at both these schools and moved once again to found Hickory Log Town School in 1829, which was short-lived as a result of western emigration.[59] The Triennial Convention declared the school officially closed in 1831, and thus ended Jesse Mercer's active involvement with Native American missions. O'Bryant's decade of active teaching is reasonably well documented in his reports to Mercer and the latter's subsequent reports to the Triennial Convention.

The following description of Tinsawattee was written by an observer in 1821:

> [Tinsawattee] is designed to instruct the Indian youth, but not to board, clothe, and lodge them. A comfortable school house, and a dwelling house for the master, horse stable and smoke house, have been procured at very little expense; and there is a prospect of a considerable number of scholars. . . . The pupils are very attentive to learning, and appear capable of as great improvement as any children in the world. They are affable, docile, amiable and mild. They already say to those who stay at home, 'you will be of no account if you do not go to school.' Their improvement in singing is remarkable, and their attention to worship is unremitting.[60]

The next year, a Tinsawattee student illustrated the success of the school when funds were requested of a Georgia Baptist group. One eyewitness described the student, believed to be James Wofford, at length:

> He has attended the school . . . for some months, and can read the English language fluently. He read verses in . . . the New Testament, without hesitating. He knows the stops and marks used in writing, and gave many proofs, that though he has a red skin, he has a strong and vigorous intellect. He sang several hymns which he had committed to memory and others from the

book. . . . He and [Humphrey] Posey sang . . . a hymn descriptive of the millennial day—'Slight tinctures of skin shall no longer engage,' &c. and, 'When white men and Indians united shall praise, / One vast hallelujah shall raise,' [which] excited much interest and feeling.[61]

Having relied upon local donations since its founding, the school was adopted by the Triennial Convention in 1824. With its sponsorship, the Department of War promised an annual stipend of $250 for the support of O'Bryant, who in turn was closely monitored by a Convention-appointed committee chaired by Mercer. Not surprisingly, Baptist mission efforts drew the interest of the Office of Indian Affairs (OIA), a branch of the Department of War. OIA director Thomas McKinney questioned the Triennial Convention especially about the Tinsawattee School in 1824 and apparently received a satisfactory report.[62] The next year Mercer wrote, "There are two reasons why we should keep up this Station. The reform of the nation is one; and the spiritual good of the poor children of the forest is the other."[63]

Hymn singing was part of the curriculum at Tinsawattee, and in 1825 Meeks reported that during a worship service in the school building, "I frequently heard them singing, praying, and exhorting, in their own tongue. I baptized one aged woman, a native Cherokee; and several more have a hope in Christ."[64] In an 1828 letter to Mercer, O'Bryant reported receiving nineteen copies of Susanna Harrison's hymnal entitled *Songs in the Night,* a rare mention of specific texts used in mission activities with Native Americans.[65] Hymns by a female author would have special significance among Native American converts. "In tribes where matriarchal traditions remained strong, as with the Cherokees and Iroquois, the chief of the council of matrons had divine authority and was thought to speak for the Great Spirit when she addressed the warrior chiefs."[66] This elevated status of women may explain the choice of Harrison's hymns for the Native American schools; hymns beginning "But Why Did Martha Take This Load?" and "Thus Ruth Received the Kindness of Her Friend" might have endeared the collection to influential females in the Native American communities. Not surprisingly, both sexes were welcome at these mission schools; Hickory Log Town's attendance in 1830 comprised twenty males and sixteen females.[67]

The single 1810 *Cluster* hymn known to be of Native American origin was written by a Mohican who was converted by George Whitefield and eventually ordained as a Presbyterian minister. Samson Occum's 1774 *Choice Collection of Hymns and Spiritual Songs* was first published in New London, Connecticut, but Mercer may have learned of this often reprinted text from a camp-meeting songster. "Awak'd by Sinai's Awful Sound" was excluded from later *Cluster* editions.

Conclusion

Although Jesse Mercer did not document his selection process for any of the 199 texts comprising the 1810 *Cluster*, his motivations may be extrapolated by analyzing the facts of his life. The idea that Mercer considered slave tastes as he compiled the 1810 edition is not far-fetched, given his background of worshipping with Africans as a youth and his inclusion of acknowledged slave favorites such as "O When Shall I See Jesus." Even as they outwardly welcomed slaves into the fold, however, these musical moments brought no true respite from the aching reality of slavery. Slaves with sufficient command of the English language would have noticed the irony of implied interclass solidarity suggested by some hymnic language. In the anonymous "Lo! Behold How Unexpected," the term "slave" indicates that death is "no respecter of persons."[68] John Newton's "Begone Unbelief" describes being enslaved by sin, again at least verbally equalizing the term.[69] Mercer's apparent efforts to represent slave tastes in the *Cluster* of 1810 suggest important contexts for the collection, but the societal condition that brought those African descendants in contact with Mercer must be remembered and lamented.

Women could feel valued in Mercer's church because positive attributes such as wisdom and mercy were consistently represented with feminine pronouns, and some hymns even stressed God's motherly characteristics. In "Hark! My Soul, It Is the Lord" by William Cowper, the "tender care" of a human mother is a benchmark against which Divine steadfastness is measured.[70] Christianity's debt to the mother of Jesus and to motherhood in general is mentioned prominently in Joseph Hart's "Let Us All with Grateful Praises."[71] In choosing these hymns, Mercer gave females the opportunity to celebrate in church the very attributes that distinguished them from their male counterparts.

Admittedly, Native Americans in Mercer's Georgia are scarcely represented by a single *Cluster* hymn of Mohican authorship. Assuming Mercer knew that the author of "Awak'd by Sinai's Awful Sound" was Native American, the text was probably no more than a token of successful conversion efforts among aboriginals. Mercer's passion for "Christianizing the heathen" and subsequent supervisory role in the Tinsawattee mission nevertheless create a conundrum. Hymns were sung at this mission and Mercer's involvement there gave him another potential audience for the *Cluster*, but no record suggests even the presence of a *Cluster* edition at the school, much less its use. Likely as not, Harrison's *Songs in the Night* were a donation made to support Native American missions, and Mercer never considered a like donation of his popular hymnal as a sound financial step. Therefore, the Native Americans are connected to Mercer's 1810 *Cluster* only generally, through the minister's mission activity and the fact that hymns were sung in the missions.

Thus are the complexities of race, class, and gender reflected, to varying degrees, in an early nineteenth-century hymnal. Paradoxical as it may seem, the antebellum South abounded with self-proclaimed "prophets" such as Mercer who endeavored to improve their society's ills by spreading the message of divine redemption. How could a man so committed to pursuing virtue still be a player in the tragically unjust systems of his day? It was not the lack of passion or commitment that distinguished the "good" man such as Mercer from an Abraham Lincoln. Instead, Mercer exhibited a common weakness—the acceptance of the status quo as a necessary condition—that carried with it devastating implications. His documented opinions on slaves, women, and Native Americans often belied a relatively considerate treatment of his disadvantaged fellow Georgians. This dichotomy must always remain in the foreground, even as we entertain the wish that someone with Mercer's potential to defy his society's greatest ills would have acted definitively to do so.

Notes

1. This paper reproduces in part my work on *Baptist Offspring, Southern Midwife—Jesse Mercer's Cluster of Spiritual Songs: A Study in American Hymnody*, Detroit Monographs in Musicology/Studies in Music, no. 34 (Warren, Mich.: Harmonie Park Press, 2002).

2. Eileen Southern, *The Music of Black Americans,* 2d ed. (New York: W. W. Norton, 1983), 150.

3. Dickson D. Bruce Jr., *And They All Sang Hallelujah: Plain-Folk Camp-Meeting Religion, 1800–1845* (Knoxville: University of Tennessee Press, 1974), 5. Bruce's characterization of plain folk offers a useful context for Mercer's world.

4. "They were, nonetheless, objects of a great deal of interest to early Baptist and Methodist evangelists." Bruce, *And They All Sang,* 5.

5. When war finally came, well-educated Confederate majors and generals fought for the elitist way of life, but their troops, illiterate and poor, fought for the autonomy of their homeland. For this disadvantaged majority of Southerners, "The War of Northern Aggression" described a cause worth dying for.

6. Albert H. Stoddard, "Origin, Dialect, Beliefs, and Characteristics of the Negroes of the South Carolina and Georgia Coasts," *Georgia Historical Quarterly* 28 (September 1944): 186.

7. The "Gullah" (Gola, i.e., Angolan) dialect still in use by some black residents of coastal South Carolina is a rare survivor of African regional speech patterns transplanted by the eighteenth-century slave trade.

8. Carol V. R. George, *Segregated Sabbaths: Richard Allen and the Emergence of Independent Black Churches, 1760–1840* (New York: Oxford University Press, 1973), 15.

9. Ibid.

10. Stoddard, "Origin, Dialect, Beliefs," 191.

11. Quoted in C. D. Mallary, *Memoirs of Elder Jesse Mercer* (New York: John Gray, 1844), 402.

12. Jesse Mercer's will, 25 quoted in Don Mercer Papers, Main Library, Mercer University, Macon, Ga.

13. Quoted in Mallary, *Memoirs,* 403.

14. Jesse Mercer, letter to Lucius Bolles, October 21, 1840; quoted in Mallary, *Memoirs,* 208–9. Emphasis in original.

15. The first two stanzas only are Burdsall's, taken from his hymn "Now Christ He Is Risen, The Serpent's Head Is Bruised." John Julian, *A Dictionary of Hymnology, Setting Forth the Origin and History of Christian Hymns of All Ages and Nations,* 2d and rev. ed. with a New Supplement (London: 1907; reprint, New York: Dover, 1957), 1555. The hand that first added the subsequent stanzas of "The Voice of Free Grace" is unknown. Allen printed four verses only; Mercer's fourth stanza is an addition.

16. Dena J. Epstein gives an extensive account of Sea Islands inhabitants and events leading to the publication of *Slave Songs of the United States* (1867) in "The Port Royal Experiment," chapter in *Sinful Tunes and Spirituals: Black Folk Music to the Civil War* (Urbana: University of Illinois Press, 1977).

17. Epstein, *Sinful Tunes and Spirituals,* 255–56. Government interest in Port Royal's largest cotton crop in years at a time when the commodity was withheld from Northern markets may have initiated the relief effort. The fact that the cotton was, indeed, harvested annually calls Union motivations into question. Volunteer workers joining the "experiment" had little to gain beyond humanitarian rewards, nonetheless.

18. William Francis Allen, Charles Pickard Ward, and Lucy McKim Garrison, compilers, *Slave Songs of the United States* (New York: A. Simpson, 1867), x–xi.

19. Ibid., xl.

20. George Pullen Jackson, *White and Negro Spirituals: Their Life Span and Kinship* (New York: J. J. Augustin, 1943), 145–227.

21. Margaret Ripley Wolfe, *Daughters of Canaan: A Saga of Southern Women* (Lexington: University Press of Kentucky, 1995), 75.

22. Bertram Wyatt-Brown, *Southern Honor: Ethics and Behavior in the Old South* (New York: Oxford University Press, 1982), 54; quoted in Wolfe, *Daughters of Canaan,* 3.

23. Linda Grant Depauw and Conover Hunt, *Remember the Ladies: Women in America, 1750–1815* (New York: Viking Press, 1976): 16.

24. Lee Ann Caldwell Swann, "Land Grants to Georgia Women, 1755–1777," *Georgia Historical Quarterly* 61 (spring 1977), 24.

25. "Tobacco and corn cost as much when purchased from a woman farmer as when purchased from a man." Depauw and Hunt, *Remember the Ladies,* 63.

26. Sara M. Evans, *Born for Liberty: A History of Women in America* (New York: Free Press, 1989), 41–42 and 57–58; quoted in Wolfe, *Daughters of Canaan,* 34.

27. Mallary, *Memoirs,* 57.

28. The apostle Paul sent an egalitarian message to the Corinthians: "The unbelieving husband is sanctified through his wife, and the unbelieving wife is sanctified through her believing husband" (I Corinthians 7:14). Earlier in the same chapter, however, Paul suggests marriage primarily as an alternative to sin for both sexes: "I wish that all men were even [unmarried] as I myself am. . . . For the unmarried and . . . widows it is good for them if they remain even as I. But if they do not have self-control, let them marry; for it is better to marry than to burn." *New American Standard Bible* (La Habra, Calif.: Lockman Foundation, 1973).

29. Jesse Mercer, Circular Letter of 1806; quoted in Mallary, *Memoirs,* 145. Emphasis in original.

30. Connie D. Garmon, "The Role of Women in Georgia Baptist Life, 1733–1840," *Viewpoints: Georgia Baptist History* 12 (1990): 11–21. As pastor of

several churches, moderator of the Georgia Baptist Association, and editor of *The Christian Index* from 1833 until 1840, Jesse Mercer figures prominently in surviving documentation.

31. Church membership could be transferred "by letter" to another congregation when a family moved to another region. Church minutes from Phillips Mill, February 10, 1821, and June 17, 1837, are summarized in Garmon's article.

32. Minutes, Phillips Mill, March 12 and August 13, 1814; summarized in Garmon, "Role of Women," 15.

33. Phillips Mill, March 7, 1798, and July 13, 1799, quoted in Garmon, "Role of Women," 15.

34. Georgia Association Minutes of 1833, 3; summarized in Garmon, "Role of Women," 16.

35. Again quoting Paul: "For the husband is the head of the wife, as Christ also is the head of the church, He Himself being the Savior of the body." *New American Standard Bible*, Ephesians 5:23.

36. The fifteen verses of "Let Christ the glorious lover have everlasting praise" appeared first in Joshua Smith's 1784 edition of *Divine Hymns, or Spiritual Songs* (Norwich, Conn.: T. Hubbard, 1794). Smith is considered the author.

37. J. R. Huddlestun and Charles O. Walker, *From Heretics to Heroes: A Study of Religious Groups in Georgia with Primary Emphasis on the Baptists* (Jasper, Ga.: Pickens Tech Press, 1976), 98.

38. Beverly Bush Patterson, *The Sound of the Dove: Singing in Appalachian Primitive Baptist Churches* (Urbana: University of Illinois Press, 1995), 30.

39. Paul wrote to the church at Corinth (ca. 47–60 CE): "Let the women keep silent in the churches; for they are not permitted to speak, but let them subject themselves, just as the Law also says. And if they desire to learn anything, let them ask their own husbands at home; for it is improper for a woman to speak in church." *New American Standard Bible*, I Corinthians 14:34–35.

40. Quoted in Robert G. Gardner, Charles O. Walker, J. R. Huddlestun, and Waldo P. Harris III, *A History of the Georgia Baptist Association: 1784–1984*, rev. ed. (Atlanta: Georgia Baptist Historical Society, 1996), 15.

41. Quoted in ibid.

42. Quoted in Mallary, *Memoirs*, 447.

43. Mercer as editor, *The Christian Index*, September 9, 1834; paraphrased in Garmon, "Role of Women," 13.

44. Bruce, *And They All Sang*, 132.

45. "Anne Steele's hymns were canonized by British Nonconformists from the late 1700s and by American evangelicals throughout the 1800s." Mary De

Jong, "'Theirs the Sweetest Songs': Women Hymn Writers in the Nineteenth-Century United States," chapter in Susan Juster and Lisa Macfarlane, eds., *A Mighty Baptism: Race, Gender, and the Creation of American Protestantism* (Ithaca: Cornell University Press, 1996), 160.

46. C. Ray Brewster, *"The Cluster" of Jesse Mercer* (Macon, Ga.: Renaissance Press, 1983), 224–25.

47. Mercer discarded the hymn after the 1810 edition and never reinstated it.

48. James Cecil Downey, "The Music of American Revivalism," Ph.D. diss., Tulane University, 1968, 106.

49. Lucy Allen, *Hymns on Various Subjects* (Windsor, Vt.: Alden Spooner, 1795); quoted in Downey, "Music of American Revivalism," 108. A professor of religion in this case refers to one who professes Christianity, not to an academic.

50. William Bartram, *Travels through North and South Carolina, Georgia, East and West Florida: A Facsimile of the 1792 London Edition* (1791; reprint, London: J. Johnson, 1792; reprint Charlottesville: University Press of Virginia, 1980), 323.

51. Missionary activities eroded Native American autonomy in a more subtle but perhaps no less devastating way than geographical encroachment. Still, bloodshed was never associated with missionary efforts in Georgia.

52. Mallary, *Memoirs*, 188.

53. *New American Standard.*

54. Jesse Mercer, *History of the Georgia Baptist Association: Compiled at the Request of That Body* (Washington, Ga.: 1838); quoted in Gardner et. al, *History*, 40.

55. Gardner et. al, *History*, 190. Jesse Mercer served as clerk of the Georgia Association from 1795 until 1816, under the moderatorship of his father, Silas.

56. Ibid., 191.

57. Robert G. Gardner, *Cherokees and Baptists in Georgia* (Atlanta: Georgia Baptist Historical Society, 1983), 9, 26–27. Mercer was a leader in the Triennial Convention and was, at that time, serving as moderator of the Georgia Baptist Association. Treaties of 1817 and 1819 already had given Native Americans in Georgia the choice of removal to the West or adaptation to agriculture and "the arts of civilization" if they remained on their ancient lands.

58. Ibid., 28.

59. Duncan O'Bryant also founded Tinsawattee Baptist Church in 1825, which remained active until November 1831, when he accompanied members of his congregation to Oklahoma. The fascinating, and at times, controversial story of this remarkable missionary is told in greater detail by Gardner, *Cherokees and Baptists*, 73 ff. Their 1831 departure spared O'Bryant and his congre-

gants the Trail of Tears and established Baptist mission work among the Western Cherokees.

60. Humphrey Posey, letter to William Staughton, undated, reproduced in *Latter Day Luminary* (May 1821); quoted in Gardner, *Cherokees and Baptists*, 38.

61. *Columbian Star* (Washington, D.C.), November 30, 1822, 2; quoted in Gardner, *Cherokees and Baptists*, 44–45. The hymns excerpted in this passage do not appear in the 1810 *Cluster*.

62. Gardner, *Cherokees and Baptists*, 47.

63. Jesse Mercer, letter to William Staughton, April 26, 1825; quoted in Gardner, *Cherokees and Baptists*, 49.

64. Littleton Meeks, letter of April 1825; quoted in Gardner, *Cherokees and Baptists*, 60.

65. The author received Gardner's transcription of O'Bryant's letter from the Main Library, Mercer University (Mercer correspondence, letter 15). Susanna Harrison (1752–84), *Songs in the Night by a Young Woman, under Heavy Afflictions*, 1st American ed. (from the 4th London ed.), with a supplement (Exeter, N.H.: Ranlet, 1802). The frequently reprinted collection comprised 133 hymns in a main section, another sixteen in an appended "Meditations," and a supplement of eighteen hymns. None of Harrison's hymns reappeared in the *Cluster* of 1810, but Mercer clearly was aware of her collection.

66. Depauw and Hunt, *Remember the Ladies*, 70.

67. Jesse Mercer, letter to Lucius Bolles, April 27, 1830; quoted in Gardner, *Cherokees and Baptists*, 56.

68. "Kingdoms countries, and their cities, / Kings, their councils, and their slaves, / There's none of them, he ever pities; / He brings them all into their graves."

69. "Determin'd to save, he watch'd o'er my path, / When Satan's blind slave, I sported with death."

70. "Can a woman's tender care / Cease towards the child she bare? / Yes, she may forgetful be, / Yet will I [Jesus] remember thee."

71. "Long had Satan reign'd imperious / 'Till the woman's promis'd seed / Born a babe, by birth mysterious / Came to bruise the Serpent's head."

3

"Old Favourites" or "New Style"

Creating the Hymnal of the Presbyterian Church in Canada

Barbara Murison

In 1878 the Presbyterian Church in Canada,[1] recently created from a union of four distinct Kirk and Secession bodies, resolved to provide an official volume "for such congregations as desire the use of a Hymn Book in their service of praise."[2] It was a momentous decision, and one not easily reached; the discussion occupied three sessions of the General Assembly, and the contributors to it were so numerous that the length of the speeches had to be severely limited. The debate had long been anticipated and, in some quarters, dreaded, for the issue had been a divisive one in the four constituent churches, where efforts had often been made to avoid rather than to confront it.[3] The drafters of the 1875 *Basis of Union* of the four Presbyterian churches were careful to state that the present practices of congregations in public worship were to be allowed and any changes were to be "left to the legislation of the united church."[4] It was safest to "hasten slowly." Even so, when the *Basis of Union* was sent down to the presbyteries and synods, it was this clause on worship to which most exception was taken. The question of the "Headship of Christ" might still exercise the veterans of the Disruption of the Church of Scotland in 1843, the fate of the substantial financial resources possessed by some of the constituent churches had vital implications for the future of the united church, and the college issue (for would there not be a surfeit of Presbyterian colleges?) also had significance—but for the bulk of the Presbyterian laity, the basic question was whether their Sunday service would change after union. Because, as a correspondent of the *British American Presbyterian* pointed out,[5] the prejudices of many church members were so deep-rooted that the mere suggestion of the *possibility* of change was regarded almost as heresy, it was clear that the hymnal committee ultimately appointed at the end of the hymnody debate of 1878 had a delicate task ahead.

The historical origins of the difficulties of the hymnal committee lay in Scotland, the country of origin of the majority of the members of the Canadian Presbyterian churches, or of their immediate forebears. Hymns were originally alien to Presbyterian worship, and only very gradually did they gain acceptance. It was not that music was regarded as unimportant; the exclusion of hymns from services and the lack of choirs and organs in Presbyterian churches until the nineteenth century derived not from indifference but from fiercely held principles. Every participant in public worship, whatever his or her musical abilities, had the duty (and the right) to offer praise to God; no choir or organ should be allowed to lessen that responsibility. Moreover, in accordance with Calvinist teaching, the service contained only what was sanctioned by scripture. This meant that the Psalms of David were alone worthy of use and thus the first Scottish Psalter was published in 1564. Calvinist ideas were again upheld in the *Westminster Directory of Worship* (1645) and received expression in the *Scottish Psalter* of 1650, which contained "the Psalms of David in Meeter . . . more plain, smooth and agreeable to the Text than any heretofore."[6] This Psalter was authorized as the only version of the psalms to be used by the Kirk and soon gained an enthusiastic following; for centuries it remained the basis of Presbyterian praise. The first collection of tunes to accompany it was published in 1666 and, by 1700, many Scots had come to believe that these twelve common-metre melodies were, in fact, the original work of that accomplished harpist, King David.[7]

The methods used in singing the psalms simultaneously assumed a prescriptive force. The musical parts of the Presbyterian service would be led by a precentor or "uptaker of the psalms," who sat below the pulpit and indicated on a tuning fork or pitch pipe the key to be used for each psalm. It was also standard practice for the precentor to "line the psalms," intoning the line of each psalm first so that those who were illiterate or who lacked psalm books could join in. The worshippers, seated, would then "grace the tune," adding various individual decorations between the basic notes as a means of aiding their meditation on the sacred words.

Any efforts to make alterations to the traditional practices could cause dissension. It took 131 years for the Kirk to accept a supplement to the Psalms and to allow further portions of Holy Scripture to be rendered into verse on the model of the 1650 Psalter and then to be issued as the *Scottish Paraphrases* (1781).[8] Over time, these scriptural paraphrases assumed the same high status as the Psalms and the Twelve Tunes. Five years after the Paraphrases were issued, the minister of Anderston Relief Church, Glasgow, published, on his own initiative, a collection of hymns for the use of his congregation.[9] It was the first hymn book compiled for the use of any Scottish Presbyterians, but it would be some years before any *official* hymnal would be issued by Secession synods, and even longer before the Kirk gave permission for the use of a small selection of hymns (1861).[10]

Each step was hard fought, and there accumulated a long history of troubling episodes connected with efforts to "modernize" Presbyterian music; some of the reasons for eighteenth- and nineteenth-century Presbyterian secessions were musical ones. *The Statistical Account of Scotland* (1791–99), which contains reports from the ministers of the more than nine hundred Kirk parishes in Scotland, provides plentiful evidence of walkouts from the parish church when efforts were made to "improve" the singing. In one Berwickshire congregation, the precentor, hoping to achieve a higher quality of music in his church, omitted to "read the line" one Sunday afternoon and instead led the singing together with a group of musical friends. The innovation "so shocked many of the hearers, that they never afterwards could be reconciled to the Established Church."[11]

It was only natural that concerns about the music of the services should cross the Atlantic with the Scottish immigrants to British North America; as Dr. Samuel Johnson once observed of some Highland emigrants, "They change nothing but the place of their abode."[12] Lack of Psalm books reinforced traditional prejudices regarding the necessary functions of the precentor,[13] and the illiteracy of some settlers, particularly of the Highlanders settled in such areas as Cape Breton and Zorra, Upper Canada, also suggested the utility of continuing the practice of "lining." Even in areas such as Halifax, Montreal, and York [Toronto], where literacy was much higher and Psalm books more plentiful, there still existed a strong desire for the old forms of worship. Whereas the transplanted Highlander longed for Ross's Gaelic Psalm book, William Lyon Mackenzie, immigrant from

Dundee and later to achieve fame as the leader of the 1837 rebellion in Upper Canada, insisted that only the Scots versions of the Psalms and Paraphrases, and tunes such as "Dundee," "Elgin," and the "Old Hundred," would do for the Presbyterian Church of York. His admiration for old school Presbyterianism was reinforced when he visited New York in 1829 and attended a service where the "old and solemn tunes" had not yet made way for "ballad rhymes" and the "single line of old Scottish Psalmody" was given out "in truly national style."[14]

If the music question had been divisive in the relatively homogeneous society of Scotland, it became a great deal more so in British North America, the chief destination of Scottish emigrants, because of the diverse nature of many colonial congregations; one of the first observations made by the Reverend William Proudfoot on reaching York in 1832 was that all the churches there contained "very incongruous materials."[15] There were substantial numbers of American and Irish settlers whose ideas on music in worship frequently diverged from those of the Scots, themselves splintered into various Presbyterian groups, each having distinctive ideas on the subject. Thus the New Englanders who settled Yarmouth, Nova Scotia, thwarted the efforts of their minister, the Reverend John Ross, to impose on them the authorized Scottish Psalter. These Americans, of mixed Presbyterian and Congregational background, had brought with them the habit of using the psalm versions of Isaac Watts, and Ross's Session reported that any attempt to meddle with the music currently in use in the congregation was "too dangerous an experiment to be hazarded."[16]

Reinforcement of the ideas of the different Presbyterian groups was provided by missionaries sent from the mother countries. The Kirk's Glasgow Colonial Society was active throughout British North America in the second half of the nineteenth century, and the American Home Mission Society made substantial efforts in the Niagara peninsula area of Upper Canada in the 1830s. The intransigence of the various protagonists on the music question is easily illustrated. Three ministers of the American Home Missionary Society, applying for membership in the Presbytery of York (in connection with the Church of Scotland) were told in no uncertain terms by the Moderator that their use of Watt's *Hymns and Sacred Songs* was "a *sin*," and one that the Presbytery would not tolerate.[17] Such remarks were not merely hyperbolic; they represented strongly held views. A basic conservatism governed the discussion of musical issues; when Nova Scotia Presbyterians were considering adopting the Scottish United Presbyterian Hymn Book of 1852, the debate "did not turn upon the merits of the book in question," because most of its opponents confessed that they either had not seen it or had examined it very superficially.[18] Their minds were already made up. Positions once taken (or inherited) were given up only with reluctance; indeed, there were cases of individuals becoming members of congregations "under protest" against hymns and paraphrases being used in the church services in addition to the Psalms.[19] As *The Presbyterian* noted, "That which from infancy we heard our parents sing . . . and as we grew up, sang ourselves" was generally accepted without criticism.[20] Undoubtedly, the various participants in the Canadian Presbyterian union of 1875 entered it with substantial musical baggage.

The official starting positions for the General Assembly hymnody debate of 1878 were as follows. Those former members of the two constituent churches that had been "in connection with the Church of Scotland" had made some small progress in assembling a small selection of hymns for their use, but then, in 1870, had thankfully embraced the idea of sanctioning the use of the *Scottish Hymnal,* officially accepted by the Kirk in that year. The two other constituent churches had had serious thoughts about a hymnal from the 1860s on, but had delayed; these two churches were themselves the product of unions between Free Presbyterians and United (Secession) Presbyterians, some Free Presbyterians adhering to the use of Psalter and Paraphrases only, whereas the United Presbyterians had "gone in advance" and started to use a large selection of hymns, not necessarily founded on passages of scripture.[21] The Canada Presbyterian Church had considered, but then retreated from, the idea of compiling a hymnal for its congregations in the early 1870s, fearing "discomfort and dispeace" between its former Free and United Presbyterian sections, the former very conservative in its worship practices, the latter highly progressive.[22]

The drafters of the various arrangements for the Presbyterian unions before and during 1875 had taken the position that present practices should be followed in modes of worship, provided that there was general conformity with the directions contained in the *Westminster Directory of Worship,* part of the general standards to which all Presbyterians adhered. Church leaders well knew that, below the minister-dominated assemblies, synods, and presbyteries, there were hundreds of congregations where an immense variety of worship practices existed, yet whose members firmly believed that they were worshipping God in precisely the way that He intended. Not surprisingly, then, there was trepidation as the hymnology debate began; even the Reverend Robert Campbell, in his prize-winning essay on Presbyterian union, a work as sunnily optimistic as the pro-union organizers of the contest could ever have hoped for, had admitted that "the matter of hymnology might occasion a little difficulty" for the united Church.[23] Indeed it did. There would be many congregations that, like that of MacNab Street Presbyterian Church, Hamilton, found the hymn question much more controversial than the matter of union itself.[24]

The debate began when an overture from the presbytery of Ottawa advocating the preparation of a hymn book was brought up for consideration by the General Assembly. The synod of Montreal and Ottawa was also backing the proposal, and similar overtures were put forward by the presbyteries of Hamilton, Miramichi, Paris, and Whitby and by the synod of Hamilton and London. We are fortunate to possess excellent and detailed accounts of the debate, for reporters from the public press were out in force.[25] Presbyterians controlled the influential *Toronto Globe*, the *Halifax Presbyterian Witness*, and the *Montreal Witness* and regaled a wide reading public with every detail of the hymnody dispute.[26]

Two major questions emerged: Should there be hymns at all in Presbyterian worship, and, if so, what *kind* of hymns should there be? Masterminding the attack on the whole principle of using hymns was Dr. Robb of Cooke's Church, Toronto; his first ploy was to attempt to get a ruling that it was unconstitutional to raise the question at all.[27] Support for this motion came from unlikely quarters, for even some who favored the use of hymns in public worship felt that it would be dangerous and divisive to discuss the question and that the church "had better leave the whole question alone."[28] When such motions failed, Dr. Robb, using arguments that could as well have been made in 1778 as 1878, advised the General Assembly, in an impassioned speech, that the church should not commit itself to any hymnology except that provided and prescribed by God himself. That could only mean the Psalms,[29] and if Presbyterian psalmody was in a deplorable state, it was the users of "uninspired" hymns who were to blame. People and ministers, he declared, hard of heart and dead of intellect, had allowed hymns when they should never have done so. His supporters, ministerial and lay, argued similarly; if the Psalms "satisfied Apostolic piety and primitive purity: why should they not satisfy us?" "Hymns are very poor and trashy" was the simple verdict of one Elder.[30] However, the antihymn contingent was a minority, if a vocal one; the battle for the exclusive use of the Psalms, or perhaps for the exclusive use of the Psalms and the Paraphrases, had largely been lost already at the congregational level. In the main, the feeling of the Assembly was in favor of hymns, in part for practical reasons. As the Reverend Mr. Rogers, the proposer of the overture from the presbytery of Whitby, remarked, it would be difficult—indeed impossible—to stop the use of hymns entirely, yet it was also undesirable to let things continue as they were, for a huge variety of hymn books was in use (another speaker claimed twenty-six or more),[31] and some churches were even using collections prepared in the *Wesleyan Bookroom* in Toronto! A good Presbyterian collection ought therefore to be prepared under the Assembly's supervision.

What, however, constituted a "good" collection? What, indeed, constituted a "good" hymn? Hymns could be applauded (or criticized) on many grounds: doctrinal purity, theme, emotional tone, and imagery. "Length, rhythm, phraseology and sentiment" were all matters of significance.[32] The suitability of the hymn tune was an equally complex affair, and there were special concerns about children's hymns and even about the ideal size of a hymn book.[33] It was a little naive then to suggest, as did the *Presbyterian Record,* that it would be an easy matter to make a judicious selection.[34]

The church that had put D. J. Macdonnell (member of the hymnal committee, 1878–95) on trial for heresy was not a church indifferent to doctrinal issues.[35] Presbyterians in nineteenth-century Canada were, in particular, highly sensitive to the threat posed by the "pestilential heresy" of Arianism, by the creeping influence of Arminianism, by Ritualism, and by Unitarianism;[36] one of the critics of hymns in the 1878 debate pointed out that "an Arminian, a Unitarian, a Ritualistic can get Hymns to suit him" and then proceeded to quote a couplet from the well-known communion hymn "'Twas on that night when doomed to know" as an example of heretical Sacramentarianism. ("Oh, hear, hear, and hisses" were the response to this, the last indicating some perturbation at the idea that Paraphrase 35, based on St. Matthew's Gospel, should be regarded as heretical.)[37] Another Assembly member pointed out that one of the Sabbath Schools had been using a hymn book containing views of Scripture radically different from those held by the Presbyterian Church. "Arminianism and Arianism might be inculcated so far as the Assembly knew."[38] Indeed, the worry that good Presbyterian folk might be "singing heresy" was one reason put forward for the compilation, under General Assembly supervision, of a hymnal for the general use of the newly united Presbyterian Church.[39]

This was a "hymn-book-making age."[40] The production of a number of new Presbyterian hymnals in England and Scotland in the 1850s and 1860s, some of which were to be adopted for use by individual Canadian congregations, provided ample opportunities for Canadian Presbyterians to consider not just the doctrinal content of hymns but also their imagery, themes, and phraseology; the reviewers of such works as the *English Presbyterian Hymn Book* (1867) and the *Scottish Hymnal* (1870) found much on which to comment. One reviewer of the latter work in *The Presbyterian* felt that certain hymns should have been "shut out": Heber's "The Son of God goes forth to war" he regarded as unfit for public worship, remarking that only two of the eight stanzas could be appropriately sung by a general congregation under any circumstances.[41] (It would not be included in the *Hymnal of the Presbyterian Church in Canada*.) Other hymns ought to have been included in the Scottish collection: for example, John Wesley's translation from the German of Paul Gerhardt's "Commit Thou All Thy Griefs" and Dryden's "Creator Spirit by Whose Aid." Surely, too, no collection was complete without Addison's "Traveller's Hymn," "How Are Thy Servants Blest O Lord." (All of these would be included in the Canadian hymnal.) Furthermore, complained the reviewer, some alterations had been made from the originals of certain hymns, which "marred their beauty." For example, the line "My *dear* Redeemer's praise" was not equal in strength to the line as it was left by the Wesleys, "My *great* Redeemer's praise." (The *Hymnal of the Presbyterian Church in Canada* would choose the original version.)[42] The ideal compiler had to be familiar with the original text of hymns,

to be aware of unauthorized changes made in certain lines and cou-
plets, and must know what changes, if any, had been introduced by
the authors themselves in later editions of their works.[43] Another reviewer castigated the inclusion of certain hymns whose imagery was
too exuberant and style too florid. Heber again received criticism:
however lovely his "Brightest and Best of the Sons of the Morning,"
a hymn addressed to a star had no place in a good Presbyterian hymnal. (It, in fact, would be omitted from the *Hymnal of the Presbyterian
Church in Canada*.)[44] All these matters, and many others, would have
to be pondered by the ten-man hymnal committee appointed at the
end of the 1878 General Assembly hymnody debate.[45]

Its initial instructions were to make a selection of hymns from the
four main hymn books already in use in a number of congregations[46]
and to send down their compilations to the presbyteries for consideration so that a report could be made to the next General Assembly.
The committee met at once and decided that every member should
prepare an individual list of hymns and that a general meeting would
then be held wherein the lists would be compared, with the hymns
common to all members having priority.

It took the better part of a year for the members to make their
selection; as the committee's secretary, W. B. McMurrich, a prominent Toronto lawyer, observed, great care had to be taken to secure
hymns "not only the best but suitable for congregational use, [and]
above all filled with true worship and devotion."[47] In all, 489 hymns
were submitted by the members of the committee, 39 of them by all
ten members. On the other hand, a breathtaking 211 were recommended by only one member, which perhaps serves to emphasize the
range of taste of the members, who were drawn, of course, from
the four constituent branches of the Presbyterian Church in Canada.
The final number of hymns selected was 349, and there were fourteen
doxologies.

The contents were arranged on a thematic basis, with the first section dealing with God: His attributes and works. Dr. Gregg, joint
convenor of the hymnal committee and a member of the subcommit-
tee for the arrangement of the index, had particularly stressed, during
the hymnody debate, that a weakness of many hymns in use was their
failure to give prominence to the many attributes of God, particularly
to His justice.[48] The next two sections dealt with Jesus Christ and the

Holy Spirit, and others contained hymns on the Christian life, the church, and death, resurrection, and heaven. Finally, there was a Miscellaneous section that included a few children's hymns and special occasion hymns. Each hymn was prefaced by a Biblical text but, in the customary manner, there was no reference to the author. As the Reverend R. W. Almond had noted in the preface to an English hymnal of 1819, "The names of Authors are properly omitted, as having a tendency to call off the attention from the subject to the Writer of the Hymn."[49] Only at the back of the Canadian hymnal were the authors' names cited, and then not in full; Robert Murray, a member of the hymnal committee and himself a hymn writer, modestly chose to appear as "M."[50]

There were two indices, one of first lines and one of tunes. The former may seem obvious enough to require no comment, but we should note that early Scottish hymnals had frequently been indexed only by topic. The first hymn book used in a Scottish Church (Anderston, 1786) began its index with "Affliction, Hope in," progressed through "Backslider, His Return," and so to "Zion, Asking the Way to."[51]

What can we learn from an analysis of the thirty-nine hymns selected by all ten members of the hymnal committee? First we should note that the committee members were united in their approval of evangelical hymns, with their emphasis on grace and the salvation of the individual. They had no qualms in approving hymns, or specific verses of hymns, that others might have thought too personal; a stanza of Lyte's "Abide with Me," omitted from the influential Anglican collection *Hymns Ancient and Modern* (1860), on those very grounds, was retained in the version included in the *Hymnal of the Presbyterian Church in Canada*.[52] Rather, it was "unreal, artificial, empty [and] shallow" hymns, "glittering hymns that have a temporary popularity" with which they had no patience.[53]

Five of the thirty-nine hymns were the work of the eighteenth-century evangelical poet William Cowper; they included "Hark My Soul! It Is the Lord," which the Bishop of Oxford had found overly sentimental when he noted its presence in *Hymns Ancient and Modern*, and "O For a Closer Walk with God," whose inclusion in the *Scottish Hymnal* had been castigated by one Canadian reviewer (although it was a "fine hymn") because it dealt too plainly with the personal experiences of the poet.[54] Another of Cowper's hymns, "There Is a Fountain Filled with Blood," contains, as a modern commentator points out, language almost shocking in its imagery, but is firmly based on scriptural texts, a fact that was bound to appeal to Presbyterians.[55] They were also impressed by Cowper's collaborator in the famous *Olney Hymns* of 1779, John Newton, who restricted himself to biblical texts for his hymns. Lionel Adey writes somewhat scathingly of "the half-educated Newton," but his "How Sweet the Name of Jesus Sounds," with its testimony of "I" and "me," was a firm favorite with nineteenth-century congregations.[56] One each of the "rude and homely compositions" of Joseph Hart and John Cennick[57] were also unanimous committee choices, as was another old evangelical favorite, Augustus Toplady's "Rock of Ages, Cleft for Me." This intense and dramatic hymn, the consolation of Prince Albert in his dying hours and a hymn "justly prized by the Christian Church" in the opinion of the authors of *Our Hymn Writers*, a small volume of biographical sketches of the authors of the hymns in the Canadian hymnal,[58] was nonetheless shorn of some of its wilder excesses when it was published; the line "When my eye-strings break in death" was toned down to the more genteel "When my eyelids close in death," and the stanza beginning "O precious Side-hole's cavity, I want to spend my life in thee," which has been interpreted by a modern commentator as a classic example of Freudian womb-regression, is omitted altogether.[59]

Although Cowper accounted for the largest number of hymns in the thirty-nine, with five, his contemporary, Charles Wesley, and the early nineteenth-century "Sheffield Poet," James Montgomery, ran him a close second with four apiece. W. E. Gladstone once described Wesley's hymns as overrated,[60] but the enthusiasm of the authors of *Our Hymn Writers* knew no bounds: they placed Wesley's hymns "first in the whole history of Christian literature."[61] Wesley's evangelical pedigree was, of course, impeccable; one of the contributors to the hymnody debate had indeed suggested that if a minister were to read out to his people Wesley's "Jesus Lover of My Soul," they would find as much of the gospel in it as there was in many of the sermons that were preached from Presbyterian pulpits.[62]

Montgomery, too, strongly appealed to evangelicals. In North America especially, his great hymn on death, "For Ever with the

Lord," achieved great popularity; it was a natural choice for the hymnal committee. It was not just Presbyterians who thought highly of Montgomery; as the preface to the 1836 English Congregational Hymn Book put it, "He must be a bold man, if not a wise one, who would attempt to improve the compositions of Mr. Montgomery."[63] The hymnal committee proved equal to that task, however: two stanzas in "Hail to the Lord's Anointed," touching on social problems that Montgomery, editor of the radical Sheffield newspaper the *Iris,* was anxious to address, were excised from the version printed in the *Hymnal of the Presbyterian Church in Canada.* The interpolation of a rarely used verse beginning "Arabia's desert ranger" allowed this hymn to be put in "The Church: Its Missions" section of the hymnal. Other Montgomery hymns, accusing priests of oppression and the wealthy of hypocrisy, are altogether missing from the collection.[64] It was not Montgomery's radical ideas, but his evangelical introspection and his vision of the church as a part of the communion of saints, practicing on Earth for what they would do in heaven, which appealed to the hymnal committee members. As J. R. Watson observes, it is a view that looks back to those of Isaac Watts and the seventeenth-century Dissenters.[65]

The Watts hymn particularly favored by the committee members was one of his psalm versions, "Jesus Shall Reign Where'er the Sun" (Psalm 72); its popularity had increased as the age of Foreign Missions advanced. It was one of two missionary hymns in the thirty-nine (three if we allow Montgomery's "Hail to the Lord's Anointed"), the other being Heber's "From Greenland's Icy Mountains," a hymn that had been used in many earlier Canadian Presbyterian hymn collections.[66] But Watts's enthusiasm did not necessarily make *all* his hymns acceptable; "There Is a Land of Pure Delight" was omitted from the hymnal, possibly on the same grounds as those that later gave the proprietors of *Hymns Ancient and Modern* pause, the problem of having a hymn that had you die and go straight to heaven rather than wait for the Day of Resurrection.[67]

It should be noted that the Presbyterian Church in Canada's search for good hymns was not confined to the work of evangelicals, still less to the work of Presbyterians or of Scots. To be sure, the hymnal of a church whose members in the main had Scottish forebears was bound to take notice of the hymns of the Scottish politician Sir Robert

Grant, whose "O Worship the King, All Glorious Above" well justifies his reputation as the finest Scottish hymn writer of the Romantic period,[68] and of the Scottish Presbyterian ministers Horatius Bonar and Robert Murray McCheyne. One hymn by Grant, two by Bonar, and one by McCheyne appeared in the lists of all ten hymnal committee members. Although the Canadian reviewer of the English Presbyterian hymn collection of 1867 bluntly stated that the hymns by McCheyne and, particularly, Bonar did not come up to the required standard, remarking of the latter hymn writer that although a "good Presbyterian name" might have led the editors astray, the public does not always follow where the critic leads.[69] Quite a few of Bonar's hymns were firm Victorian favorites by the time the hymnal committee set about its work, and "I Heard the Voice of Jesus Say" had been one of the great hits of *Hymns Ancient and Modern*.[70] Its inclusion in the *Hymnal of the Presbyterian Church in Canada* was never in doubt.

Although the English Presbyterian hymnal could be castigated for putting the denomination before everything else, the Canadian hymnal was more measured in its attitude. Thus the Anglican Sir Robert Grant's "Saviour, When in Dust, to Thee," each stanza of which ended with "Hear our solemn *litany,*"[71] was included despite the possible affront to Presbyterian sensibilities. Indeed, a great many hymns by Anglicans found a place there, including some by members of the Oxford Movement;[72] John Keble's "Sun of My Soul, Thou Saviour Dear" was a unanimous choice of the hymnal committee. A number of hymns by Catholic converts from Anglicanism also found their way into the collection. "Jesus, The Very Thought of Thee," a translation of a twelfth-century hymn by St. Bernard, was suggested by all committee members, despite the fact that it came from Edward Caswell's "strongly Romish" *Lyra Catholica,*[73] and the work of Matthew Bridges and Frederick William Faber was also represented in the hymnal. Included too was John Henry Newman's "Lead, Kindly Light," although whether through Presbyterian prudence or poor proofreading, this Victorian favorite, the work of the most famous apostate from Protestantism of his day, was noted in the index as by that great evangelical, Newton![74] As the chairman of the Church of Scotland's hymn committee noted in 1885, those who desired to bring hymns by Catholics into Presbyterian hymnals had had to fight with much "vulgar and stupid bigotry."[75]

No bigotry, however, was displayed toward female hymn writers, for the writing of hymns, like the teaching of Sunday school or Bible class, was regarded in the nineteenth century as an eminently respectable activity, for which women's tenderness and sensitivity to suffering particularly fitted them. Many female hymn writers were themselves invalids, and a sense of resignation permeates their work. Such was the case with the two women whose hymns appear in the lists of all the members of the hymnal committee. There was Charlotte Elliott, granddaughter of Wesley's friend Henry Venn, with "My God and Father, While I Stray" and "Just As I Am, Without One Plea," a hymn so popular in the nineteenth century that it was published separately with illustrations and an exposition; and there was Sarah Adams, a Unitarian whose "Nearer, My God, to Thee" ranked high in the Victorian top ten and was welcomed into the Canadian Presbyterian hymnal in the hope that it would be sung "with a believing reference to Christ."[76]

Elliott and Adams, in common with most of the writers represented in the *Hymnal of the Presbyterian Church in Canada*, were from the British Isles; there was merely a scattering of the work of North American writers. Only three (or possibly four) Canadian writers were included in the collection, although, to be sure, the work of one of them, Joseph Scriven's children's hymn "What a Friend We Have in Jesus" had already attained immense popularity on both sides of the Atlantic.[77] No Canadian hymns were featured in the hymnal committee's thirty-nine, and only one American hymn appeared. This was "My Faith Looks Up to Thee," the composition of the contemporary New York Congregational minister Ray Palmer. Its plain and earnest tone appealed to serious-minded Presbyterians and indeed many of Palmer's hymns, as the author of *Our Hymn Writers* pointed out, were "justly prized on both sides of the Atlantic."[78] It was certainly their content and seriousness that were the attraction, and not their U.S. origin; apart from the small presbytery of Stamford, Canadian Presbyterianism had had few close contacts with the United States, and a certain anti-Americanism informed Canadian discussions of hymns and also of their music. As the author of the preface to a Maritime collection of sacred Presbyterian songs assembled in the 1860s remarked, certain American publishers had made "slight . . . but *vicious* alterations in melody and harmony" to the finest tunes introduced

from Great Britain.[79] It should be noted that the period of the compilation of the Canadian hymnal was also the age of Moody and
Sankey, whose celebrated tours created controversy as well as enthusiasm. Many Canadian Presbyterians shared the sentiments quoted
by one pamphleteer that Moody and Sankey were "simply Yankee ad-
venturers of the Barnum type,"[80] whose "gospel songs" were unsuitable if not positively dangerous for Presbyterian congregations. As
Dr. Robb acidly remarked during the hymnody debate, if the newspapers reported that the General Assembly of the Presbyterian Church
in Canada opened by singing a song of praise, no one would suppose
that it began its proceedings with a song of the Moody and Sankey
variety.[81] Nonetheless, one or two "Gospel Hymns" did find their way
into the Canadian hymnal.

There was hostility not merely to the *sentiments* of the Moody and
Sankey songs ("threatening, sadistic, bullying, regressive, self-centred"
are but some of the adjectives applied to them by a modern critic)[82]
but also to their music; tunes were not an unimportant afterthought,
but meant to emphasize the spiritual effects of particular words. The
choice of tunes for the 349 hymns of the *Hymnal of the Presbyterian
Church in Canada,* then, was another potential minefield for the hymnal committee. In the years before the union of 1875, there were criti-
cisms made of the dismal standard of congregational singing,[83] but
there was no unanimity concerning the cure. Was the solution to return to the practices of a perhaps idealized past when the tune "Elgin"
was often sung three times in one day,[84] or should modern tunes,
choirs, and organs be introduced? The musical debate was as vigorous
as the textual, and the same basic division between traditionalists and
modernists existed.

The former certainly had the best of it in the pages of the Canadian *Presbyterian,* where a review of the English Presbyterian hymnal
praised its preference for "simple, quiet, and stately" tunes, of the type
that "used to delight our fathers," and the Church of Scotland *Psalm
and Hymn Tune Book* was similarly praised for its "restoration of noble
old tunes."[85] Many correspondents of the *British American Presbyterian* similarly emphasized the need to use "standard" hymns and tunes
and to avoid "highly seasoned refrains" that would soon pall and tend
to lead to a constant demand for new music.[86] There was no need for

a church to rival "theatres, concert-rooms and other places of amusement," and the effects of hiring a professional quartet or a prima donna who might have sung in the theatre the Saturday night before could only be pernicious.[87] All this was connected by one writer, in a fit of anti-Catholic hysteria, to stained glass, elaborate cathedral architecture, and other aspects of ritualism. A decline to Puseyism and popery was predicted.[88] The question of a congregation's readiness for innovation was also raised, for too many new tunes might cause people to give up. The hazards of fugue arrangements and part-singing were also forcefully expressed. The minister and congregation advised in turn by soprano, alto, tenor, and bass to "Take Thy Pil-, take Thy Pil-" were presumably relieved to have the line finished as "Take Thy Pilgrim to his home."[89]

The hymnal committee was well aware that the acceptability of the new hymnal would to some extent depend on the nature of the tunes selected; yet the members well knew that individual positions on specific hymn tunes were not necessarily the product of any logical process. Dr. Robb, leader of the anti-Hymnal group in the 1878 debate, led the singing at the closing of the General Assembly having chosen a repeating and fugue tune, which, suggested hymnal committee member Robert Murray, "would have deeply distressed and horrified some of the godliest men I ever knew."[90] Hymns were often sung at the committee meetings to test their suitability for congregational use; that this kind of testing was no chore is suggested by a comment in the obituary of a member of the Kirk synod's committee on hymnology in preunion days, referring to happy evenings spent amidst a heap of hymn books of all kinds, when time was forgotten and discussions with fellow enthusiasts went on long into the morning.[91]

Donald Macdonnell, whose knowledge of music was, so his fellow-committee member Robert Murray averred, "always helpful," was made the convenor of the Sub-Committee on Music and by the end of 1880 was able to report that its work was ready for revision and that it recommended that the task be put in the hands of Dr. Edward J. Hopkins, the English Anglican organist of the Temple Church, London, a hymn-tune writer of note and a veteran in the field of musical editorship.[92] The completed manuscript was forwarded to him in 1881, and in the summer Macdonnell traveled to England to discuss the final arrangements. There were days spent in Dover with Hopkins, the work of going over the tune book being varied by dips in the sea, walks along the chalk-cliffs, and a visit to Canterbury Cathedral.[93]

The music finally selected was an interesting combination of "Old Favourites" and "New Style." Not surprisingly, Hopkins himself was strongly represented, with nineteen tunes, one specially written for this collection.[94] Interestingly, however, the composer with the largest number of tunes, at twenty-three, was John Bacchus Dykes, whose "lush chromatic harmonies" and partiality for repeated notes might have been thought insufficiently severe for some Presbyterian tastes but who had achieved widespread popularity by the 1870s.[95] Dykes's work appears in almost every hymn book of the late nineteenth century; indeed, such tunes as "Melita" for "Eternal Father, Strong to Save" and "Hollingside" for "Jesus, Lover of My Soul" seemed to have been indissolubly wedded by "those cunning old match-makers," the compilers of *Hymns Ancient and Modern*.[96] Seven of the eight men in Bradley's "first division" of Victorian English composers together contributed eighty-five tunes to the *Hymnal of the Presbyterian Church in Canada*; his "second division" contributed twelve.[97] In contrast, modern Scottish composers were poorly represented—hardly surprising, perhaps, given the history of church music in Scotland since the Reformation.[98] Contemporary American composers, with more than a dozen tunes, did rather better; Lowell Mason headed the field with ten contributions, including "Missionary Hymn" for Heber's "From Greenland's Icy Mountains," his "best air" in the view of one Canadian Presbyterian.[99] In sum, almost half of the tunes in the *Hymnal of the Presbyterian Church in Canada* were of the nineteenth century, with the majority of them being products of the Anglican choral revival of the period. Composing tunes for hymns was a popular pursuit for both professional and amateur musicians, some of the latter being of the highest rank; the two tunes composed by Prince Albert, "Albert" and "Gotha," both found a home in the Canadian hymnal.

It was a very strong showing for the modernists; how did the traditionalists fare? Almost twenty tunes were drawn from sixteenth and seventeenth Psalters, including the Scottish Psalters of 1615 and 1635, various Genevan, French, and English Psalters,[100] the Welsh Psalter of Archdeacon Prys (1621), and other assorted Swiss and German collections. From Germany there also came more than forty additional tunes, again mainly of the sixteenth and seventeenth centuries. There were five by Luther, or based on his melodies, two each by Neander and Crüger,[101] single tunes by a handful of other German composers and a large number of tunes simply identified as "German" or "from an old German chorale." This was symptomatic of a renewed interest in German hymns[102] and their music in the nineteenth century, a revival appreciated by Presbyterians—or, at least, their ministers—who found in Germany "a field strangely neglected for a long time, but which promises now to furnish us with many noble tunes of the very kind we prefer and need."[103] Perhaps so: but the meters of these hymns were often cumbrous, and some of the hymns put in on the "well, they must go in, whatever the people think" basis.[104] One wonders just how often "Penuel," a Leipzig melody set to one of Catherine Winkworth's translations from the German, "I Will Not Let Thee Go," with a meter of 12.8.10.6.6.10.6 was actually sung by congregations.[105] There was also a small number of "Ancient Tunes"[106] and more than a dozen tunes by well-known composers including Bach, Beethoven, Handel, Purcell, Mendelssohn, and Mozart.[107] The music of the hymnal was completed by a scattering of what were clearly folk tunes, including an "Indian Melody" set to the children's hymn composed by the nineteenth-century Scot, Andrew Young, "There Is a Happy Land."

Although the members of the hymnal committee had undoubtedly cast their net wide in the selection of hymns and tunes and had been careful to solicit the views of the presbyteries, they did not have an entirely easy time of it at the various General Assemblies that discussed their work. Dr. Gregg reported to the 1879 Assembly that the committee had followed the church's instructions and, from approximately one thousand different hymns in the four main hymn books being used as models, they had selected 253.[108] From other sources they had selected twenty-five, and they had also added eleven hymns for the young and eleven doxologies. Sixteen presbyteries had expressed general approval of the selection, two disapproved, seven recommended a year's delay, three expressed no general opinion but remitted some alterations and additions, and six had not yet sent in any report. Furthermore, Gregg continued, in compliance with the recommendations of the presbyteries, several hymns had been omitted, together with a number of verses of other hymns; verbal alterations had been made in some of those remaining. (We should note, however, that the statistics indicated that only a third of the presbyterial suggestions had actually been followed.) The committee report brushed aside criticism of the small number of children's hymns by pointing out that the collection was not one designed for Sunday schools and attempted to deflect Presbyterian concerns about difficult meters by citing figures indicating that only thirty-four were "peculiars" likely to be new to many.

The report did not go unchallenged; an overture from the London and Hamilton Synod recommended that more time was needed to give proper consideration to the hymn book and that the committee ought to be enlarged. Supporters of the overture talked of too few Psalm translations, and one speaker felt that there was such an overreliance on the English Presbyterian *Hymn Book* that the volume might just as well have been adopted in toto. By promising to be ready to receive written suggestions, however, the committee defeated its opponents; the proffered resignations of the coconvenors were rejected.[109]

By the time of the 1880 General Assembly, a words-only edition had been copyrighted and printed, and the music selection was well underway. Old Dr. Cook of St. Andrew's Church, Quebec, might rail at the "namby pamby" nature of many of the hymns and express concern over the dangers of giving six hundred ministers freedom to roam among the numerous hymns of the new collection (now increased to 349), but the committee had essentially presented the Assembly with a fait accompli.[110] Cook's was the sole dissentient vote; the *Hymnal* was approved and commended and the final work on the music was to go ahead, enabling a words and music edition to be published in 1881. Sales were impressive; seventy-five hundred copies at ninety cents each were sold in the first year.[111] It was a vote of confidence in a committee that had succeeded in steering a thoughtful course between the traditional and modern, even if it was apologetic for having deviated at times from stern Presbyterian principles. It had bowed to popular tastes, acknowledging that in a few cases hymns "of a lower order of merit" and tunes "not of the highest class" had been retained.[112]

The *Hymnal* was complete: but not, of course, forever. Soon a separate children's hymnal was published, and there were calls for an edition bound with the Psalms and the Paraphrases and, within a very few years, for general enlargement and revision. There was even a scheme for a common hymnal for all Presbyterian Churches in the empire. The *Hymnal of the Presbyterian Church in Canada*, in common with hymn books of other denominations, turned out to possess a shelf life disproportionately short in comparison to the effort expended by its compilers. And the old arguments certainly continue. A headline in the *London Times* for October 5, 1999, read: "And what has replaced our great hymns? Dumbed-down ditties and lachrymose lullabies. 'Morning Has Broken' makes me shiver."[113]

Notes

1. The phrases in the chapter title are used in the preface to *The Choir: Music for the Use of the Congregations and Families of the Presbyterian Church of the Lower Provinces, British North America* (Halifax: A. and W. Mackinlay, 1879).

2. *Acts and Proceedings of the Fourth General Assembly of the Presbyterian Church in Canada* (Toronto: Presbyterian Print Office, 1878), 88. The four constituent churches were the Canada Presbyterian Church, formed in 1861 from a union of Free and United (Secession) Presbyterian churches (Canada in this title meaning the province of that name, i.e., the modern Ontario and Quebec), the Presbyterian Church of Canada in connection with the Church of Scotland (i.e., the Kirk, to this day the general term in Scotland for the Church of Scotland in the province of Canada), the Presbyterian Church of the Lower Provinces, formed in 1860 from a union of Free and United (Secession) Presbyterian churches, and lastly the Presbyterian Church of the Maritime Provinces in connection with the Church of Scotland.

3. Thus, for example, when the Presbyterian Church of Nova Scotia was considering adopting the Scottish United Presbyterian Hymn Book of 1852, the discussion was deferred until the second week of Synod, when many of the members, both clerical and lay, had already left for home. It was then shelved: see the account of Synod proceedings in *The Missionary Record of the Presbyterian Church of Nova Scotia* 4 (1853): 119.

4. *Basis of Union*, 1875, Canadian Institute for Historical Microreproductions, no. 58897.

5. *British American Presbyterian* 1 (November 15, 1872), letter from "Bar-

rister." This periodical, published weekly, circulated mainly among the members of the Canada Presbyterian Church.

6. John Julian, *A Dictionary of Hymnology* (London: John Murray, 1892), 1023, quoted in Hugh D. McKellar, "150 Years of Presbyterian Hymnody in Canada," *Canadian Society of Presbyterian History Papers* (1986): 2.

7. McKellar, Not until 1868 did the Church of Scotland issue a new, authorized collection of tunes; Julian, *Dictionary of Hymnology*, 1025.

8. On these, see "The Scotch Paraphrases," *The Presbyterian* 22 (1869): 268–71. Five hymns were included with the Paraphrases, including three by Joseph Addison, one by Isaac Watts, and one by Bruce or Logan: see Julian, *Dictionary of Hymnology*, 1033. (*The Presbyterian* represented the views of Presbyterians in the province of Canada who were in connection with the Church of Scotland.)

9. Rev. James Steuart, *Sacred Songs and Hymns on Various Passages of Scripture, Selected for the Congregation at Anderston* (Glasgow: David Niven, 1786). The Relief Church had been formed in 1761 as the result of a secession from the Kirk.

10. A convenient tabular summary is available in Rev. John Young, "Scottish Hymn Books Antecedent to The Church Hymnary," *The Hymn Society of Great Britain and Ireland Bulletin* 3, no. 4 (1952): 59.

11. Sir John Sinclair, ed., *The Statistical Account of Scotland* (Edinburgh: William Creech, 1791–99), 14, 581.

12. Samuel Johnson, *A Journey to the Western Islands of Scotland* (Oxford: Oxford University Press, 1924), 87.

13. E. A. K. McDougall and J. S. Moir, eds., *Selected Correspondence of the Glasgow Colonial Society, 1825–1840* (Toronto: Champlain Society, 1994), 50, 82, 191.

14. Charles Lindsey, *Life and Times of William Lyon Mackenzie* (Toronto: P. R. Randall, 1862) 1:162.

15. Diary of Rev. William Proudfoot, November 15, 1832, J. J. Talman Regional Collection, University of Western Ontario, London, Western Libraries.

16. Minutes of the Presbytery of Halifax, November 19, 1841, United Church Archives, Toronto.

17. For an account of this case and others, see John Banks, "American Presbyterians in the Niagara Peninsula, 1800–1840," *Ontario History* 57, no. 3 (1965): 136–37.

18. *Missionary Register of the Presbyterian Church of Nova Scotia* 4 (1853): 119.

19. *The Presbyterian Record of the Dominion of Canada* 1 (1876): 318.

20. *The Presbyterian* 22 (1869): 83.

21. Rev. Robert Campbell, *On the Union of Presbyterians in Canada* (Mon-

treal: F. Grafton, 1871), 21. A Scottish United Presbyterian Hymn Book had been issued in 1852: see note 3.

22. Editorial in the *British American Presbyterian* 1 (May 31, 1872, June 21, 1872). A detailed exposition of Free Church attitudes can be found in James Begg, *Anarchy in Worship: Or Recent Innovations Contrasted with the Constitution of the Presbyterian Church and the Vows of Her Office-Bearers* (Edinburgh: Lyon and Gemmell, 1875). The work contains sections on such topics as "The Presumptuous and Blasphemous Innovator," "The Popularity Hunting Innovator," and "The Politic and Scheming Innovator."

23. Campbell, *On the Union*, 21.

24. (No author), *The Presbytery of Hamilton, 1836–1967* (Hamilton: Presbyterian Church in Canada, 1967), 78. The worship problems at MacNab Street Church were aired in full at the 1878 General Assembly: see the *Toronto Globe* report, June 17, 1878.

25. The official *Acts and Proceedings* of the General Assembly are brief and dispassionate.

26. George Brown edited the *Globe*, Robert Murray, shortly to be appointed a member of the General Assembly's hymnody committee, edited the *Presbyterian Witness,* and John Dougall, the *Montreal Witness.* Presbyterian periodicals also covered the Assembly's doings, although publications such as the *Presbyterian Record of the Dominion of Canada,* which stated in its very first number (January 1876) that there would be "no place found in its columns for controversy," was hardly likely to convey the full flavor of many discussions.

27. The argument was that the Presbyterian Church had never affirmed the principle of altering and regulating the worship of the church.

28. Principal Grant of Queen's, reported in the *Globe,* June 17, 1878.

29. The fact that Robb's own congregation used the Paraphrases in addition to the Psalms was thus rather surprising: see the editorial comments in the Halifax *Witness,* June 29, 1878.

30. *Globe,* June 17, 1878; *Presbyterian Witness,* June 29, 1878. The speakers here were the Reverend James Thompson, West River, and Mr. Charlton, M.P. The Reverend Andrew Wilson of Kingston also raised the practical issue that some ministers were shut out of pulpits because of their views on hymns.

31. *Globe,* June 17, 18, 1878.

32. *The Presbyterian* 27 (1879): 39.

33. The great Dr. Candlish of Free St. George's Church in Edinburgh once suggested to the Free Church Assembly that twenty-five was the ideal number for a collection of hymns; quoted in *The Presbyterian* 21 (1868): 246. The English Presbyterian Hymn Book of 1867 contained some five hundred.

34. *The Presbyterian Record of the Dominion of Canada* 1 (1876): 30.

35. For a sympathetic account of Macdonnell, see J. F. McCurdy, *Life and Work of D. J. Macdonnell* (Toronto: W. Briggs, 1897); a more judicious assessment is contained in Francess G. Halpenny, ed., *Dictionary of Canadian Biography* (Toronto: University of Toronto Press, 1966) 12:615–18. The trial took up much time in the Presbyterian courts between 1875 and 1877.

36. Arians denied the divinity of Christ; Arminians opposed Calvin's teaching on predestination; Ritualists, with their emphasis on ceremony in the church, were accused in the pages of *The Presbyterian* 24 (1871): 68–69, of proceeding headlong down the road to Rome.

37. The remarks of the Reverend Andrew Wilson, and the Assembly's reactions, were reported in the *Globe,* June 19, 1878, and the *Halifax Witness,* June 29, 1878. The couplet quoted was "my broken body thus I give / For you, for all, take, eat and live." On Protestant fears regarding doctrinally unsuitable communion hymns, see Ian Bradley, *Abide with Me: The World of Victorian Hymns* (London: SCM Press, 1997), 65.

38. Remarks of Mr. Scott, *Globe,* June 17, 1878.

39. Remarks by Mr. Campbellton of New Edinburgh, *Globe,* June 17, 1878.

40. Letter to the *English Churchman,* August 14, 1862, cited in Bradley, *Abide with Me,* 54.

41. *The Presbyterian* 22 (1869): 84. The work could be reviewed in 1869 because a thousand copies had been printed for private circulation and possible comment before the General Assembly of the Church of Scotland gave its approval.

42. Hymn no. 78. All references are to the 1881 words and music edition of the *Hymnal of the Presbyterian Church in Canada* (Toronto: James Campbell and Son); *The Presbyterian* 22 (1869): 84–85. On the "appalling instability" of hymn texts, see J. R. Watson, *The English Hymn: A Critical and Historical Study* (Oxford: Oxford University Press, 1997), 9–10.

43. *The Presbyterian* 22 (1869): 83–84.

44. *The Presbyterian* 22 (1869): 184–85.

45. The members were Drs. Jenkins and Gregg (joint convenors), Professor Mowat, Dr. James, Donald McRae, John Thomson, D. J. Macdonnell, J. S. Black, Robert Murray, and W. B. McMurrich (secretary).

46. The Church of Scotland's *Scottish Hymnal* (1870), the English *Presbyterian Hymn Book* (1867), the United Presbyterian *Hymn Book* (1852, revised edition 1876), and the Free Church *Hymn Book* (1873).

47. W. Barclay McMurrich, *Historical Sketch of the Hymnal Committee of the Presbyterian Church in Canada* (Toronto: Henry Frowde, 1905), 8.

48. Reported in the *Globe,* June 17, 1878, and the *Halifax Witness,* June 22, 1878.

49. R. W. Almond, *Hymns for Occasional Use in the Parish Church of St.*

Peter in Nottingham (Nottingham: H. Barnett, 1819): xi, cited in Watson, *English Hymn,* 267.

50. On Murray, editor of the *Halifax Presbyterian Witness,* see Halpenny, *Dictionary of Canadian Biography* XIII, 755–57. There are six hymns by Murray in the *Hymnal of the Presbyterian Church in Canada.*

51. See note 9.

52. Hymn no. 182. The stanza reads: "Thou on my head in early youth didst smile; And, though rebellious and perverse meanwhile, Thou hast not left me, oft as I left Thee, On to the end, O Lord, abide with me."

A & M, as it is generally known, in many ways set the agenda for hymn discussion in all the Protestant churches.

53. Robert Murray, discussion of the attitudes of his fellow committee member, D. J. Macdonnell, cited in McCurdy, *Life and Work of D. J. Macdonnell,* 187.

54. The bishop's comment is cited in Bradley, *Abide with Me,* 64. For the review comment, see *The Presbyterian* 22 (1869): 185.

55. Watson, *English Hymn,* 295.

56. Lionel Adey, *Class and Idol in the English Hymn* (Vancouver: University of British Columbia Press, 1988), 33. A distinguished team of theologians was consulted by the editors of *Hymns Ancient and Modern* in 1874 on the propriety of retaining the word *husband* in this hymn; Bradley, *Abide with Me,* 67. The hymnal committee did not tamper with it.

57. Joseph Condor, preface to *The Congregational Hymn Book* (n.p.: London, 1836), vii, cited in Watson, *English Hymn,* 335.

58. No author (preface has initials "J. C."), *Our Hymn Writers, Being Biographical Notices of the Hymns, Selected by the Hymn Book Committee of the Presbyterian Church in Canada* (Toronto: James Campbell and Son, 1880), 35. The work appears to have been a product of the hymnal committee.

59. Hymn no. 128, *Hymnal of the Presbyterian Church in Canada.* Gordon Rattray Taylor's interpretation is cited in Susan Tamke, *Make a Joyful Noise unto the Lord: Hymns as a Reflection of Victorian Social Attitudes* (Athens: Ohio University Press, 1978), 38.

60. "He wrote more than Homer; 7,000 hymns of thirty lines each, say; do the sum, gentlemen, and be appalled"; cited in Bradley, *Abide with Me,* 193.

61. *Our Hymn Writers,* 37.

62. *Globe,* June 19, 1878.

63. Joseph Condor, cited in Watson, *English Hymn,* 334.

64. On Montgomery's social reform ideas, see Tamke, *Make a Joyful Noise,* 106–07. The Arabia verse was found only in a few hymn collections: see Julian, *Dictionary of Hymnology,* 480.

65. Watson, *English Hymn,* 316.

66. In the second edition of *The Harmonicon: A Collection of Sacred Music* (Pictou, Nova Scotia: James Dawson, 1841) this hymn is identified as *the* missionary hymn, and its words are given separately at the beginning of the volume. Lowell Mason's later tune for it was simply called "missionary hymn." For modern assessments of this much-discussed (and much-criticized) hymn, see, for example, Tamke, *Make a Joyful Noise,* 125–26, and Watson, *English Hymn,* 322–23.

67. On this problem, which is not confined to Watts, see Bradley, *Abide with Me,* 67.

68. Watson, *English Hymn,* 502. Grant was a member of the Anglican evangelical Clapham sect.

69. *The Presbyterian* 21 (1868): 247–48.

70. Bradley, *Abide with Me,* 77, where Bonar is also identified as "incomparably the greatest Scottish hymn writer"; but see Eric Routley's suggestion that most Bonar hymns have "at least one appalling line," *Hymns and Human Life* (London: John Murray, 1952), 165, 324. It was ironic that Bonar's own church, Chalmers Memorial Free Church, Edinburgh, did not accept the use of hymns in services for some years after the publication of the Free Church Hymn Book of 1882.

71. Italics mine. See *The Presbyterian* 22 (1869): 186 for worries regarding the attitude of "old Presbyterian pillars" to this hymn.

72. The Oxford Movement was a high Anglican movement that aimed to repel liberal attacks on the church and to restore its ancient rituals.

73. The phrase is Bradley's: see *Abide with Me,* 23.

74. It also appeared exactly as written by Newman. For a brilliant discussion of this hymn and of its textual vicissitudes, see Owen Chadwick, *The Spirit of the Oxford Movement* (Cambridge: Cambridge University Press, 1990), chap. 4.

75. Letter from A. H. K. Boyd to the proprietors of *Hymns Ancient and Modern,* July 7, 1885, cited in Bradley, *Abide with Me,* 77.

76. *Our Hymn Writers,* 1; Bradley, *Abide with Me,* 90.

77. The three Canadians were Robert Murray (see note 51); Charles Cameron, a minister from Ottawa (see *Our Hymn Writers,* 10); and Scriven, whose name does not appear in the list of authors at the back of the hymnal, "What a Friend" being attributed simply to "Faith Hymns." The first ascription to Scriven was in a hymn collection published in 1886. On Scriven, see *Dictionary of Canadian Biography* XI: 803–04. The probable fourth Canadian is "J," who may well be Dr. Jenkins or Dr. James of the hymnal committee, just as "M" is Murray.

78. *Our Hymn Writers,* 30.

79. Italics mine. Preface to *The Choir.*

80. George Sexton, *An Impartial Review of the Revival Movement of Messrs Moody and Sankey* (London: n.p., 1875), 4, cited in Watson, *English Hymn,* 491.

81. *The Globe,* June 18, 1878. We should note, however, the strong impact of Moody and Sankey's Scottish tour of 1873 and the close, if somewhat unlikely, friendship that grew up between Sankey and the distinguished Free Church minister and hymn writer Horatius Bonar; the first gospel song tune Sankey ever wrote was for Bonar's "Yet There Is Room"; see Bradley, *Abide with Me,* 181–82. Furthermore, Scriven's "What a Friend We Have in Jesus" (Hymn no. 144 in the *Hymnal of the Presbyterian Church in Canada*) was popularized by Ira Sankey, while "Jesus of Nazareth Passeth By" (Hymn no. 43), the work of the American Eta Campbell, was also a favorite Sankey solo.

82. Watson, *English Hymn,* 493.

83. See, for example, James Croil, *A Historical and Statistical Report of the Presbyterian Church in Canada in Connection with the Church of Scotland for the Year 1866* (Montreal: J. Lovell, 1868).

84. Letter from "An Old Scotsman" to the *British American Presbyterian* 2 (1873): 5.

85. *The Presbyterian* 21 (1868): 249; 22 (1869): 338. "Dundee," "Elgin," and the "Old Hundred," the very tunes desired by William Lyon Mackenzie back in the Upper Canada of the 1820s, were specifically mentioned. See note 14.

86. *British American Presbyterian* 1 (December 6, 1872): 5.

87. Some leading New York churches were said to pay as much as $1500 to their leading lady singers; *British American Presbyterian* 1 (December 20, 1872), 2 (January 10, 1873).

88. *British American Presbyterian* 2 (January 10, 1873). Edward Pusey was a leader of the Oxford Movement.

89. *British American Presbyterian* 1 (November 29, 1872). For other examples of ludicrous effects, such as "And catch the flee—And catch the flee—And catch the fleeting hour," see Percy A. Scholes, *The Oxford Companion to Music,* 9th ed. (London: Oxford University Press, 1956), 503.

90. *Presbyterian Witness,* June 29, 1878.

91. *The Presbyterian* 27 (1874): 39, obituary of Francis Nicol. For Bradley's comments on the pleasures of compiling hymn books, see *Abide with Me,* 54.

92. On Hopkins, see Sir Sidney Lee, ed. *Dictionary of National Biography, Twentieth Century: 1901–1911* (Oxford: Oxford University Press, 1912), 301. Hopkins had already edited the hymnal of the Scottish Free Church. Bradley, *Abide with Me,* 148, notes that many other Protestant churches turned to Anglican composers for tunes and musical editorship. For Murray's comment on Macdonnell, see McCurdy, *Life of D. J. Macdonnell,* 187.

93. McCurdy, *Life and Work of D. J. Macdonnell,* 188.

94. This was "Gloria in Excelsis," for Hymn 349. McMurrich, *Historical Sketch,* 18, notes Hopkins's generosity in donating the use of his hymns to the committee.

95. To dismiss Dykes (together with Henry Gauntlett, John Stainer, and Arthur Sullivan) as "trivial and sentimental ear-ticklers" seems, as Bradley suggests, an overly harsh judgment; see *Abide with Me,* 227, citing Kenneth Long, *The Music of the English Church* (London: Hodder and Stoughton, 1971), 359.

96. Bradley, *Abide with Me,* 72, 147.

97. The "first division" comprised John Bacchus Dykes, Joseph Barnby (none of whose tunes was included in the hymnal), Henry Gauntlett, Henry Smart, Edward Hopkins, Arthur Sullivan, William Henry Monk, and John Stainer. The "second division" comprised Samuel Sebastian Wesley, Richard Redhead (only one contribution, but that one the famous "Petra," for "Rock of Ages"), George Elvey, Charles Steggall, John Goss, and Herbert Oakeley.

98. Scottish tunes included John Turnbull's "Torwood" for "I Heard the Voice of Jesus Say," Alexander Ewing's "Ewing" for "Jerusalem the Golden" and "Kilmarnock," the work of Neil Douglas, the blind precentor of Greenock, for "How Are Thy Servants Blest, O Lord!"

99. *The Presbyterian* 21 (1868): 280; the writer was commenting on its unfortunate omission from the English Presbyterian *Hymn Book.* On Dr. Mason, see Scholes, *Oxford Companion to Music,* 609.

100. For example, the "Old Hundredth" was drawn from Marot and Beza's Geneva Psalter of 1551.

101. On Joachim Neander and Johann Crüger, see Julian, *Dictionary of Hymnology,* 271–72, 790–92.

102. Women were particularly prolific in providing translations from the German; several examples by Frances Cox and Catherine Winkworth appear in the hymnal.

103. *The Presbyterian* 21 (1868): 249.

104. This was a comment on the large number of German hymns in the *Scottish Hymnal: The Presbyterian* 22 (1869): 184.

105. Of the meters in the hymnal, the three "ordinary" meters, Common (8.6.8.6), Short (6.6.8.6), and Long (8.8.8.8) are outnumbered by other meters approximately two to one. For a thoughtful discussion of hymn singing and meter, see Watson, *English Hymn,* chap. 2.

106. See, for example, "Palestine," Old Latin, seventh century.

107. It must be said that "Thanksgiving," a tune "from Mozart's Figario" [*sic*], was not a happy choice.

108. This description of the 1879 General Assembly is based on the *Acts*

and Proceedings of the Presbyterian Church in Canada (Toronto: Presbyterian Print Office, 1879) and the *Globe,* June 21, 1879.

109. *Globe,* June 21, 1879.

110. *Acts and Proceedings of the General Assembly of the Presbyterian Church in Canada, 1880* (Toronto: Presbyterian Print Office, 1880), appendix, cxxxiv–v. In the end, 223 were taken from the most recent United Presbyterian *Hymnal,* 135 were from the old one, 213 were from the English *Presbyterian Hymn Book,* 165 were from the *Scottish Hymnal,* and 75 were from the *Free Church Hymn Book,* nearly the whole of this last collection.

111. McMurrich, *Historical Sketch,* 29.

112. Note by the Committee on Tunes, prefaced to the *Hymnal of the Presbyterian Church in Canada.*

113. Norman St. John-Stevas.

4

In the Shadow of Calvin and Watts

Twentieth-Century American Presbyterians and Their Hymnals

Darryl G. Hart

Arguably one of the best books ever written on congregational and liturgical song is Thomas Day's *Why Catholics Can't Sing*.[1] If not the best, it is the funniest, such as when Day describes a memorable scene in which his friend is trying to pass the peace to an elderly woman who is absorbed with her rosary beads during Mass at Philadelphia's Cathedral. The response from the woman to "may the peace of the Lord be with you" cannot be found in any Christian liturgy nor is it repeatable in polite company.[2] But it wonderfully captured the problem Day set out to explain, namely, why it was that Catholic congregations' participation in the liturgy, especially in congregational singing, was about as warm as this hoary Catholic woman's response to the Handshake of Peace. Here is how Day described the difficulty: "Today, a large number of Roman Catholics in the United States who go to church regularly—perhaps the majority—rarely or barely sing any of the music. . . . [T]his stands out as a most curious development in the history of Christianity."[3]

What is interesting about Day's book for what follows is the contrast he draws between Catholics and Presbyterians. While in graduate school Day worked as a substitute organist, playing in Catholic and Presbyterian churches. The difference between these two services, especially because the congregations sometimes sang the exact same hymn, was, in Day's estimate, amazing. "Why," Day asked, "did the small Presbyterian church make such a joyful noise, while the Catholics sounded almost in pain?" It was not because Presbyterians alone were such good singers. Day also acknowledged that he had been in Episcopalian churches where fifty church members produced "more volume than three hundred Roman Catholics."[4] From Day's perspective this indicated that Protestants are healthier than Catholics. "When hundreds of parishioners packed into a church do not even make an attempt to sing "Silent Night" . . . you have a religious, social, and cultural breakdown of astounding proportions."[5]

The history of Presbyterian hymnody and its twentieth-century hymnals might prompt Day to revise his assessment of Protestant singing. To be sure, Day is correct to observe that Presbyterians, both mainline and sideline, sing well, often, and with gusto. But after examining their thick hymnals with short shelf lives, along with Presbyterian writing about corporate worship, one could legitimately ask whether Presbyterians know why they sing. In other words, the volume of singing alone may not be a reliable index of liturgical well-being, just as the consumption of large quantities of food does not make one a gourmet. What believers sing is just as important. And the history of Presbyterian hymnals in the last century indicates that the liturgical heirs of John Calvin and John Knox have acquired an undiscriminating taste for congregational song. At the same time, Presbyterians do not complain much. Presbyterians are likely to sing whatever hymns their denominational committees offer.

This may not in itself be a lamentable condition, and it is by no means one that Presbyterians bear alone. But it does provide a useful gauge to measure the direction of Presbyterian worship practices. In fact, recent developments in Presbyterian hymnody indicate the liturgical thin ice on which American Presbyterians tread every time they gather for worship. Over the past 250 years, Presbyterianism, and the Reformed tradition more generally, has not distinguished itself as fertile ground for the making of hymns, especially compared to other Protestant traditions. Lutherans have Bach, Episcopalians have Ralph Vaughan Williams, Methodists have Charles Wesley, and Pentecostals have Jack Hayford. The closest Presbyterians have come to making a contribution to Protestant hymnody is Louis F. Benson, perhaps the twentieth century's leading student of hymns, but not much of a producer of song for corporate worship. Part of the trouble for Calvinists is the legacy of exclusive psalmody. As Benson himself put it in the Stone Lectures he gave at Princeton Seminary in 1927, the musical bind in which Presbyterians historically found themselves was as old as the Christian Church. "Has the Church a right," he asked, "to supersede or even enlarge the hymn book that is of canonical authority? Is it not audacious to supplement inspired Psalms with handmade hymns?" Benson then went one step farther. "Even if it be lawful" to replace Psalms with hymns, "is it expedient?" This was, in his estimation, even as late as the 1920s, well after mainline American Presbyterianism had introduced hymns into corporate worship, "the issue" not just for Benson's fellow Presbyterians but for all Christians.[6]

As it turns out, what for Benson was "the issue" has not been much of a factor for Presbyterians and the hymnals they have produced. If their books of song show anything, it is that Presbyterians sing a lot but do not have much of an idea why they sing what they do. Following is an analysis of the most popular hymns (i.e., the most frequently published) in twentieth-century Presbyterian hymnals, both mainline and sideline, with some attempt to explain these preferences.[7] What this study shows is that so-called conservative and liberal Presbyterians, contrary to the oft-repeated claim that "theology matters," have roughly the same favorite hymns, still pay deference to the tradition of psalmody, and sing hymns mainly for pedagogical or homiletical reasons. The explanation for these similarities has as much to do with liturgical developments in the seventeenth and eighteenth centuries as it does with the particulars of twentieth-century American Presbyterianism. Whatever Presbyterian hymnals reveal about the liturgical health of the Reformed tradition in the United States, the Presbyterian experience illustrates perhaps the most important lesson taught by evangelical hymnody over the last century: the trend that encourages greater ecumenicity through song also functions as a generic solvent of historic liturgical and theological traditions.

Presbyterian Song before Benson

The nine hymnals that Presbyterians have produced for corporate worship over the last century must be regarded first in the context of Calvin's Anglo-American descendants' inexperience with hymns.[8] Here it is important to remember that American Presbyterians did not create their first hymnal until 1831, and they were among the first in the Reformed tradition to do so. In other words, only after 125 years of Presbyterian history in the New World did the Reformed branch of the Protestant Reformation officially embrace hymnody. By

1831, American Presbyterians apparently felt the need to make up for lost time, producing nine different hymnals over the rest of the nineteenth century. With the addition of eight more during the twentieth century, American Presbyterians have, since 1831, gone through seventeen official denominationally sponsored hymnals for use in corporate worship. This pattern averages at a staggering rate of a new Presbyterian hymnal every decade.[9]

One of the major reasons that American Presbyterians have apparently rushed into the business of making many hymnals may be that, coming out of the Protestant Reformation, the prospects for Presbyterian hymnody were grim. The gravity of worship and the fear of blasphemy made the Calvinistic wing of the Reformation extremely wary about what went on during the course of a service. As a result, two positions emerged: one propounded by the churches in Zurich under the direction of Ulrich Zwingli and Heinrich Bullinger, the other articulated by the churches in Geneva, led by John Calvin. Although Zwingli was likely the best musician among the Reformers, he removed song from worship, in part because of its potentially destructive power and also because he found no biblical warrant for singing in worship. He acknowledged that the apostle Paul did in fact teach Christians to sing (e.g., Colossians 3:16), but countered that this instruction did not necessarily address corporate worship. In fact, Paul's meaning was for believers to sing "in their hearts," not necessarily with their mouths. Consequently, aside from removing organs from Zurich's churches, Zwingli went one better and left song out of Reformed worship. Nowhere is this liturgical point more evident than in the *Second Helvetic Confession,* written by Zwingli's successor, Bullinger, who made congregational singing optional. Chapter 23 of the confession reads, "If there be any churches which have faithful prayer in good manner, without any singing, they are not therefore to be condemned, for all churches have not the advantage and opportunity of sacred music."[10]

In Geneva things were not as austere for worshipers gifted with good voices. Calvin did eliminate organs, like Zwingli, not because he despised music, but because he understood its attraction and potential for abuse, especially without words. But Calvin departed from Zwingli's spiritualizing of the Pauline writings about song. Believers should really sing, both with voice and heart. The question, then, was what to sing. Calvin's answer was simple—the Psalms. He believed this was the pattern of the early church, which picked up the practice of worship in the synagogue. Calvin also thought song's function in worship was a form of prayer. What better words to use in praying to God than the ones he had inspired? Calvin's understanding of song prompted the Geneva churches to commission the production of a Psalter from Clement Marot, Theodore Beza (who supplied the verse), and Louis Bourgeois (who wrote the tunes). The Geneva Psalter went through seven editions in Calvin's lifetime (1539, 1541, 1543, 1545, 1551, 1554, and 1562), with the final edition including all 150 Psalms, with 125 tunes and 110 different meters.[11]

For Presbyterians and Puritans (Reformed also, for that matter) who sided with Calvin over Zwingli, the way to sing in congregational worship was from a Psalter. Indeed, the seventeenth century witnessed little deviation from Calvin's norm, whether in the Church of England, the Church of Scotland, or the dissenting Protestant churches. For Anglicans, Sternhold and Hopkins, a Psalter produced during the reign of Edward VI, or Tate and Brady's version published in 1696 were the only Psalters authorized for use in public worship.[12] The Scottish Kirk produced a Psalter as early as 1564, before Andro Hart issued another in 1615, which in 1635 was reissued and updated by Hart's heirs.[13] When Presbyterians began in the early eighteenth century to show up in the North American British colonies in numbers large enough to merit a denomination, they carried their Psalters with them. In fact, the Old Side-New Side controversy that led to the first rupture of American Presbyterianism in 1741 may have been as much about rival Psalters as it was about George Whitefield's revivals and subscription to the Westminster Confession of Faith and Catechisms. The stodgier old side used *The Psalms of David in English Meter*, prepared in 1643 by Francis Rous, a Presbyterian-turned-Independent and member of the Westminster Assembly, or that of another Puritan, William Barton's *Book of Psalms in Metre* (1644). The more innovative New Side preferred Tate and Brady.[14]

What also contributed to the Old Side-New Side struggle was the introduction of a new type of song to churches where metrical psalms had been the norm. The source of this novelty was Benjamin Franklin's publication in 1729 of the first American edition of Isaac Watts's *The Psalms of David Imitated*. To be sure, Watts's songs were not full-blown hymns such as the ones he wrote for *Hymns and Spiritual Songs* (1707), which were compositions based on scriptural thoughts as well as the fullness of biblical revelation in the New Testament. In his imitations of the Psalter, Watts was simply trying to present psalms in a way "accommodated to modern Gospel worship."[15] Even so, Watts's Christianizing of the psalms was an explicit break with the tradition of metrical psalmody that had prevailed among Presbyterians and Reformed Christians since Calvin.[16]

Watts's renovated psalmody slowly gained a foothold among colonial Presbyterians during the revivals for which George Whitefield became the cause celebre. The initial publication of Watts in 1729 would have to wait until 1741 for a second edition.[17] The New Side who supported Whitefield tended to be the ones buying copies of Watts's gospel psalms. As early as 1746, Whitefield's Presbyterian sympathizers in Newburyport began to use Watts, and soon thereafter the presbytery of Boston followed suit.[18] Whitefield himself actively promoted Watts's *Hymns* and *Psalms*, which, according to Henry Wilder Foote, the revivalist "greatly admired." Foote also states that Whitefield prompted Jonathan Edwards to introduce Watts into public worship at his Northampton church.[19] In the South, as early as 1752, Samuel Davies, an itinerant evangelist in Virginia, introduced not only Watts's psalms but also his hymns. When Davies left Virginia to preside over the newly founded College of New Jersey, a New Side institution, his successor, John Todd, petitioned his presbytery to approve the use of Watts's psalms and hymns because the churches "have received great advantage" from the writer's "excellent compositions, especially his sacramental hymns."[20]

During the seventeen years that the Old Side Presbyterian Church ministered separately from the New Side, Watts's imitations never became an issue. The ethnic composition of the Old Side helps to explain this absence. As a communion that was predominantly Scotch-Irish, the Old Side churches were devoted to Rous's version of the psalms and fully prepared to resist innovation. So adamant could the Scotch-Irish be in their opposition to new songs that in 1756 New York's "Scotch Church" withdrew from the synod of New York (a New Side body) to align with the Associate Presbytery, a communion composed of secessionist churches from the Church of Scotland. By 1765, after the reunion of the old and new sides, the issue was hardly settled, even though banning Watts was impossible to enforce. In a dispute over the proper content of song in worship, the synod of New York and Philadelphia ruled that "the inspired Psalms in Scripture" were "proper matter to be sung in Divine worship, according to their original design and the practice of the Christian churches." At the same time, the synod refused to "forbid" those "whose judgment and inclination lead them to use the imitation of psalms."[21]

From 1765 until 1831, American Presbyterians were truly conflicted over congregational song. Watts gained in popularity as his work came out in newer and better editions. At the same time, many Presbyterians continued in their attachment to Rous's version. Even though a denominationally approved hymnal would have to wait until the fourth decade of the nineteenth century, the first General Assembly of American Presbyterians in effect settled the controversy when, in 1788, it adopted its first *Directory for the Worship of God*. Instead of saying that the "duty of Christians was to praise God publiquely by singing Psalms," as a first draft had it, following the lead of the Westminster Assembly's *Directory*, the General Assembly stated instead that the duty of believers in public praise was to sing "psalms and hymns."[22] Because for Presbyterians in the new nation the words *hymns* and *Watts* were synonymous, Watts's *Hymns*, according to Louis Benson, "may be called the first hymn book of American Presbyterians."[23] Until 1831, Watts and Rous would be the texts that Presbyterians used in corporate worship.[24]

The primacy of Watts and metrical psalmody, then, is the best framework for trying to make sense of the many hymnals that Presbyterians have published. The Anglo-American liturgical descendants of John Calvin have felt a duty to show allegiance to metrical psalms even while they may prefer to sing the Christianized verse of Watts. The very first official Presbyterian hymnal of 1831 reflected this tension. It began with an entire metrical Psalter, and to it the committee added 531 hymns, 199 of which were by Watts.[25] Although the numbers have changed, twentieth-century Presbyterian hymnals display a similarly high proportion of psalms and Watts. This is true even after accounting for theological differences among mainline and sideline Presbyterians. No matter whether Presbyterians are sympathetic to J. Gresham Machen or Eugene Carson Blake, chances are their hymnals will look similar to that of their Presbyterian great-grandparents.

In other words, twentieth-century theological conflicts and ecclesiastical separations among Presbyterians in the United States have done little to change the pattern established once American Presbyterians first chose to add Watts's imitations to the metrical versions of King David's real Psalms.

Presbyterians Prefer Watts

In his book on Protestant church music, Robert Stevenson makes the astute observation that Isaac Watts is the favorite among Presbyterians, Charles Wesley among Methodists, and the Anglican high-churchman, John Mason Neale, the choice of Episcopalians.[26] In fact, Stevenson's calculations are accurate even if his presentation of them slightly misrepresents the numbers. Watts is undoubtedly the most frequently included author in Presbyterian hymnals. Of the eight hymn books produced in the twentieth century, Watts accounts for 155 separate titles, and these make up 295 of the grand total of hymns in Presbyterian hymnals (which is roughly six percent of the 4,871 total hymns). The runners up to Watts are Charles Wesley appearing with 137 total hymns in all the hymn books, the translations of German hymns by Catherine Winkworth appearing 119 times, Neale's translations and hymns appearing 109 times, and the Scottish Free Church minister Horatius Bonar appearing with 80 hymns in the eight hymnals. Another way of putting it is to say that the average twentieth-century Presbyterian hymnal has thirty-seven hymns by Watts, seventeen by Wesley and Neale combined, fifteen by Winkworth, and ten by Bonar. A sampling of other Reformed, Lutheran, and Episcopal hymn books supports Stevenson's contention about Presbyterians' preference for Watts. In these other collections, Neale is the most popular, accounting on average for eighteen per hymnal; next is Wesley, who averaged seventeen; followed by Watts at sixteen, Winkworth at fifteen, and Bonar at seven.[27]

These numbers represent for the twentieth century something of a decline in Watts's popularity compared to nineteenth-century patterns. For instance, as early as 1834, Watts accounted for one-third of the hymns in the German Reformed Church's *Psalms and Hymns*. At the end of the century, a survey of 750 hymn books in 1891 revealed that two-fifths of the hymns printed were written by Watts. And seven years later a study of the thirty-two most popular English hymns included five by Watts. These statistics may explain the composition of the first two Presbyterian hymn books of the twentieth century, the southern Presbyterian Church's *New Psalms and Hymns* (1901) and the northern Presbyterian Church's 1911 revision of *The Hymnal* (1895). Southern Presbyterians had 127 Watts hymns from which to choose in contrast to the forty-nine available to northern Presbyterians. By 1990, when Great Commission Publication revised *The Trinity Hymnal,* the favorite among the sideline denominations, the Presbyterian Church in America and the Orthodox Presbyterian Church, Watts was still holding strong with thirty-six hymns, whereas the mainline Presbyterian Church, U.S.A.'s hymnal of the same year had only thirteen Watts hymns (seven behind the most frequent author, Neale). One of the obvious reasons for Watts' decline over the twentieth century has been the growing awareness of Christian hymnody and efforts by denominations to reflect an ecumenical posture in congregational song. This also accounts for the disparity of Watts hymns between the northern and southern churches' hymn books of 1901 and 1911. The northern church's 1911 hymnal relied on the efforts of Louis F. Benson, whose knowledge of the variety of hymns was vast and so did not feature Watts to the same degree as his peers to the south.

Despite the steady decline of Watts's hymns throughout twentieth-century Presbyterian hymnals, he continues to receive the most attention from Presbyterian authors writing about worship. According to Hughes Oliphant Old, a mainline Presbyterian pastor and professor of homiletics at Princeton Seminary, Watts "exemplifies the Reformed doxological tradition at its best." His "hymnody springs from the psalmody" and its "devotional quality" is "unsurpassed."[28] Old's comments are worth highlighting because they come from a book that may well rank as one of the most thoughtful arguments for historic Reformed worship written in the last 150 years. And yet, even among the proponents of liturgical conservation, what were innovative practices by sixteenth- and seventeenth-century standards now provide the best resources for congregational song.

The affinity between Watts and twentieth-century liturgical traditionalists finds additional support in the work of Horton Davies, longtime professor of religious history at Princeton University and a

Congregationalist minister. In his monumental study of Puritan worship, Davies curiously presents Watts as the culmination of psalmody among the Puritans. By Watts's "brave defence of the right to paraphrase the songs of the Old Dispensation in the interests of the New," Davies asserts, "he was delivering the Puritans from the Bibliolatry of the literalists." Davies even goes so far as to say of Watts's hymns and paraphrases that "they are the finest flowers of Puritan piety."[29] Considering how long it took for Watts to gain a following among the Puritans' Presbyterian and Congregationalist heirs, Davies's attempt to hitch the father of English hymnody to the wagon of traditional metrical psalmody could arguably be deemed a stretch. But after two centuries of Presbyterian congregational singing, trying to tell the difference between Watts and historic Reformed practices in congregational song has become almost impossible.[30] This may explain Stevenson's biting remark that "in our day Calvin's precepts on church music are more honored in the breach than in the observance."[31] More winsome but equally apt is Louis F. Benson's remark "that the hymns of this innovator should thus become a badge and symbol of orthodoxy and conservatism in the churches that once disputed his way is an illustration of personal influence not easy to parallel."[32]

Davies's and Old's evaluations may reflect a certain form of Presbyterian naiveté about Protestant hymnody, but Benson, perhaps the leading student of hymns and a Presbyterian in his own right, provides ample justification for Watts's importance to Presbyterians. Benson did not always regard Watts's hymns as the best and, in fact, argued that the English Independent's popularity may have retarded the development of Presbyterian hymnody. During the early nineteenth century, for instance, when revivals spawned "fresh" and "new types" of hymns, Presbyterians remained stuck with Watts, which, according to Benson, seemed "like a step backward."[33] Even so, the contribution of Watts was in its context "so glaringly original" that Benson, in his lectures at Princeton Seminary in 1927, gave Watts a place equal to that of the early church, Greek and Latin hymns, Luther, and Calvin. "The fetters, whether of obligation, or of prudence, or of use and wont, that held the Church's songs so close to the letter of Scripture," Benson summarized, "were in the minds and habits of English-speaking Christians finally severed by Dr. Watts."[34] In a backhanded way, Benson explained the appeal of Watts to Presbyterians. The quality of his hymns may not have been as good as other authors, but by inaugurating a new era of congregational song, especially for communions that only sang metrical psalms, Watts became for Presbyterians the way to justify singing hymns, a justification that would always tip the scales in favor of Watts's compositions.

The popularity of Watts, however, did not prevent the Wesley brothers, especially Charles, from establishing a discernible presence in twentieth-century Presbyterian hymnals. In fact, of the ten hymns to appear in every Presbyterian hymnal produced over the last century, Charles Wesley wrote twice as many as Watts. The most popular Wesley hymns among Presbyterians have been "Christ, Whose Glory Fills the Skies"; "Hark! The Herald Angels Sing"; "Come, Thou Long-Expected Jesus"; "Ye Servants of God, Your Master Proclaim"; "Rejoice, the Lord Is King"; and "Love Divine, All Loves Excelling."[35] The three by Watts to be printed in every hymnal are "Our God, Our Help in Ages Past"; "Joy to the World, The Lord Is Come"; and "When I Survey the Wondrous Cross." Rounding out the top ten Presbyterian hymns of the twentieth century is one by Horatius Bonar: "Here, O My Lord, I See."[36]

In the category of hymns to appear in all but one of the Presbyterian hymn books, Watts wrote two: "Alas! And Did My Savior Bleed?" and "From All That Dwell Below the Skies." Wesley wrote one "O For a Thousand Tongues to Sing."[37] The third most popular group of hymns, that is, the ones to appear in all but two of the hymnals, totaled six, with four by Wesley ("Jesus, Lover of My Soul"; "Soldiers of Christ, Arise"; "Jesus Christ Is Risen Today"; and "Lo! He Comes, With Clouds Descending") and one by Watts ("Jesus Shall Reign Wher'ere the Sun") and one by Bonar: "Blessing and Honor and Glory").[38] Part of the explanation for Wesley's popularity among lovers of Watts is the sheer volume of the Methodist's hymns, which numbered more than 6,000 compared to Watts's combined effort of approximately 700 hymns and psalm imitations.[39]

Still, the Presbyterian use of Wesleyan hymnody is one of those liturgical curiosities that deserves some comment, especially considering that many of Charles Wesley's hymns pertained to the Christian life and that Calvinists and Wesleyans disagree fairly vigorously on sanctification. Benson contends that the reception of Wesley's hymns was gradual over the course of the nineteenth century. The reason had to do with the nature of the Methodist movement itself. Whereas Watts "moved on the social uplands of English Nonconformity," Wesley worked "behind the hedges," and so Methodists were regarded "as schismatics," "ranters," "sentimentalists," and "sensationalists."[40] So great was the isolation of Methodism and its hymnody from other Protestants that, according to Benson, when Wesley's hymns began to appear in the nineteenth century, compilers often printed them anonymously or attributed them to other authors. Even as accomplished a student of hymns as John Mason Neale was, in 1850, he could not identify the author of "Hark! The Herald Angels Sing," attributing it instead to Philip Doddridge.[41] Benson, perhaps being overly charitable to fellow Calvinists, did not believe such mistakes to be evidence of a conspiracy. "There was a common ignorance concerning Charles Wesley and his work," Benson explained. Even so, all's well that ends well, and in Benson's estimation, once other Protestants came to realize the extent of Wesley's contribution, they also recognized the "large area of Christian truth and feeling which all the Churches hold in common."[42]

This happy spin, however, could not overcome the tension that Benson himself recognized in the experiential quality of Wesley's hymns. And this tension points to the unstable compound produced when mixing Presbyterian doctrine and Wesleyan piety. For instance, in his discussion of "Jesus, Lover of My Soul" for *Studies of Familiar Hymns,* Benson could not help asking whether "a lyric so tender and deeply felt should be used in public worship or reserved for private devotion." He went on to quote an English bishop who thought Wesley's verse "inexpressibly shocking" to put such sentiments "into the mouths of a large and mixed gathering of people." Benson even noted that "actual investigations" found this hymn to be one of the three favored by "English tramps." To the defensive response of noting that the apostle John, who lay on the bosom of the Lord, could have penned these lines, Benson replied, "We are not all St. Johns."[43]

This line of criticism dovetailed with Benson's general assessment of Wesley's "hymnody of the Methodist revival." Unlike Watts, who broke the back of the Psalter's reign within congregational singing, Wesley's chief contribution was twofold, aside from raising a new literary standard for hymnody. First, he introduced the genre of evangelistic hymn "as we use that term to-day."[44] These hymns were designed "to bring the unchurched and saved within the sound of the gospel" and lead to conversion. For Benson, this explained why the first section of the original collection of Methodist hymns was titled "Exhorting and Entreating to Return to God." Second, Wesley turned hymnody in the direction of Christian experience. In fact, Benson thought Wesley conceived of hymnody primarily as a "manual of spiritual discipline." The experience that Wesley charted may too often have been his own. And Benson had reservations about the autobiographical nature of the Methodist's hymns, namely, whether the individual author's experience was "fitted to be a norm of Christian experience in general," or whether such expression made the one singing guilty of "religious insincerity." Nevertheless, Wesley's hymns charted "with firmness and precision" the entire scope of "the operations of the Spirit in the heart."[45]

Although Benson appeared to be assessing Wesley more from the perspective of his own study (and possibly preferences) as a hymnologist rather than as a Presbyterian churchman, his objections may in fact help to account for the Presbyterian adoption of Wesleyan hymnody. Ever since the First Great Awakening, the division between Old and New Side Presbyterians in 1741, and their subsequent reunion in 1758, American Presbyterians have embraced the revival as a beneficial means of reaching new converts and invigorating old ones.[46] In other words, Presbyterians in the mainstream American denominations would not necessarily have had objections in principle to the evangelistic purposes or experiential piety involved in Wesley's hymns. Presbyterians did take a while to include his compositions in their hymnals. But even if their confession and catechisms articulated a piety that was oriented more toward the objective character of Christianity than to the subjective experience of the Christian, Presbyterian history from 1750 to 1900 made Presbyterians susceptible to Wesley's intimate and soul-wrenching sentiments.[47]

Even so, the attraction of Wesley for Presbyterians may have very well stemmed from their reliance upon Watts. Indeed, Watts's hymns of "divine love" delved into matters of the heart in ways that many of his contemporaries and later commentators would find unprecedented. For instance, John Wesley, who omitted his brother's "Jesus,

Lover of My Soul," from the Methodist Collection of hymns, wrote that Watts offended him "in a more gross manner than in anything which was before published in the English tongue." He faulted Watts especially for inserting "coarse expressions" in "spiritual hymns." "How often," Wesley complained, "in the midst of excellent verse, are lines inserted which disgrace those that precede and follow."[48] Robert Stevenson more recently commented on the amorous quality of the English Dissenter's verse, such as when Watts refers to Christ's "sweet Lips" and "Heavenly Look" that "seek my kisses and my Love." Stevenson also noted that Watts's use of the word *die,* such as in a line about the believer dissolving in the arms of Christ like "the Billows [that] after Billow rolls to kiss the Shoar, and Dye," had perhaps not the most fitting of connotations in the context of eighteenth-century romantic poetry.[49]

Explaining Bonar's popularity among twentieth-century Presbyterians is less difficult than accounting for Wesley's, because the appeal turns out to be similar. A minister in the Free Church of Scotland, first in Kelso and later in Edinburgh, Bonar (1808–89) was, at least by Benson's reckoning, "the greatest of Scottish hymn writers."[50] He is also, according to Benson, the only answer to the charge that Presbyterians have not written hymns of lasting value for congregational song.[51] That attribute alone may explain why Bonar has the number of hymns found in twentieth-century Presbyterian hymnals. It is just as likely that Benson was correct when he asserted that the denominational identity of hymn writers is insignificant. "We choose our hymns for what they are," he wrote, thus making "the modern hymn book" the best expression of "church unity so far achieved."[52]

An explanation of Bonar's appeal to twentieth-century Presbyterians is the emotional character of his lyric. According to Benson, one bishop in the Church of England thought Bonar's hymns belonged "to the class known as 'subjective hymns' or 'hymns of inward experience.'"[53] Benson himself concluded that Bonar was more like the "writers of the Evangelical Revival" than any other group, though in this case the theology was of a sterner Calvinistic sort. Actually, Bonar's premillennialism may account for the predominance of pilgrimage as a theme in his hymns. For instance, in his most popular hymn, "I Heard the Voice of Jesus Say," Christ is a source of comfort to the weary pilgrim, offering him rest, water, and light. The world, accordingly, offers no delights of its own, nor does God work through his creation to meet the needs of his children. Instead, Bonar's piety is absorbed with the immediate ministry of Christ as an escape from the toil, tedium, and darkness of this life. Bonar's verse, according to Benson, was so escapist that one "High Church lady" thought the Scottish hymn writer was actually a medieval saint.[54]

Bonar's appeal, then, like that of Wesley and Watts to a lesser degree, confirms the legacy of revivalism for Presbyterian hymnody. The authors most frequently included are those who either gained prominence during revivals or whose verse evokes the piety of revivalism. It might even be fair to claim that, if it had not been for the First and Second Great Awakenings, Presbyterians would still be singing the songs that Calvin prescribed, namely, the Psalms. In fact, during the twentieth century, the one period in American Protestantism lacking a clearly identifiable awakening comparable to those of the eighteenth and nineteenth centuries that split the Presbyterian Church, metrical psalmody has made a comeback, and Presbyterian hymnals bear that out.[55]

The Return of the Psalter

As much as Watts continues to be a dominant influence on Presbyterian congregational song, another chapter of the story of twentieth-century hymn books is the recovery of psalm singing, though this development has been largely a post–World War II phenomenon. During the first half of the twentieth century, metrical psalmody was a small percentage of the songs available for Presbyterian congregations to sing. In the southern Presbyterian Church's 1901 hymnal, for instance, 102 of the 715 hymns could be classified as metrical psalms.[56] But of these psalms, sixty-four were by Watts, meaning that only thirty-eight came from other sources and authors. And most of these were like Watts's, paraphrases of the Psalms by such authors as James Montgomery, Henry Lyte, and John Newton. Indeed, few of the 1901 hymnal's psalms came from old Psalters. The health of metrical psalmody was even worse in the northern Presbyterian Church, where the revision of 1911 contained only forty-seven

psalms out of the 734 total hymns, twenty-three of which were paraphrases by Watts. In 1933, the northern church's hymnal contained
forty-one psalms out of 513 total hymns, twelve by Watts. The all-
time low in psalm output came with the ill-fated 1972 *Worshipbook* by
the northern Presbyterian Church. Of the 373 hymns, a manageable
size but arranged mechanically in alphabetical order, thirty-three were
fashioned after the Psalms, with Watts being the source of six.

The 1972 hymnal, however, was the exception among post-1950
Presbyterian collections. Prospects for metrical psalms brightened considerably with the 1955 *Hymnbook*, an initiative of the southern Presbyterian Church that enlisted cooperation from the northern Presbyterian Church, as well as the Associate Reformed Presbyterian Church,
the United Presbyterian Church of North America, and the Reformed
Church in America. This hymnal included eighty-three psalms, only
nine of which were from Watts, out of the 600 total hymns. Then,
in 1961, the Orthodox Presbyterian Church kept up the pace in its
Trinity Hymnal, producing 146 psalms out of 730 total hymns, 15 of
which were Watts's paraphrases. The revision of this hymnal in 1990,
sponsored jointly by the Orthodox Presbyterian Church (OPC), the
Presbyterian Church in America, and Great Commission Publications,
included the most psalms out of all twentieth-century Presbyterian
hymnals, 154 out of 742 total hymns, with 15 by Watts. For some in
the OPC and Presbyterian Church of American (PCA) the new hymnal did not have enough psalms and, in 1991, Great Commission Publications issued the *Trinity Psalter*, a condensed version of the Reformed Presbyterian Church in North America's Psalter, containing
all canonical psalms without music.[57]

But arguably just as significant for the recovery of psalm singing
among American Presbyterians was the 1990 *Presbyterian Hymnal*,
which features a section much like older Psalter hymnals, designated
for metrical psalms, though unlike many of those earlier hymnals, the
psalms follow a section of hymns for use during the Christian year—
the church calendar being foreign to the Presbyterian and Reformed
fold before the late nineteenth century, when Christmas and Easter
emerged as both religious and commercial holidays.[58] Even though the
total number of psalms, ninety-six out of 564 total hymns, is not as
great as the new *Trinity Hymnal*, the *Presbyterian Hymnal* uses fewer

paraphrases of Watts (five) and introduced new metrical versions of the psalms, many of which were commissioned by the hymnal committee.[59]

Part of any explanation for the twentieth-century recovery of metrical psalmody has to include the *1912 Psalter*. This project began in the late nineteenth century under the efforts of the United Presbyterian Church of North America (UPCNA), which invited all Presbyterian and Reformed denominations to cooperate in the compilation of a new Psalter. Nine denominations accepted the invitation—only the southern Presbyterian Church and the German Reformed declined —and the *1912 Psalter* became, in the words of Emily R. Brink, "the most widely used and influential metrical psalter of the twentieth century."[60] It became the official *Psalter of the United Presbyterian Church*, and the Christian Reformed Church used it as the basis for its 1914 *Psalter*. How the other Presbyterian denominations used it is unclear, because individual congregations are free to choose whatever songs they prefer. None of the other denominations adopted it officially, however.[61]

Even if the hymn singing denominations may have initially slighted the *1912 Psalter*, by 1955 it had emerged as the reliable source for recovering metrical psalmody. Of the eighty-three psalms in *The Hymnbook* (1955), fifty-three came originally from the *1912 Psalter*. The OPC's *Trinity Hymnal* (1961) selected eighty-four psalms out of its total 146 from the *1912 Psalter*. And the revised *Trinity Hymnal* used seventy from the 1912 collection out of its total 154 metrical psalms. Only in the *Presbyterian Hymnal* (1990) does the influence of the *1912 Psalter* begin to subside, with twenty of the ninety-six psalms coming from the earlier book of praise. Part of the reason for this decline was a concerted effort by the Presbyterian Church USA (PCUSA) to find metrical versions of the psalms from within the denomination.[62] Even so, the United Presbyterian Church of North America's *1912 Psalter* arguably deserves the most credit for reviving the tradition of metrical psalmody.

Of the psalms sung (at least printed) with the most frequency, perhaps the biggest surprise is Psalm 103, which appeared twenty-five times in all the hymnals, only five behind the ever-popular Psalm 23. The first lines of the three most popular versions may indicate the reason for Psalm 103's popularity. Watts's version, "O, Bless the Lord,

My Soul," and the *1912 Psalter*'s "O, Come My Soul, Bless the Lord," make this psalm an easy one to use in that part of the service calling for praise. At the same time, "The Tender Love a Father Has," from the later verses in the Psalm, as rendered in the *1912 Psalter*, make it an attractive way to sing of God's faithfulness, much like Psalm 23. Psalm 119 was the third most frequently used, though its length may explain part of its appeal, as well as the general Protestant high regard for God's word, the subject of the Psalm. Psalms 84, 19, 72, and 100 appeared twenty, nineteen, eighteen, and seventeen times respectively. The themes of these metrical psalms are diverse, from the Lord's House to the Law of God, the reign of Christ, and God's sovereignty, and serve a variety of purposes in worship. Of the last three Psalms rounding out the ten most frequently printed, 46, 91, and 148, all appearing fourteen times in all the Presbyterian hymnals, the only surprise may be that Psalm 46, originally versified by Luther as one of the great hymns of the Reformation, did not inspire more metrical versions. The other two, Psalms 91 and 148, treat God's faithfulness and the work of creation. Drawing any conclusions about the theological or liturgical preferences from this top ten list of metrical psalms would be ill-advised, though it is important to consider which psalms do not appear in any of the hymnals. Twenty-four in all (Psalms 7, 21, 26, 28, 35, 49, 52, 53, 54, 57, 58, 59, 64, 70, 74, 75, 81, 101, 105, 109, 111, 112, 120, and 140) have not been available for Presbyterians to sing. The likeliest explanation for a number of these is their imprecatory nature.[63]

The one conclusion that may be drawn responsibly, aside from noting the recovery of metrical psalmody among twentieth-century Presbyterians, is a point made by Louis F. Benson during his Stone Lectures. The modern Presbyterian disposition on the question of what to sing in corporate worship is "the natural result of its own experimenting with the double standard of 'Psalms and Hymns' set up by Dr. Watts."[64] To be sure, American twentieth-century Presbyterians still reserve a great deal of space for Watts even while adding a bevy of other hymns to their repertoire. And the most recent generation of Presbyterians appears to be willing to sing more psalms than its grandparents. Nevertheless, the staples of Presbyterian congregational singing, if twentieth-century hymnals are any indication, are Watts and King David as advocated by Calvin. In the words of James

Rawlings Sydnor, "The two men who had the most profound influence on Presbyterian congregational song" were Calvin and Watts.[65] Twentieth-century Presbyterian hymnals prove that point.

Why Presbyterians Sing

The continuing preponderance of Watts and the recovery of psalmody are no doubt reassuring to Presbyterians and outsiders who might think them odd. Watts may not be the greatest of hymn writers, but he is certainly not the worst, and so Presbyterians cannot be faulted for going to an obscure or poor source for their hymnody. Furthermore, metrical psalms have the advantage of antiquity as well as the appeal of being native to the Reformed tradition, and so the Presbyterian rediscovery of the Psalter has a laudable, nostalgic ring to it. Yet, as reassuring and as mainstream as the results of this survey are, several other factors need to be remembered, ones that are less flattering about Presbyterian liturgy and singing.

As suggested earlier, Presbyterians are drowning in a flood of hymns and metrical psalms. Not only have mainstream and sideline Presbyterian denominations produced hymnals roughly every twenty-five years, the average length of which is 621 hymns, with the northern church's revised hymnal of 1911 being the longest at 734 hymns, and the PCUSA's 1972 *Worshipbook* being the most brief with only 373 selections.[66] These figures do not include hymnals that the denominations sponsored for evangelistic purposes and youth activities.[67] Nor do they take into account the individual congregations that choose to use a hymnal other than the one provided by the denomination.

What such variety and numbers indicate is that, contrary to the popular perception that hymns are a great way to learn theology (more following), the size and frequency of Presbyterian hymnals may actually hamper such instruction. For instance, any congregation that sought to learn the theology of its hymnal would take nearly four years to sing through it only once (e.g., singing three new hymns per week would mean learning only roughly 150 hymns per year, which is a quarter of the average number of hymns in each hymnal). And then after the congregation had sung through the hymnal six times, they would have to adjust to the next hymnal to be produced by denominational officers. On the positive side, the size and frequency of Presbyterian hymnals helps to cut down on controversy over songs, because it would be difficult to know when an old favorite is missing, let alone develop a group of favorites given the sheer number of hymns a congregation may sing any given week.

Many think the diversity of hymns and number of hymnals to be a sign of musical vitality and ecumenical zeal. To be sure, Presbyterian hymnals reflect a pattern among all denominational hymnals, namely, that they increasingly lack liturgical or theological particularity and look the same. In the words of James F. White, denominational hymnals "have become an anomaly, the contents becoming more and more identical with each revision. . . . [D]enominational labels are no longer important."[68] Morgan F. Simmons thinks Presbyterians "are richer for sharing in the wealth of expression that comes from all branches of Christendom."[69] James Rawlings Sydnor concurs, adding that "the quality and scope" of Presbyterian hymnals has "improved and expanded."[70]

Others, however, see such diversity as harmful. Louis F. Benson, who may have started the trend of including more hymns from diverse sources, concluded his Stone Lectures with the observation that "the church hymnal has become cumbersome . . . too encyclopedic and utilitarian to appeal to the heart." The problem was that pastors required "all sorts of hymns for all sorts of purposes," thus padding the hymnals "with so much that is dull." "This encyclopedic range," Benson concluded, "may be a pastoral convenience but it is a spiritual blunder."[71] Erik Routley has also expressed reservations about the virtue of variety in hymns. Contrary to the notion that Lutheran hymnody is superior to Presbyterian congregational song because of its longer history of development, Routley suggests that a quantitative increase of chorales among Lutherans had the opposite effect. It introduced a "sorry confusion" that detracted from the "original clarity" of Lutheran song, whereas the original canon of the Genevan psalms "propagated" a healthy species in Britain and America.[72] Routley's comments concern the music of hymns, but they may be equally applicable to the text, especially if, as so many claim, the value of hymns is their pedagogical function.

One way to illustrate some of this confusion is to look at the placement of some of the most popular hymns. For instance, Watts's "Our God, Our Help in Ages Past," could likely be placed in any section covering the attributes of God or in one covering God's love and faithfulness. This is the general way the hymnals situate Watts's hymn, but they also reflect uncertainty about the author's meaning. Three of the hymnals (1911, 1933, and 1955) group this hymn in the section on God's love and fatherhood. Two (1961, 1990a) put it in the section on God's eternity, and one (1901) places it in a section on the fatherhood of God. (The other two give it no topical placement; 1972 arranged everything alphabetically, and 1990b situated it in the metrical psalm section.) Even greater uncertainty surrounds the placement of Wesley's "Love Divine, All Loves Excelling." Three (1933, 1955, and 1990b) place this hymn in a section on life in Christ, though two (1933, 1955) of these hymnals further divide this section into the various aspects of such life, putting Wesley in the love group. Meanwhile, three hymnals (1901, 1961, and 1990a) include this hymn in the section on sanctification. Finally, one hymnal (1911) places Wesley's hymn in the section on forgiveness of sins. Bonar's "Here, O My Lord, I See" is more straightforward and serves best to be sung in connection with the Lord's Supper, which is where five of the hymnals (1901, 1911, 1933, 1955, and 1990b), all mainline Presbyterian, put it. But the OPC and PCA editors responsible for the editions of the *Trinity Hymnal* (1961, 1990a) chose to place it in the section on the opening of worship.

Despite such ambiguity about the instruction of individual hymns, Presbyterians continue to insist that the primary purpose of congregational song is instructional. This is most evident in the way Presbyterians organize their hymnals. With the exception of two, all of the hymnals arrange the songs according to a thematic structure that begins with God, the Trinity, and his attributes, moves to the church, and then concludes with different themes from the Christian life and special occasions. The two exceptions are the 1972 *Worshipbook,* again with its alphabetical arrangement, and the 1990 *Presbyterian Hymnal,* which includes a section on the church year and metrical psalms before moving into the conventional Presbyterian topical arrangement. Such thematic patterns follow the arguments made in most of the Presbyterian writing on worship, hymns, and congregational song. According to James Rawlings Sydnor, "People absorb a great deal of Christian truth from the hymns which they sing," namely, "the great foundation doctrines of our faith."[73] Even more emphatic is a PCA church musician, Leonard R. Payton, who insists that the biblical role of singing is as a partner to preaching. Hymns, accordingly, "teach" and "admonish."[74]

Perhaps if Presbyterians had not been historically so liturgically wooden,[75] they might recognize the other purposes for which song is legitimately used. Calvin, for instance, argued, that corporate worship consisted of three elements—word, sacrament, and prayer—and regarded song as a form of prayer.[76] Likewise, Benson distinguishes among three categories of hymns: those of praise, edification, and liturgy. The first are designed to express praise of God, the second for the nurture of the singers, and the third for use in the church's order of worship.[77] In his history of the English hymn, Benson places Presbyterians via Watts squarely in the second category, namely, the tradition of doctrinal hymnody that edifies by reinforcing the sermon. Watts "designed his hymns to meet the demand from the pulpit for hymns that would illustrate and enforce the sermon themes." It is no wonder that Presbyterians preferred Watts, especially because his hymns were, in Benson's words, "Calvinistic in tone and often in detail."[78] This may also explain the variety and size of Presbyterian hymnals, because sermons vary according to biblical text and theme. But the homiletical purpose of Presbyterian congregational song is vulnerable to being replaced by superior forms of theological reinforcement, such as skits, readings, or even the sacraments. What is more, poetry has not been the way the reformed church has usually taught propositional truth. Catechisms were considered a better form of instruction. And if the congregation does not understand a hymn, or if they understand that singing hymns is part of the church's pedagogy, song in corporate worship threatens to become little more than a time for worshipers to stretch their legs and lungs.[79]

At this point, Presbyterians might well learn from their liturgical Christian counterparts who use set forms and defend them as laudable. Communions that use set liturgies or books of prayer have an easier time figuring out what a song does because it performs a specific function in worship, usually as a response to the means of grace. It

is, in other words, a way for the congregation to express praise, peti-
tion, or thanksgiving to God. Liturgy, then, undergirds congregational song. With a clear sense of what the order of worship does and
how the pieces fit together, figuring out which hymns to sing and
why becomes a much easier task. As Paul Westermeyer argues, "When
the public liturgical bones of communal worship are dismissed, the
church's song is left in a free fall."[80] What is more, liturgical coherence
could help to reduce the volume of songs in Presbyterian hymnals.
To be sure, Lutheran and Episcopalian hymnals are by no means lean,
but they are published less frequently because these traditions are less
hostile to the notion of repetition and ritual. Presbyterians, however,
ever since the debates and fights in seventeenth-century Britain over
the *Book of Common Prayer*, have avoided liturgy as a sign of either
episcopal tyranny or dead formalism.[81] As such, the number of hymns
and hymnals available to Presbyterians in the twentieth century has
been inversely proportional to the number of Presbyterian church
members—which is another way of saying that the liturgical confusion reflected in Presbyterian hymnals may be a factor in the loss of
Presbyterian identity both within the churches and among individual
members.[82]

In *Why Catholics Can't Sing*, Thomas Day observed the connection
between liturgy, hymns, and religious identity. In his closing advice
to priests and parishes, Day wrote, "Good congregational singing begins with a sense of beloved familiarity and the best way to develop
that familiarity is with an outstanding hymnal/service book which
will stay in the pews for more than a generation."[83] Day's logic would
not seem to work for Presbyterians because they sing well despite
the constant change of hymnals. But for Day, good congregational
singing is not just about volume, but also involves liturgical good
sense. Repetition, familiarity, and habit, even in congregational song,
"humbles" the minister and the congregation by instilling the idea
that corporate worship is bigger than any single individual or faction
in the church.[84] Musical variety in turn may encourage the idea that
worship is more about the style or taste of the church than about
serving God. Day's point is that liturgical uniformity and a limited
range of songs best keeps the emphasis of worship on the creator
rather than his creatures. After all, Christian worship historically has

been chiefly about serving God, not those involved in the service. One would think that Presbyterians, whose Shorter Catechism has it that man's chief end is to glorify God, would understand the direction and purpose of worship. Ironically, it may very well be their hymnals, which are supposed to teach doctrine, that have helped to obscure this basic point.

Notes

1. Thomas Day, *Why Catholics Can't Sing: The Culture of Catholicism and the Triumph of Bad Taste* (New York: Crossroad, 1990).
2. Her exact words were, according to Day, "I don't believe in that shit." Ibid., 6.
3. Ibid., 1.
4. Ibid., 1, 4.
5. Ibid., 3.
6. Louis F. Benson, *The Hymnody of the Christian Church* (1927; reprint, Richmond: John Knox Press, 1956), 57–58.
7. The hymnals surveyed here run chronologically as follows: General Assembly of the Presbyterian Church in the U.S., *The New Psalms and Hymns* (Richmond: Presbyterian Committee of Publication, 1901); General Assembly of the Presbyterian Church, U.S.A., *The Hymnal*, rev. ed. (Philadelphia: Presbyterian Board of Publication and Sabbath-School Work, 1911); General Assembly of the Presbyterian Church, U.S.A., *The Hymnal* (Philadelphia: Presbyterian Board of Education, 1933); Presbyterian Church, U.S., et al., *The Hymnbook* (Richmond: John Ribble, 1955); Committee on Christian Education, Orthodox Presbyterian Church, *The Trinity Hymnal* (Philadelphia: Great Commission Publications, 1961); Joint Committee on Worship, *The Worshipbook* (Philadelphia: Westminster Press, 1972); Great Commission Publications, *The Trinity Hymnal* (Philadelphia: Great Commission Publications, 1990); and Westminster/John Knox, *The Presbyterian Hymnal* (Louisville, Ky.: Westminster/John Knox, 1990). There is one additional hymnal, the PCUS's 1927 *Presbyterian Hymnal*, which was not included in this survey because its indexes are so poor and because its editors failed to attribute hymn texts to biblical (e.g., Psalm) sources. For this reason it cannot be meaningfully compared to the other hymnals, though where possible, such as favorite hymn writers, I have compiled appropriate statistics. Because Morgan F. Simmons, "Hymnody: Its Place in Twentieth-Century Presbyterianism," in *The Confessional Mosaic: Presbyterians and Twentieth-Century Theology,* ed. Milton J. Coalter

et al. (Louisville: Westminster/John Knox, 1990), 174, concludes that this was a "very mediocre hymnal," its absence from this study may be for the best.

8. Nine, counting the 1927 *Presbyterian Hymnal.* This number will be assumed hereafter.

9. On the history of Presbyterian hymnals, see Louis Fitzgerald Benson, *The English Hymn: Its Development and Use* (Philadelphia: Presbyterian Board of Publication, 1915), 177–95, 372–89, which is unsurpassed on practically all Protestant traditions of hymnody. See also James Rawlings Sydnor, "Sing a New Song to the Lord: An Historical Survey of American Presbyterian Hymnals," *American Presbyterians* 68 (1990): 1–13, and Simmons, "Hymnody," 162–86.

10. On Reformation developments in hymnody, see Paul Westermeyer, *Te Deum: The Church and Music* (Minneapolis: Fortress Press, 1998), 141–60, and on Zwingli and Zurich specifically, 149–52; Rochelle A. Stackhouse, *The Language of the Psalms in Worship: American Revisions of Watts' Psalter* (Drew Studies in Liturgy, no. 4, Lanham, Md.: Scarecrow Press, 1997), 29–70; and Erik Routley, *The Music of Christian Hymnody* (London: Independent Press, 1957), chaps. 2–4.

11. Westermeyer, *Te Deum,* 153–58. Westermeyer concedes that Calvin's practice was closer to the early church but different in that Geneva's worship was more restrictive lyrically and musically. The early church was not limited to Psalms, and they chanted, a practice that Calvin thought unintelligible to Geneva's Christians.

12. Robert Stevenson, *Patterns of Protestant Church Music* (Durham: Duke University Press, 1953), 120.

13. Routley, *Music,* 42.

14. On colonial Presbyterian developments, see Westermeyer, *Te Deum,* 179–80, 252–53, and Benson, *English Hymn,* 177–95.

15. Benson, *English Hymn,* 101. Stevenson, *Patterns,* 107, raises questions about Watts's Christianization of the psalms, because the hymn writer's views on the deity of Christ were "peculiar" and "dangerous."

16. Benson, *Hymnody,* 88, writes of Watts: "In the light of its immediate surroundings it was so glaringly original . . . I think we shall come to feel more and more that to a larger view, it was hardly more than a dislodgment of the Calvinistic settlement in favor of a reaffirmation of Luther's."

17. Westermeyer, *Te Deum,* 204.

18. Benson, *English Hymn,* 180.

19. Henry Wilder Foote, *Three Centuries of American Hymnody* (Cambridge: Harvard University Press, 1940), 147, 148.

20. Benson, *English Hymn,* 182.

21. Ibid.

22. Ibid., 191.

23. Ibid., 193.

24. On these developments, see also Foote, *Three Centuries*, 152–56. For a good background on American Presbyterian worship in the eighteenth and nineteenth centuries, see Julius Melton, *Presbyterian Worship in America: Changing Patterns since 1787* (Richmond: John Knox Press, 1967), chaps. 1–3.

25. Sydnor, "Sing a New Song," 4.

26. Stevenson, *Patterns*, 139.

27. I have decided not to treat Neale or Winkworth because their significance is harder to determine than that of an author of specific hymns. This pattern holds for the southern Presbyterian Church's 1927 hymnal. There Watts had the most with twenty hymns, next were Wesley and Bonar with sixteen, then Neale with seven, and finally Winkworth with two.

28. Hughes Oliphant Old, *Worship That Is Reformed According to Scripture* (Atlanta: John Knox Press, 1984), 55.

29. Horton Davies, *The Worship of the English Puritans* (1948; reprint, Clear Spring, Md.: Soli Deo Gloria, 1997), 178, 179.

30. See, for instance, James Rawlings Sydnor, *The Hymn and Congregational Singing* (Richmond: John Knox Press, 1960), 28–29, 52, who associates Watts with historic Reformed worship. In contrast, James Hastings Nichols, *Corporate Worship in the Reformed Tradition* (Philadelphia: Westminster Press, 1968), 125–26, links Watts to pietism and revivalism.

31. Stevenson, *Patterns*, 13.

32. Louis F. Benson, *Studies of Familiar Hymns* (1903; reprint, Philadelphia: Westminster Press, 1921), 129.

33. Benson, *English Hymn*, 195–96.

34. Benson, *Hymnody*, 88, 93.

35. The 1927 Presbyterian Hymnal includes all of these hymns except for "Rejoice, the Lord Is King."

36. All of these by Watts and Bonar appear in the 1927 *Presbyterian Hymnal*.

37. "From All That Dwell Below the Skies" does not appear in the 1927 *Presbyterian Hymnal*.

38. The 1927 *Presbyterian Hymnal* does not include "Jesus Christ Is Risen Today" or "Blessing and Honor and Glory."

39. For estimations about the number of hymns Watts and Wesley wrote, see Benson, *English Hymn*, 114–16, 245.

40. Ibid., 258.

41. Ibid., 259–61.

42. Ibid., 261.

43. Louis F. Benson, *Studies of Familiar Hymns,* 2d series (1923; reprint, Philadelphia: Westminster Press, 1926), 43.

44. Benson, *English Hymn,* 248, 252.

45. Ibid., 248–49, 250.

46. On the importance of revivalism to eighteenth-century American Presbyterianism, see Leonard J. Trinterud, *The Forming of an American Tradition: A Re-examination of Colonial Presbyterianism* (Philadelphia: Westminster Press, 1949); and Leigh Eric Schmidt, *Holy Fairs: Scottish Communions and American Revivals in the Early Modern Period* (Princeton: Princeton University Press, 1989).

47. For other assessments of Wesley and Watts, see Bernard L. Manning, *The Hymns of Wesley and Watts: Five Informal Papers* (London: Epworth Press, 1942); J. Ernest Rattenbury, *The Evangelical Doctrines of Wesley's Hymns* (London: Epworth Press, 1941); Harry Escott, *Isaac Watts, Hymnographer* (London: Independent Press, 1962); Rochelle A. Stackhouse, "Changing the Language of the Church's Song circa 1785," *Hymn* 45 (July 1994): 16–19; and E. K. Simpson, "Isaac Watts: A Rounded Life," *Evangelical Quarterly* 21 (1949): 190–202. Presbyterian receptivity to the emotionalism of Watts and Wesley could also well account for the way some congregations today have welcomed the genre of praise songs and choruses, even though it also makes less defensible the so-called traditionalist position of defending "standard" hymns in the contemporary worship wars.

48. John Wesley, *The Works of the Rev. John Wesley,* vol. 2 (New York: n. p., 1856), 443, quoted in Stevenson, *Patterns,* 105.

49. Isaac Watts, *Horae Lyricae, Poems Chiefly of the Lyric Kind* (London: n. p., 1706), 80, 83, quoted in Stevenson, *Patterns,* 106.

50. Benson, *Studies,* 2d series, 209.

51. Ibid., 218, 219. Benson adds the following names to the list of Presbyterian hymn authors of note: from Scotland, "Bruce, Logan, Morison, J. D. Burns, Norman MacLeod, Matheson, Miss Borthwick and Mrs. Findlater, Brownlie, Mrs. Cousin and the Duke of Argyll"; from Canada, Robert Murray; and from the United States, "Davies, J. W. Alexander, Duffield, Dunn, Hastings, Mrs. Prentiss, Wolfe, Hopper, March, Mrs. C. L. Smith, and van Dyke."

52. Ibid., 219.

53. Ibid., 216.

54. Ibid., 211. Bonar has not received much attention in the historical literature, but Kenneth R. Ross, "Calvinists in Controversy: John Kennedy, Horatius Bonar and the Moody Mission of 1873–1874," *Scottish Bulletin of Evangelical Theology* 9 (1991–92): 51–63, is helpful for placing Bonar's views about revivalism and thus adds another link connecting hymns and evangelistic piety.

55. For an argument that the twentieth century has experienced a Great Awakening, two even, see William G. McLoughlin, *Revivals, Awakenings, and Reform* (Chicago: University of Chicago Press, 1978).

56. For this study I counted as metrical psalms only those where the attribution for the song explicitly mentioned a Psalm or portion of one, as opposed to the later custom in many hymnals of quoting a line of Scripture at the very top of the page that the hymn is supposed to be reinforcing or teaching. The scriptural indexes of many hymnals include these biblical references even when the hymn itself is not a versification of the cited text.

57. See *Trinity Psalter: Psalms 1–150: Words Only Edition* (Pittsburgh: Crown and Covenant Publications, 1994).

58. On the rise of Christmas and Easter observance among Protestants adverse to the church calendar, see Leigh Eric Schmidt, *Consumer Rites: The Buying and Selling of American Holidays* (Princeton: Princeton University Press, 1995).

59. For some of the background on *The Presbyterian Hymnal,* see LindaJo H. McKim, *The Presbyterian Hymnal Companion* (Louisville: Westminster/ John Knox, 1993).

60. Emily R. Brink, "Metrical Psalmody in North America: A Story of Survival and Revival," *The Hymn* 44 (October 1993): 21.

61. On the *1912 Psalter,* see Bertus Frederick Polman, "Church Music and Liturgy in the Christian Reformed Church of North America" (Ph.D. dissertation, University of Minnesota, 1980), 60–67; and Simmons, "Hymnody," 171–73.

62. On the metrical psalms commissioned by the PCUSA, see McKim, *Presbyterian Hymnal Companion,* 159, 164, 177. Some of the other Psalters used in the recovery of metrical psalmody were the United Presbyterian *1871 Psalter,* the Associate Reformed Presbyterian *1931 Psalter,* and the Reformed Presbyterian *1940 Psalter.*

63. On the imprecatory Psalms Watts left out, as well as the ones the *Lutheran Book of Worship* does not include, see Paul Westermeyer, *Let Justice Sing: Hymnody and Justice* (Collegeville, Minn.: Liturgical Press, 1998), 34–38. For considerations of how psalms were selected and sung in Geneva, see John D. Witvliet, "The Spirituality of the Psalter: Metrical Psalms in Liturgy and Life in Calvin's Geneva," *Calvin Theological Journal* 32 (1997): 273–97.

64. Benson, *Hymnody,* 91.

65. Sydnor, "Sing a New Song," 1.

66. The 1927 *Presbyterian Hymnal* weighed in with 486 hymns.

67. On the hymnals designed for schools, evangelistic purposes, and informal occasions, see Simmons, "Hymnody," 168–69, 177–78.

68. James F. White, "Public Worship in Protestantism," in *Altered Land-*

scapes: Christianity in America, 1935–1985, ed. David W. Lotz (Grand Rapids: Eerdmans, 1989), 113.

69. Simmons, "Hymnody," 183.

70. Sydnor, "Sing a New Song," 12.

71. Benson, *Hymnody,* 276.

72. Routley, *Music,* 35.

73. Sydnor, *Hymn,* 18.

74. Leonard R. Payton, "Congregational Singing and the Ministry of the Word," *Reformation and Revival* 7 (1998): 121. See also S. T. Kimbrough Jr., "Hymns Are Theology," *Theology Today* 42 (1985–86): 59–68. One of the revealing aspects of Presbyterian writing about worship is how little is written on song in discussions of liturgy. See, for instance, Paul E. Engle, *Discovering the Fullness of Worship* (Philadelphia: Great Commission Publications, 1978); Donald Macleod, *Presbyterian Worship: Its Meaning and Method* (Richmond: John Knox Press, 1965); and Robert Johnston, *Presbyterian Worship: Its Spirit, Method, and History* (Toronto: Publisher's Syndicate, 1901). Even in a book about music explicitly, John M. Frame, *Contemporary Worship Music: A Biblical Defense* (Phillipsburg, N.J.: P&R Publishing, 1997) says almost nothing about the purpose of singing in worship. In contrast, see the variety of views on congregational singing from sixteenth- and seventeenth-century Reformed Christians and Presbyterians in David W. Music, *Hymnology: A Collection of Source Readings* (Studies in Liturgical Musicology, no. 4; Lanham, Md.: Scarecrow Press, 1996), 51–81.

75. See Davies, *Worship of the English Puritans,* for sources of American Presbyterian liturgical tone deafness.

76. On Calvin's views on song, see Charles Garside Jr., *The Origins of Calvin's Theology of Music: 1536–1543* (Philadelphia: American Philosophical Society, 1979); and Calvin's preface to the *Genevan Psalter,* reprinted in Music, *Hymnology,* 63–68.

77. Benson, *Hymnody,* lect. 4.

78. Benson, *English Hymn,* 208–9.

79. For one expression among contemporary exclusive psalm singers on the function of song in corporate worship, see Michael Bushell, *The Songs of Zion* (Pittsburgh: Crown and Covenant Publications, 1980), 115–20, where he argues that song does not fulfill the function of prayer, partly in an effort to overcome the objection that if song is like prayer, why not allow for non-canonical songs in the same way that public prayers are not required to use words from the Bible.

80. Westermeyer, *Te Deum,* 209. See also Edward Dickinson, *Music in the History of the Western Church* (1902; reprint, New York: Haskell House, 1969), 401, who wrote, "Music, however beautiful, loses something of its effect if

its accompaniments are not in harmony with it. . . . One great advantage of an ancient and prescribed form is that its components work easily to a common impression, and in course of time the ritual tends to become venerable as well as dignified and beautiful."

81. On Puritan objections to the *Book of Common Prayer*, see Davies, *Worship of the English Puritans*.

82. For one of the best recent efforts to assess the place of song in worship in the context of the debates about praise songs and hymns, see Paul Westermeyer, "Church Music at the End of the Twentieth Century," *Lutheran Quarterly* 8 (1994): 197–211.

83. Day, *Why Catholics Can't Sing*, 170.

84. Ibid., 140–44.

5

The Anatomy of Immigrant Hymnody

Faith Communicated in the Swedish Covenant Church

Scott E. Erickson

Swedish immigrants in the United States expressed their religious identity in relation to other denominations as 1.3 million of them arrived on American shores from the 1840s to the 1940s. They organized churches and established schools to give expression and institutional support to a developing form of Swedish American religion. The Swedish Mission Covenant Church (presently the Evangelical Covenant Church) was one denomination established by the immigrants. The founding of this church body was an important component in the development of religious identity among evangelical Swedish immigrants. The hymns and music used in local congregations were major components of an organic theology and a significant means by which these evangelical Christians communicated faith. The study of hymns used by people in the Covenant Church enriches the general story of evangelical Protestant hymnody by showing that Americans with ethnic origins were very selective in how they chose texts and music and then adapted these into the worship life of their communities. In many ways, Swedish immigrant communities were separated by choice, in that they carefully selected what they wished to incorporate. Immigrants employed both ethnic and religious criteria as they defined their theology in a new homeland and discussed which English-language tunes and texts could be used in their churches. Some American hymn texts were translated into Swedish and sung during revival meetings and in Sunday worship services. Other American hymns were picked up and sung in English, especially as the English-speaking second generation began to make decisions about the choice of hymn texts and tunes.

A rich hymn tradition was also brought with the immigrants from Sweden, even though some of the texts and music were translated into English as the immigrant community made the difficult language transition. This meant that Swedish evangelicals would move their communities forward in a "Swedish" manner. The first generation of Swedes in America—that is, those who emigrated from the homeland—were reluctant to move into an English-language sphere. This resulted in a certain level of isolation, which means that the vibrant nature of local Swedish communities could easily have been overlooked or misunderstood. In the first—and even second—generation in their adopted country, Swedish evangelicals within the Covenant context were not singing the hymns most often reprinted in the evangelical hymnals of the era. "All Hail the Power of Jesus' Name" and "Jesus Lover of My Soul" did not have the resonance among Swedish evangelicals as these texts and tunes had among purely English-speaking American evangelicals.

But this very point provides the opportunity for an interesting study: How did ethnic metaphors and religious themes converge as Swedish evangelicals sought to understand American Protestant hymnody? Even if texts and tunes have few points of convergence, what themes and metaphors are similar or dissimilar? And why? There was certainly an effort among Swedish immigrant leaders to discover the Protestant hymn ethos and then to express a unique form of it through selection and adaptation into the foreign-language worship life in the ethnically dominated Covenant Church. Similarities and dissimilarities are part of an intriguing local history in specific Swedish communities, which, after all, is where people were living and working and singing about their faith. This was a rich theological and musical culture that was beginning to take shape in the latter half of the nineteenth century and in the early decades of the twentieth century.

Before they migrated, many of these Swedish evangelicals had participated in efforts to revitalize the state-established Church of Sweden, while at the same time keeping themselves apart from religious bodies more directly inspired by Anglo-American influences, for example, the Baptists and Methodists. In 1856, they were involved in the establishment of Evangeliska Fosterlands Stiftelsen (the Evangelical National Foundation), a national organization that coordinated evangelical activities in Sweden and was an official, yet voluntary association within the bounds of the state church.[1] The leaders of the foundation, among them Hans Jakob Lundborg and Carl Olof Rosenius, perceived this organization as their ideal of a church within a church. Although they generally supported the state church's Lutheran devotion and theology, members of the foundation were skeptical of any church policy that employed birthright membership as a means whereby God's grace was mediated. Instead, they considered religious conversion as the "one thing needful" for salvation.[2] In the 1870s some Mission Friends began more strongly to question church tradition, doctrine, and confession, as well as state-established religion. Paul Peter Waldenström challenged the Church of Sweden's atonement doctrine in 1872–73 and argued for a nonconfessional stance. In 1878, Carl Johan Nyvall and Erik J. Ekman proposed the founding of an association more independent than the Evangelical National Foundation, and the Mission Covenant Church of Sweden was born.

In America many Swedish immigrants were associated with the Lutheran Augustana Synod. Founded in 1860 and generally consisting of Swedish (and, until 1870, Norwegian) Lutherans, the synod adhered strictly to the Augsburg Confession and developed clear guidelines on membership and doctrine.[3] Mission Friends, most of whom arrived in America after the Civil War, wished to express their religion in a manner different than those who founded the Augustana Synod. Events in Sweden had re-charted the religious map in the homeland and among Swedish immigrants. Waldenström's ecclesiastical challenges in the 1870s initiated questions about theological freedom, and many Mission Friends in America supported Waldenström's views, whereas confessional Augustana leaders and ministers generally did not. Non-Lutheran groups, for example, the Baptists and Methodists, also undertook active missionary work among Swedish Americans.[4] In 1885, in an effort to unite around a common mission among their compatriots in their adopted country, the evangelical Mission Friends established a formal network, a denomination, when the Covenant Church was organized in Chicago.

The story of local singing among Swedish evangelicals in America takes us into the lives of the evangelist Erik August Skogsbergh (1850–1939)[5] and his music director Andrew L. Skoog (1856–1934).[6] Skogsbergh was called "the Swedish Moody" because of his reputation as a revival preacher among Swedish evangelicals. Immigrants called Skoog "the Swedish Sankey" because of the song leader's work with and relationship to the powerful Swedish evangelist. The story is centered in the Swedish evangelical enclave—or better, the Swedish evangelical ghetto—of Minneapolis. Here, one can explore the anatomy of immigrant hymnody as it was related to the breadth of American Protestant hymnody in theme and structure, if not in the usage of specific texts and tunes.

How was faith communicated to and among Swedish evangelicals in America? In his autobiography, Carl V. Bowman wrote that E. A. Skogsbergh often described Minneapolis as a "glorious city" where great possibilities existed for Christian ministry and for the building of Swedish American institutions. Bowman, who served as president of the Mission Covenant Church from 1927 to 1933, remembered that Skogsbergh described the Twin Cities as the "center of the universe."[7] For a large number of Swedish immigrants during the latter part of the nineteenth century, the Twin Cities had become a new home and a lively center of activity. Earlier Swedish American rural settlements had been supplemented by these urban enclaves. Common religion, politics, culture, language, and traditions allowed Swedish Americans to express ethnicity in their immigrant community and through institutional form.

Thus, as migration from Sweden increased to high levels in the 1880s, many Swedish immigrants who arrived in the Twin Cities were concerned about religion and the communal expression of their Christian faith. Mission Friends often sought out conventicle, or small group, meetings held in homes throughout Minneapolis and St. Paul. They were inspired by Rosenius to gather for Bible studies and prayer. They were not dramatically anti-Augustana, as their devotional life was generally Lutheran, but were caught up in the currents of theological freedom and remained unsure about the necessity of formal church membership. In 1874, a group of Minneapolis Mission Friends gathered to organize a non-Augustana body, the Swedish Evangelical Lutheran Mission Church, which would later become the Minneapolis Swedish Tabernacle Church and is presently First Covenant Church.[8]

The establishment of immigrant communities and Swedish American churches is related to the central problem that confronted all immigrant groups, that is, identity. Ethnic institutions, including churches, were the result of immigrants' desires to preserve Swedish heritage while somehow relating to the adopted country. One cannot blame them for seeking mutual contact in homes, stores, secular associations, historical societies, churches, and schools. After all, prevailing rhetoric and societal pressure suggested that immigrants could indeed be uprooted from their homeland and integrated rapidly into American culture, that is, melted into the diverse American pot.[9] Working against these pressures, immigrants were active in communities where there was a lively interaction of people and innovation of ethnic traditions. Even if a majority of them did not write eloquently about ethnicity, many were involved in the process of defining a common ethnic identity. Music played a key role in ethnic identity and in helping Swedish Americans in the Twin Cities develop a shared immigrant vocabulary.[10]

Immigrant leaders who mediated between their Swedish compatriots and those outside Swedish American enclaves often shaped communal expression of religion and Swedish American ethnicity. John Higham has written that ethnic leaders worked with the "consolidation and maintenance of [America's] ethnic groups" and served a "mediating function, weaving a web of ethnic mutuality on the one hand and encouraging their people to reach beyond it on the other."[11] In the same line of thinking, Victor Greene has called ethnic leaders "mediating brokers" between immigrant communities and American society.[12] Like conduits, these leaders conveyed information and influenced their people to define ethnic and religious identity through a shaping of community life, rather than allow their identity to disintegrate into the chaos of melting pots and unavailing assimilation.

Skogsbergh and Skoog, as evangelical and musical leaders, found their way to Skogsbergh's "center of the universe." Skoog, the future song leader, was first to arrive. His father preceded the family across the sea, and, in 1869, Andrew immigrated to the Twin Cities with his mother and siblings. His education was very basic and sporadic, for his assistance was required in the family's tailoring business. He also studied music, but this too was intermittent. Skoog had time for only twelve lessons on a small reed organ; his other tasks did not allow for much formal training.[13]

In 1876, Skogsbergh arrived in the United States. He had accepted a call to serve as preacher at the North Side Mission Church on Franklin Street in Chicago, a position that required him to emigrate from Sweden, which he agreed to do following many weeks of indecision. He first collaborated with J. M. Sanngren, pioneer preacher and president of the Mission Synod, an association of non-Augustana congregations that was organized in 1873. The ailing Sanngren sought Skogsbergh's assistance with his ministry among Swedes in the Chicago area. Before long, Skogsbergh was known as a stunning preacher and great evangelist, and the church building on Franklin Street was deemed too small for the crowds he attracted. He therefore asked the American revival preacher Dwight L. Moody if his large auditorium could be used for a Swedish service on Sunday afternoons. This request was granted, and Skogsbergh began preaching to large crowds in the ten-thousand-seat church. Thereafter nicknamed "the Swedish Moody," Skogsbergh was leading a Swedish-language revival that approached the success of Moody's services in English.[14]

Skogsbergh's revival was increasingly unlike the Swedish evangelical form, which was identified by small conventicle meetings in candlelit homes and chapels. In contrast, Skogsbergh was a lively, busy evangelist who attracted much attention in his new country, as evidenced by the large worship spaces he required. He soon convinced his own congregation to construct a tabernacle for Swedish immigrants on the south side of Chicago.[15] Skogsbergh noted that his revival "success" in Chicago would not have been possible in Sweden. He reflected later that he appreciated the spontaneity found in American cities, including the positive aspects that allowed for a wealth of possibilities and the negative aspects that forced him to confront a complex and foreign society. Skogsbergh was seldom dismayed because, he wrote, "everything is successful in America."[16]

But the popular evangelist could not long avoid the "center of the universe." Less than a year following his arrival in Chicago, he sought to take a vacation from his preaching duties. This opportunity for rest turned into a Macedonian call to preach in the fall of 1877. He gave up his vacation plans because he "felt a special urging toward Minneapolis" and believed that "a revival was imminent."[17] Indeed, it would have been uncharacteristic for "the Swedish Moody" to give up the opportunity to lead a religious revival. While in the Twin Cities, he noticed two difficulties that confronted Mission Friends. First, there were too few preachers to serve the Swedish communities.

This meant that they had to travel great distances among a growing number of congregations. The amount of activities and the needs on the field swamped the trained workers. Financial resources and organizational structures did not exist.[18] Skogsbergh worried that many Mission Friends were not connected to a common church life and a wider immigrant community.

Second, Skogsbergh was deeply concerned about the spiritual status of the increasing number of Swedish immigrants in the Twin Cities. He had already set ablaze dozens of revival fires in Chicago, and he sought to do the same during his crusade in the Northwest. He gained much inspiration from Moody in his desire to help as many experience a religious conversion as possible. It did not matter how they were brought to Christ as long as they got there quickly.[19] Writing about these spiritually hungry Swedish Americans, Karl A. Olsson noted that "people wanted God."[20] And Skogsbergh was prepared to convey this gospel message in a blazing manner.[21] He described the climax of his revival services as "a battlefield after a bloody engagement." Continuing, he noted, "Wherever one looked, people lay in the pews or hung like dishrags over the backs. Everywhere could be heard the weeping and sobbing of people who were asking earnestly what they could do to be saved. Believers from the various churches had learned to participate in the work for the salvation of souls."[22]

One young man who heard Skogsbergh's message and responded like so many others was Andrew Skoog, who had been living in the Twin Cities for eight years. Skoog's mother, out of concern for her son's spiritual state, entreated Skogsbergh to employ her son as organist for his worship services. She claimed that if Andrew were not used for Christ's work, he would serve the secular world through a career in the theater. Skogsbergh obliged, and Andrew soon experienced a religious conversion. The meeting of Skogsbergh and Skoog initiated a lifelong partnership. Together, they would shape religious and ethnic community life among Mission Friends.[23]

Gospel and music, as means to express Swedish evangelical faith and ethnicity, were part of the Mission Friend community in Chicago, a city to which Skogsbergh convinced Skoog to relocate in 1879, despite the fact that the song leader moved without any assurance of full-time work or salary. In the next several years, their cooperation produced a variety of results. A large Swedish tabernacle was built on the south side of Chicago; revival meetings were undertaken in other parts of the Midwest; song groups were organized; music programs were developed; a school for Swedish Americans was founded; a Swedish songbook was published (*Evangelii Basun,* 1883); and the Mission Covenant denomination was founded in 1885, the organizational meeting of which was held at the tabernacle.[24]

But Skogsbergh was not one to tarry in one place if he sensed that God was leading him to start a revival somewhere else. He believed that he best served God by establishing his evangelical revival center in Minneapolis at the beginning of 1884. By the time Skoog arrived in the summer of 1885, Skogsbergh had already initiated many activities, including a building program. After all, the preacher was inspired by an America where many things were big and busy, including revival programs and churches. He planned to erect the largest Swedish American tabernacle in existence by convincing the immigrants in Minneapolis to take the necessary financial risks. He already had "revealed" this vision during his 1877 revival, at a time when, as he later noted, "the news fell like a bomb on the people."[25] In 1884, now appointed pastor and spiritual shepherd, Skogsbergh proved his skill at raising funds within one month of his arrival, and plans were drawn under his close supervision. The ground floor was completed in 1886, and the Swedish Tabernacle was dedicated in the fall of 1887.[26] The construction of this place of worship was not an attempt to impress people with a grand and "stately temple." Rather, Skogsbergh wanted his congregation to have a "practical" American auditorium in which many could gather. Function, not style, was paramount.[27]

The preacher did not concentrate his efforts exclusively on the construction of a large tabernacle. During his pastorate of this significant church (nearly twenty-five years), Skogsbergh traveled a great deal on preaching and revival missions, seeking to establish and care for new churches while giving encouragement to his colleagues in ministry. His entrepreneurial bent, coupled with tireless journeys to every corner of the district, led him to envision many activities that joined congregations and pastors in a common mission program, and thus the Northwest Mission Association of the Covenant was formally established in 1896 in the basement of his tabernacle. Minneapolis was thought of as this association's Jerusalem, with Skogsbergh serving as bishop.

Although many were uncertain (or even jealous) of Skogsbergh's intentions and successes, and even though he often did act independently, his ambitions paved the way for many district and national organizations for evangelical Swedish immigrants.[28] He was not to be outmaneuvered by either people or conflicting events.[29] He believed that all gatherings of immigrant people were opportunities to build Swedish American religious culture—a work he believed would grow because of a vigorous revival attitude. Ethnicity and religion, as developed by first-generation immigrants, was an inheritance to bequeath proudly to second and third generations. This inheritance was not expressed in buildings, but rather through a living culture in which conversion was the "one thing needful" and living a Christian life was the objective. Skogsbergh was clear: immigrants were living a "pioneer life," and the establishment of their living culture would bear fruit in future generations.[30]

As an immigrant community leader, Skogsbergh also sought to express a shared religious vocabulary. He believed that the proclamation of the gospel was the best way to pass on a Swedish American religious inheritance.[31] Furthermore, the building of immigrant institutions was the best way to pass on a Swedish American ethnic inheritance. Erik Dahlhielm stated that Skogsbergh did this with the flurry of a "hurricane."[32] If he were too inactive, would that not look like religious idleness? Dahlhielm has provided an even more revealing interpretation when he noted one of the reasons why the preacher could carry on hurricane-like activities: "Skogsbergh supplied the ideas, the energy, the inspiration. Skoog did the work—most of the work, at any rate."[33]

Indeed, much of the time, Skogsbergh was the one to initiate and Skoog the one to implement. With great precision and attention to detail, Skoog organized his colleague's vision, ideas, and creations into workable routines. In the Twin Cities, as in Chicago, he was intimately involved with Sunday school, in its American-inspired Christian-education format. He also did most of the editorial work for *Söndagskol-Vännen* (*The Sunday School Friend*), a children's paper founded by Skogsbergh in 1886. Because of the careful administration provided by Skoog and others, the Sunday school programs in the district and denomination received timely attention and development.[34]

In 1884, Skogsbergh began publishing a Swedish American religious newspaper, *Svenska Kristna Härolden* (*The Swedish Christian Herald*), which was renamed *Minneapolis Veckoblad* (*The Minneapolis Weekly*) in the fall of 1887. Skoog published a wide variety of religious materials, and this newspaper was a major communication link for many Swedish Americans. Although it certainly had competitors, the weekly's long life (from 1884 to 1934) is a witness to the significant role its journalists played in the dissemination of information, devotional materials, and matters of interest to the immigrant community.

Skoog's publishing efforts converged with his desire to develop the musical life of Swedish Americans at the tabernacle and in the wider Mission Covenant Church. A volume of hymns was published in 1889 (*Evangelii Basun II*) and was followed a year later by a songbook for Sunday schools (*Lilla Basun*). In 1891, a book of choral music was added to the increasing number of Skoog's copyrights.[35] That same year, the Skoog Publishing Company began operations, and several books, hymnals, and choral music pieces rolled off the printing press. Skoog's music journal, *Gittit*, offered advice to church musicians and new material for their choirs and congregations.[36] This plethora of activity and productivity evidences a great versatility, one of Skoog's traits that most impressed Theodore W. Anderson, future president of the Mission Covenant Church, and many others.[37] During his years in the Twin Cities, Skoog proved himself to be an accomplished editor, translator, publisher, composer, teacher, fund-raiser, and choral leader. His music helped immigrants express their Christian faith through song, and this would bear fruit in future generations. As a community leader, Skoog developed a religious musical culture that allowed many Swedish Americans to participate in worship and relate to their Christian faith. Religion, as expressed through music, bound immigrants together within their ethnic community.

Skoog's ethnicity and religion were public, not private, issues. His published hymns were used in his own tabernacle choirs and through congregational singing at services led by Skogsbergh. Like Ira Sankey, though not as famous, Skoog wanted to encourage lively and robust congregational singing as a complement to the preaching of his colleague. Like J. S. Bach, though not as prolific, Skoog translated, transcribed, and composed music for the church. Like F. Melius Christensen, though probably not as precise, Skoog led choirs. This was a task for which he lacked training, according to his own critique. He reflected later, "I actually knew nothing about choral conducting, but I reasoned thus: First and foremost, singers need a little knowledge about sight-reading, and in any event, I was so far advanced in music that I could keep myself ahead of them." Regardless of his own feelings of inadequacy, reports of excellent singing in the filled-to-capacity tabernacle reveal that his manner of leading choirs and congregations in song was widely approved.[38] And the statistics are impressive. One of his children's choirs had five hundred members. During a festival in 1901, Skoog led a combined choir of three hundred singers. A reunion choir in 1908 had a list of four hundred names.[39] He also gave instruction in singing and lectured his choral singers on how to become skilled in "hitting the tone," as he called it.[40] Many in his choirs were not accomplished, but Skoog was undaunted. In Christian worship, according to Skoog, "spiritual tonality" was more important than absolute or perfect pitch.[41]

The spiritual tone, or faith pitch, of Skoog took on a variety of forms, and his contributions allowed Swedish Americans from different generations to sing their faith through their hymns. Two hymns that do not exist in the English-language database ("Day by Day" and "I Have a Future All Sublime") were nevertheless important for the growing generation of English speakers in the immigrant communities. To be sure, Skoog wanted the Swedish evangelical heritage to be sung by future generations, and the way to ensure this was to translate the texts into English—and to provide opportunities for singing in Swedish and English. He and many others believed (rightly) that bilingual communities would survive. In the following Lina Sandell text, translated by Skoog, the faith of Swedish evangelicals is certainly evident—a faith that Skoog certainly thought was worth translating and singing about:

Day by day and with each passing moment,
Strength I find to meet my trials here;
Trusting in my Father's wise bestowment,
I've no cause for worry or for fear.
He whose heart is kind beyond all measure

Gives unto each day what he deems best—
Lovingly, its part of pain and pleasure,
Mingling toil with peace and rest.[42]

Or note this translation by Skoog of a text and tune by the Swedish revival folk musician Nils Frykman:

I have a future all sublime,
Beyond the realms of space and time,
Where my Redeemer I shall see
And sorrow never more shall be.

A precious heritage is mine,
In heaven kept by love divine;
What serves me best, while here below,
My Father will provide, I know.

Dear Lord, I pray that I may be
More wholly yielded unto thee,
While on the way I yet remain,
Before my heavenly home I gain.[43]

Swedish evangelicals did a good deal of singing about the heavenly home for the wayward earthly pilgrim. There are literature and research that note how the immigrant experience was often referred to as a pilgrim experience. This is evident in many evangelical texts, and Swedish-language hymns were no exception. Skoog wrote this text and the accompanying music:

We wait for a great and glorious day,
As many as love the Lord,
When shadows shall flee, and clouds pass away,
And weeping no more be heard.
O wonderful day that soon may be here!
O beautiful hope the pilgrim to cheer!
Thy coming we hail in tuneful accord,
Thou glorious day of Christ, our Lord.[44]

Skoog's music often reflected the joy of the evangelical faith, as well as the hope of the evangelical life. This joy came through in the musical rhythms that gave life to the worship services in the Minneapolis Tabernacle. Skoog never had the opportunity to translate the following hymn by E. Gustav Johnson into English. He felt that it offered easy-to-sing Swedish texts for second-generation immigrants who he thought should learn to sing about their faith in Swedish:

> Praise the Lord with joyful song,
> Unite with full accord!
> For his glory and his might
> Sing praises to the Lord!
>
> Sing his praises every living thing,
> Unto him devoted homage bring,
> Of his love and goodness ever sing!
> Hallelujah! Praise the Lord!
>
> Praise him with harmonious chimes,
> With chords of joy proclaim!
> Great and holy is the Lord:
> Sing praises to his name!
>
> Sing his praises every living thing,
> Unto him devoted homage bring,
> Of his love and goodness ever sing!
> Hallelujah! Praise the Lord![45]

The following text was especially intended for revival meetings and Sunday school worship services:

> Sing the glad carol of Jesus, our Lord,
> Sing it again, Sing it again!
> No other song can such blessing afford,
> Sing it again, again!
>
> Jesus, our friend!
> Happy and blessed chorus!

Over the earth let its message extend,
Sing it again, again!

Faith and new courage are in this refrain,
Sing it again, sing it again!
Freedom it offers, it breaks every chain,
Sing it again, again!

Jesus, our friend!
Happy and blessed chorus!
Over the earth let its message extend,
Sing it again, again![46]

Perhaps this hymn best elicits the similarities between the singing in the Swedish evangelical culture and the singing in the English evangelical culture: a theology of Jesus as friend, the joy of the new life offered by Christ, and the human need for the Savior and for reconciliation. Even if specific hymns were different from one ethnic group to another (and therefore do not appear on the same database), Swedish- and English-speaking evangelicals were musically communicating similar themes about faith. They were singing what they believed, and they believed what they sang.

Numerous activities informed the traditions that Skogsbergh and Skoog helped shape among Swedish evangelicals in the Twin Cities. Thousands of people attended morning and evening services at the tabernacle, and tons of hymns and musical scores were published. Large choirs held weekly rehearsals, while hundreds of children learned to sing their evangelical faith. Numerous ministerial meetings and conferences were held together by robust singing of a faith inherited from the homeland yet modified to express a pilgrim experience in the adopted country. For many of these Swedish evangelicals, in seeking to define their identity in the New World and in perhaps realizing they were unsure exactly how to do so, the hymns they sang within their evangelical community in the Twin Cities must have seemed like a "center of the universe." And for them it was. It was their ethnic home. These evangelicals knew they were no longer living in a culture like that of their home country of Sweden. At the same time they were pilgrims who wished to express their religion and who generally valued America, but they were unwilling to accept being forced into the chaos of a melting pot, thereby losing their cultural integrity. These were a thoughtful people who knew that they could sing the Swedish revival hymns with the same vigor as the second generation, who began to appreciate the English hymnology of Bliss and Sankey. Thus life was a daily dialectic: both Sweden and America defined them. When they asked themselves if they were Swedes or Americans, they probably looked to their developing culture—to the gospel about which they sang—as the means by which they were simultaneously preserving Sweden and embracing America. The community language contained a vocabulary influenced by their hymn singing. Their evangelical faith was communicated musically from one person to another and from one generation to another. They were held together, in part, by a framework defined through their hymnology.

Notes

1. Karl A. Olsson, *By One Spirit* (Chicago: Covenant Press, 1962), 81–87.

2. Axel Andersson, *Svenska Missionsförbundet. Dess uppkomst och femtioårliga verksamhet, Inre missionen* (Stockholm: Svenska Missionsförbundets Förlag, 1928), 27–31.

3. Hugo Söderström, *Confession and Cooperation: The Policy of the Augustana Synod in Confessional Matters and the Synod's Relations with Other Churches up to the Beginning of the Twentieth Century* (Lund, Sweden: CWK Gleerup Bokförlag, 1973), 56–69. Cf. Olsson, *By One Spirit,* 181–96.

4. Carl V. Bowman, *The Mission Covenant of America* (Chicago: Covenant Book Concern, 1925), 19–32.

5. For a biography of Skogsbergh, see Erik Dahlhielm, *A Burning Heart: A Biography of Erik August Skogsbergh* (Chicago: Covenant Press, 1951).

6. For the life of Skoog, see E. Gustav Johnson, *A. L. Skoog: Covenant Hymn-Writer and Composer* (Chicago: Covenant Historical Commission, 1937); Oscar E. Olson, "A. L. Skoog: Pioneer Musician of the Evangelical Mission Covenant of America" (Master's thesis, Northwestern University, 1941); Skoog Papers 4:7, Covenant Archives and Historical Library, Chicago [hereafter identified as Skoog Papers]; and Hjalmar Sundquist, "A. L. Skoog," *Covenant Weekly,* December 4, 1934: 5.

7. Carl V. Bowman, *Son of the People: The Autobiography of C. V. Bowman* [English version] (Chicago: Covenant Publications, undated), 187.

8. Philip J. Anderson, *A Precious Heritage: A Century of Mission in the Northwest, 1884–1984* (Minneapolis: Northwest Conference, 1984), 25.

9. For example, note the terminology of J. Hector St. John de Crève-coeur, *Letters from an American Farmer* [1782] (New York: Dutton, 1957), 39; and Israel Zangwill, *The Melting Pot* [1909] (New York: Macmillan, 1910). For representative sources in which scholars suggest an older immigration histo-riography (preoccupied with the notion that Swedes quickly assimilated into or adjusted to American society), see Adolph B. Benson, "The Assimilation of Swedes in America," *The Swedish Pioneer Historical Quarterly* 7 (October 1956): 139, and Oscar A. Benson, "Problems in the Accommodation of the Swede to American Culture," *University of Pittsburgh Bulletin* 30 (1933): 47. Cf. Gene Lund, "The Americanization of the Augustana Lutheran Church" (Ph.D. diss., Princeton University, 1954), and Carl M. Rosenquist, "The Swedes of Texas" [1930], in *A Report on World Population Migrations: As Related to the United States of America* (Washington, D.C.: n.p., 1956).

10. Martin E. Marty has written that "ethnicity is the skeleton of religion in America because it provides 'the supporting framework,' 'the bare outlines or main features,' of American religion." Martin E. Marty, "Ethnicity: The Skeleton of Religion in America," *Church History* 41 (1972): 9.

11. John Higham, "Leadership," in *Harvard Encyclopedia of American Ethnic Groups,* ed. Stephan Thernstrom (Cambridge: Belknap, 1980), 642, 646. Cf. John Higham, *Send These to Me: Immigrants in Urban America* (Baltimore: Scribner, 1975), and John Higham, ed., *Ethnic Leadership in America* (Baltimore: John Hopkins, 1978).

12. Victor Greene, "'Becoming American': The Role of Ethnic Leaders— Swedes, Poles, Italians, Jews," in *The Ethnic Frontier: Essays in the History of Group Survival in Chicago and the Midwest,* ed. Melvin G. Holli and Peter d'Alroy Jones (Grand Rapids: Eerdmans, 1977), 144–75.

13. Johnson, *Skoog,* 6.

14. For discussions on Skogsbergh as "the Swedish Moody," see Anderson, *Precious Heritage,* 37, and Herbert E. Palmquist, *The Wit and Wisdom of Our Fathers: Sketches from the Life of an Immigrant Church* (Chicago: Covenant Press, 1967), 87.

15. Dahlhielm, *Burning Heart,* 56–85.

16. Erik August Skogsbergh, *Minnen och upplevelser under min mer än femtioåriga predikoverksamhet* (Minneapolis: Veckobladets Trykeri, 1923), 180.

17. Erik August Skogsbergh, *Ett tjugofemårsminne* [1899], 26. MS translation by Karl A. Olsson, E. A. Skogsbergh Papers 1:17, Covenant Archives and Historical Library, Chicago.

18. Anderson, *Precious Heritage,* 27–28.

19. Skogsbergh, *Minnen,* 149–60. Cf. Skogsbergh, *Ett tjugofemårsminne,* 26–29.

20. Olsson, *By One Spirit,* 463.

21. For a narrative about Skogsbergh's first preaching tour in the Twin Cities, see Dahlhielm, *Burning Heart,* 63–73.

22. Skogsbergh, *Ett tjugofemårsminne,* 27. Cf. Skogsbergh's description of revival meetings as "battlefields" in *Minnen,* 98.

23. Skogsbergh, *Ett tjugofemårsminne,* 160–61. Cf. Dahlhielm, *Burning Heart,* 65–66. Skoog called Skogsbergh his "spiritual father" and credited the preacher with allowing his work to bear so much fruit. Andrew L. Skoog, "Minnen från min körverksamhet," MS, Covenant Archives and Historical Library, Chicago, 17.

24. Skogsbergh, *Ett tjugofemårsminne,* 4–10.

25. Ibid., 31.

26. Skogsbergh, *Minnen,* 195–203.

27. Ibid., 208–9.

28. Anderson, *Precious Heritage,* 36–43.

29. As a matter of fact, there are very few occasions when other church leaders or members of his church outmaneuvered Skogsbergh. The eventual move of the Covenant school to Chicago, in 1894, is one occasion when Skogsbergh's view did not rule the day. For insight into aspects of Skogsbergh's personality, see Skogsbergh, *Ett tjugofemårsminne,* 9, and Anderson, *Precious Heritage,* 37.

30. Skogsbergh, *Minnen,* 167–68.

31. In his memoirs, Skogsbergh often mentions his revival work. He calls it fishing and hunting for souls, or sowing and harvesting the conversion crop. Skogsbergh, *Minnen,* 274–75. Cf. Skogsbergh, *Ett tjugofemårsminne,* 20–26.

32. Dahlhielm, *Burning Heart,* 145.

33. Ibid., 80.

34. Ibid., 112.

35. Although a good many of Skoog's texts were available in Swedish, it is interesting to note that his work went generally unnoticed in Sweden, even in Svenska Missionsförbundet (Mission Covenant Church of Sweden) circles. Concerning the American Covenant, twelve Skoog hymns were in the hymnal that was used until 1973. In the American Covenant hymnal published in 1996, four Skoog hymns and four of his translations are available. The Swedish hymnal presently used in most Mission Covenant churches, *Psalmer och Sånger,* contains only one Skoog hymn: "Snart randas en dag" ("We Wait for a Great and Glorious Day").

36. Skoog, "Minnen," 11–15. Cf. Anderson, *Precious Heritage,* 39.

37. Palmquist, *Wit and Wisdom,* 193.

38. Although Skoog lamented his lack of musical training, Skogsbergh wrote that the song leader was "born a composer." Skogsbergh, *Minnen*, 180.

39. Skoog, "Minnen," 3, 14–16.

40. Lecture by A. L. Skoog, MS, Skoog Papers 3:21.

41. Skoog, "Minnen," 9.

42. "Day by Day and with Each Passing Moment," *The Covenant Hymnal* (Chicago: Covenant Press, 1973), 381.

43. "I Have a Future All Sublime," *The Covenant Hymnal* (Chicago: Covenant Press, 1973), 609.

44. "We Wait for a Great and Glorious Day," *The Covenant Hymnal* (Chicago: Covenant Press, 1973), 230.

45. "Praise the Lord with Joyful Song," *The Covenant Hymnal* (Chicago: Covenant Press, 1973), 73.

46. "Sing the Glad Carol of Jesus, Our Lord," *The Covenant Hymnal*, 255.

6

Lifting the Joists with Music

The Hymnological Transition from German to
English for North American Mennonites,
1840–1940

David Rempel Smucker

As a Christian denomination that traces its historical origins
to sixteenth-century European Anabaptism, Mennonites have considered congregational hymn singing as an indispensable pillar of communal and personal worship. Knit together by the spiritual effects of
physically producing verbal affirmations in music, Mennonite congregations have celebrated their journey with God in Jesus Christ.

An emphasis on the spiritual enfranchisement of lay people and the
strong aversion to liturgical practices of the Roman Catholic Church
resulted in a simple, congregation-centered liturgy.[1] Anabaptist theological emphases, combined with an isolation of geography and culture, have helped to fashion a significant hymnological tradition.[2] This
tradition has been nurtured by compositions both by Anabaptist-Mennonites and, from the very beginning of the movement in the
1500s, by texts and tunes originating in other Christian groups and
tunes from secular contexts.[3]

In one sense, Christians struggle to sing what spoken words cannot
express. This singing always has a component of oral tradition conveyed unconsciously without the aid of printed materials or organized
instruction. We learn to sing hymns by singing hymns—from the
subtle cues of gesture, timbre, volume, posture, and emotional expression.[4]

Hymnals provide pale and inadequate evidence for this aspect of
the story of music. Yet prior to the age of electronic recording, hymnals are the primary evidence available for research on an aspect of
church life that was rarely described in writing. Hymnals have served
to channel aspects of the hymnological stream and to provide histo-

rians with more objective evidence than a series of isolated anecdotes, evidence by which long-term trends may be identified. This chapter centers on printed hymnals for basic evidence.

Introduction

From the first immigration of Mennonites to North America in 1683, the majority of Mennonites and Amish spoke a form of German. They encountered English from the beginning of their sojourn. For certain legal and economic situations they needed either to learn some English or to depend on fellow Germans who knew it. However, the first official hymnal in English was not published until 1847, 164 years after the first handful of Mennonites stepped ashore in Philadelphia, Pennsylvania. From 1683 into the twenty-first century, German-speaking Mennonites and Amish have immigrated to North America— each group creating, strengthening, or reviving the German-language hymn tradition in the face of the wider, and in most instances, predominant English-speaking culture. This language transition from German to English is continuing today in Canada with German-speaking Mennonites of recent origins in the former Soviet Union, South America, and Central America.[5]

This chapter focuses on the nature of the North American Mennonite hymnological tradition at four junctures of transition from German to English, the first of which began in 1847 when the first English hymnal was published. The study then progresses to the 1940s, when two hymnals—one German and one English—were published. The year 1950 also marks the endpoint of the "Evangelical Hymns Database," developed under the auspices of the Institute for the Study of American Evangelicals (ISAE) of Wheaton College, Wheaton, Illinois.[6] The ISAE Database provides a baseline historical picture of the North American Protestant textual tradition, which Mennonites confronted in their musical transition.

The timing and nature of this transition depended on a complex interplay of immigration waves from German-speaking lands in various time periods, the degree of theological/ideological separation from the wider society, the degree of geographical separation from the wider society, and the degree of anti-German sentiment in the wider society. Generalizations that precisely fit all cases are almost impossible to prove, so this chapter will focus on four representative regions, each during a particular time period from 1847 to 1940. Nine representative hymnals will be examined more closely—with two (in one instance three) hymnals for each time period. For each pair of hymnals, the antecedent one is German and the subsequent one is English. The four time periods (1737–1847; 1848–90; 1891–1927; 1928–40) each preceded the first edition of four influential English hymnals published by Mennonites—in the first two time periods for the (Old) Mennonite Church and the last two time periods for the General Conference Mennonite Church. This chapter will present its findings for each of the four time periods and regions then draw some provisional conclusions.

The four time periods and regions plus abbreviations of German and English Mennonite hymnals follow: 1) 1737–1847: Virginia (Old) Mennonites UG—*Unpartheyisches Gesangbuch* (1804) and PH—*A Collection of Psalms, Hymns, and Spiritual Songs* (1847); 2) 1848–90: Midwestern (Old) Mennonites of Indiana/Ohio/Illinois, AL—*Die Allgemeine Lieder Sammlung* (1871), DLM—*Deutsches Lieder und Melodien* (1895), HT—*Hymns and Tunes* (1890); 3) 1891–1927: Great Plains (U.S.) General Conference Mennonites, GMN—*Gesangbuch Mit Noten* (1890), MHB—*Mennonite Hymn Book* (1927); 4) 1928–40: U.S. and Canadian General Conference Mennonites, GM—*Gesangbuch der Mennoniten* (1942), MH—*Mennonite Hymnary* (1940).

The hymnals chosen for this study were the official ones produced primarily for Sunday morning worship. In general, the English language initially entered Mennonite music literature in privately published books, Sunday school songbooks, singing school books, or even later through sheet music, radio, and television. One could suggest a sequence of social locations for the transition to English: informal circle of family or friends, church gatherings other than Sunday worship, Sunday worship, and the official hymnal.[7] These are significant areas of study, but for present purposes, the focus remains on hymnals as the central rite of communal worship.

The sociology of language and foreign-language acquisition shows that children and young people more easily learn a new language than adults. This becomes clear when studying the transition to German among Mennonites in various time periods and regions. For example, the singing school among nineteenth-century Virginia Mennonites was a religious and social institution that focused on young people. It often had a key role in the introduction of English songs and hymns. The songs and hymns of the singing schools were usually not sung during Sunday worship, at least not initially. The efforts to improve and regularize singing, to introduce part singing, to teach music literacy—all opened the gate for English hymns.[8]

The title phrase "lifting the joists" comes from a metaphor used in a report in 1906 about the hymn singing of the Virginia Mennonites.[9] It points to the metaphorical impact of powerful musical vibrations on the physical structure of a church building in a worship service. To extend the metaphor, this study asks the question: Were the meetinghouse roof joists of the German-language tradition "lifted" when Mennonites sang English hymns, and, if so, did the roof structure sustain too much "damage" to allow repair? Or did the roof settle down easily and sturdily on the walls and continue to perform its proper function? That is, was the German-language hymnological tradition for Mennonites continued, transformed, or lost?

1. When Mennonites began singing hymns in English, did they appropriate the English Protestant tradition at the center of their own unfolding tradition, or did they relegate it to the periphery? a. What English text tradition(s) did Mennonites accept? b. What English-origin tune genre(s) did Mennonites accept?

2. When Mennonites began singing hymns in English, were they able to transfer or "bring along" any of their German tradition? a. Did they utilize any texts translated from German to English? b. Did they use German-origin tunes with English-origin texts?

3. Did the hymnological transition precede or follow the changes in wider church life and thought? a. What theological emphases were notable in the English texts that they appropriated? b. What was the sequence and was there any causation between the musical transition from German to English and other transitions in theology and polity?

Patterns and Methods

In a broad sense the hymnological contact between German and English, and the subsequent transition to English, can be theoretically viewed as types of responses grouped in two broad categories—heterogeneous mixtures signifying initial (and sometimes continuing) contact and homogenous mixtures signifying more mature interaction.

Heterogeneous mixture occurs where the two traditions are juxtaposed in usage; texts and tunes retain their form. The three responses concerning usage are 1) protect German and ban English, 2) use both German and English, and 3) abandon German and embrace English. When both languages are used, two additional subcategories emerge: a congregation may use both English and German hymnals or an English hymnal with a German appendix, and an English hymn text may be sung with a tune composed for a German text, or vice versa.

Homogeneous mixture occurs where the two traditions interact internally through change in form via translation or composition. The three responses under this rubric are 1) translate English text into German when the ideas based in English were brought into the "old" language, 2) translate German text into English when ideas based in the German language were transferred to the "new" language, and 3) compose tunes to either borrowed or composed English texts.

These interpretive constructs did not operate in a chronological sequence, although the homogeneous categories tended to follow the heterogeneous ones. Not every particular time period and region moved through a similar sequence. In some settings the process fixed or stopped at one category. For example, the Old Order Amish settled in the category of protecting German and banning English in worship, even though they learned English in order to converse with non-Amish. These categories provide helpful angles from which to view the interaction of hymnological traditions in two languages. I have been able to identify one or more of these constructs with the four sets of time periods/regions/hymnals.

During a period of cultural transition for an ethnic group, language is usually one of the last areas to change.[10] During a period of language transition, hymn singing is often the final or almost final element to make the transition. Along with other mimetic elements, such as scripture texts, prayers, and congregational responses, people remember hymns after other linguistic forms have been forgotten.[11] The association of a text with a particular tune creates strong signals for the memory. The final stage occurs when the younger people no longer understand the meaning of the language they sing.[12]

When a believer sings hymns in a language that he or she no longer uses in daily conversation, a certain lack of "fit" occurs, a distance between the singer and what he or she professes.[13] At this point the words in their formulaic use take on the symbolic quality of pointing less to the present and more to the past—to the parental generation. Only through skillful translation can the meaning of the texts point again to the present.

One method to ascertain the theological emphases of various hymnals is to examine the rubrics, the subject titles of the sections—their nature and order. I examined the rubrics of the hymnals and compressed the findings in a chart form. I then analyzed the order of the rubrics to identify doctrinal ordering patterns or liturgical ordering patterns. Doctrinal patterns emphasize a systematic theological order. Liturgical patterns arise from the order of the worship service, the order of the annual church calendar, or (what I call) the daily-seasonal natural order. (In the Protestant history, the former pattern is associated with the Reformed tradition and the latter with the Lutheran tradition.)[14]

Another method of ascertaining emphases is identifying most frequently used texts in a group of hymnals. From the ISAE Database I obtained four lists of first lines of hymn texts in order of frequency of use for the four time periods. I noted the first twenty most frequently used texts ("top twenty") in each time period and ascertained if those texts were used in the seven English-language Mennonite hymnals published during the period from 1847 to 1940.

Another useful comparative angle for this study is the history of North American Lutheran hymnody.[15] Many Lutherans also experienced the language transition from German to English and, in many instances, they lived in the same regions as Mennonites. It is helpful to compare and contrast Lutherans and Mennonites on the nature and timing of the hymnological transition, especially with respect to the above-mentioned heterogeneous and homogeneous categories.

For each time period I will describe the historical context, the hymnals, and the rubrics of the hymnals. Then I will answer the questions pertaining to the Anglo-American tradition, the transfer of the German tradition, and the types of heterogeneous and/or homogeneous contact. Finally, I will briefly correlate the hymnological transition with the theology influenced by North American Protestantism.

Four Time Periods and Regions

1737–1847: Virginia (Old) Mennonites

For this time period, the German hymnal chronologically antecedent to *A Collection of Psalms, Hymns, and Spiritual Songs* (PH, 1847) is represented by the *Unpartheyisches Gesangbuch* (UG, 1804), published in Lancaster, Pennsylvania. It contains significant portions of the European Anabaptist hymns from the *Ausbund,* and also texts from the European Lutheran and European Reformed traditions.[16]

For UG the order of rubrics was shaped by liturgical more than doctrinal themes. The first rubric is "For the beginning and end of gathering [worship]," that is, the worship-liturgical category. Toward the beginning of the table of contents we see a set of rubrics under the theme of church calendar-liturgical: Christmas, New Year, Passion, Easter, Ascension, Pentecost. Toward the end we see a set of rubrics under the theme of daily/seasonal-liturgical: spring, harvest, morning, evening, table grace, departure. Rubrics with the highest numbers of hymns include encouragement (9.3%), repentance (7.3%), cross and suffering (6.9%), and death and burial (6.2%)—themes that reflect the European Anabaptist and Pietist heritage. The first official English hymnal published by Mennonites in North America was PH, printed by Joseph Funk (1778–1862) in Rockingham County, Virginia.[17] Along with Joseph Wenger and David Hartman, Funk served on the committee that compiled this hymnal. The completion and subsequent printing of this book were the culmination of Funk's long career of compiling music books, leading singing schools, and publishing/printing religious works.[18]

Most of the Mennonites in Virginia had migrated from Pennsylvania in the century prior to 1847. Because many of the Pennsylvania Mennonites had come from Europe in the period between 1710 and 1750, the Virginia Mennonites of the mid-nineteenth century were removed from their European origins by as many as six generations. Although Pennsylvania Mennonites of the eighteenth century had contact with English speakers, a thriving Pennsylvania German culture enabled them to maintain significant geographical and linguistic identity. Much of this culture and religious identity was transferred to the Shenandoah Valley of Virginia, but it became more difficult to maintain both the linguistic and denominational identities, including hymn traditions, in the new setting.

The greater Shenandoah Valley contained important settlements of German-speaking Lutherans, who, like the Mennonites, underwent the language transition primarily in the period from 1820 to 1840.[19] In 1816, Funk published in this region his first music book, a German singing school book, *Die Allgemein nuztliche Choral-Music*, which was designed for Mennonites, Lutherans, and Reformed. A Lutheran financed the project and a Reformed person wrote the foreword[20]—an interdenominational effort not probable in Pennsylvania. This suggests that Funk was reducing the degree of theological separation between Mennonites and other denominations, even as he sought to satisfy the various German-speaking denominations.

Funk was concerned that significant elements of the German-speaking religious tradition would be transferred to English; consequently he translated a Mennonite confession of faith in 1837.[21] However, despite all his linguistic skill and printing ability, he did not undertake any major effort to translate the German hymn tradition of Mennonites into English. Unlike the Mennonites, the Virginia Lutherans in this era made English translations of much of their doctrinal and liturgical literature such as catechisms, hymn texts, confessions, sermons, and the liturgy. In fact, Funk himself printed the third edition of a Lutheran hymnal compiled by Paul Henkel.[22]

The 1847 hymnal appeared at the end of the language transition for Virginia Mennonites. One may infer from the preface that preaching tended to change to English before hymn singing: "It is thought expedient, as the English language has become so prevalent, to have the Word of God preached in the church, and the religious exercises in the worship of God performed in that language also."[23]

PH contains nineteen out of the twenty most frequently appearing English texts in the ISAE Database. They include nine by Isaac Watts and others by eighteenth-century British evangelicals such as Wesley, Robinson, Cennick, Cowper, and Stennett.

For PH, the order of rubrics is shaped by no discernible overall themes; small, isolated clumps exist that pertain to doctrinal, daily/ seasonal-liturgical, and worship-liturgical categories. Rubrics with the highest number of hymns include two miscellaneous ones—public worship (14%) and various subjects (18%). The third highest was prayer and supplication (7.9%). The order and nature of the rubrics of these two hymnals clearly reveal major contrasts. Also, no German-origin texts and tunes are found in this hymnal.

PH clearly draws on the Protestant Evangelical Anglo-American hymn tradition at its center. Little of the German-language hymn tradition was transferred into English. It is true, however, that in 1851 the second edition contained an appendix of twenty-seven German hymns.[24] This shows that Funk was not trying to suppress or ban the German tradition, but neither did PH promote homogeneous contact. In the final analysis, the appendix served to segregate rather than nurture the German tradition.

Many of the texts of PH indicated that they were to be sung with tunes from a singing school book, *Genuine Church Music* (1832) by Joseph Funk. This book contained only eleven German chorale tunes (5% of total), and those are set to English-origin texts, not translated German ones. A number of the tunes were from North American folk hymns.[25]

The preface of PH uses terminology and a theological emphasis that partakes of an evangelical longing for heaven as the benefit of singing hymns: "Thus they are animated and strengthened to march on in their heavenly way, through this barren wilderness, to the wished-for Canaan—the heavenly Jerusalem—there to join the company of those who were redeemed from the earth, and are harping upon their harps, and singing a new song before the throne."[26]

This is in marked contrast to the theological themes in the UG, which stress communal encouragement through obedience to Jesus Christ and his teachings, especially nonresistant love, as humbly practiced by his gathered community here on earth.[27] PH supplied the needs of Mennonites who advocated community-based singing schools, interdenominational cooperation, and Anglo-American hymns.

In striking contrast with PH is another Mennonite hymnal in English, also published first in 1847, titled *A Collection of Hymns* by John Reist, a minister of the Reformed Mennonite Church.[28] This very small and exclusivist group had fled mainstream Mennonites in 1812 in Lancaster County, Pennsylvania, to create an ethnically and theologically pure Anabaptist church. Instead of borrowing English texts or translating German ones from "corrupted" churches, Reist and other Reformed Mennonites most likely wrote all the texts so that the content could remain theologically pure. The level of poetry is quite crude. Here we see the abandonment of the German tradition in the context of a very conservative theology and polity—a church not open to the ecumenical and revivalist currents of the day. This hymnal appears to contradict the idea that only Mennonites open to broader American religious influences accepted English hymns, but the obscurity of this small group and the lack of extended studies on their hymnology makes fuller interpretation difficult.

1848–90: Midwestern (Old) Mennonites of Indiana / Ohio / Illinois

Most of the Midwestern (Old) Mennonites stemmed from the European emigration between 1710 and 1750, thus standing as much as eight generations from Europe by this time period. The Mennonites in this region and time period had, like the Virginia Mennonites, left the protective "womb" of a surrounding Pennsylvania German culture in Pennsylvania. They did not have as much geographical separation as their Pennsylvania coreligionists and possibly less than their Virginia ones.[29]

These Mennonites initiated institutional development in the church context such as Sunday schools, revivalism, publishing ventures, and mission efforts. They began to selectively appropriate techniques and institutional efforts from the wider Protestant world.[30] For example, in 1864, in Elkhart, Indiana, John F. Funk founded a printing and publishing firm and a church periodical—*Herald of Truth* in English and *Herold der Wahrheit* in German.

These Mennonites experienced a church division between the Old Order and the progressive factions in the 1870s, when the use of English became one of the bones of contention. The Old Order clearly discouraged English preaching and English hymns from their worship services. A story is told about a progressive church leader, Daniel Brenneman, in the 1860s in northern Indiana, who received criticism from a fellow Mennonite: "He sings bass and preaches in English."[31] Part singing and English preaching together were envisioned as highly undesirable by this conservative Mennonite worldview. After the Old Order and the progressive Mennonites parted ways in the 1870s in Indiana, the progressives were freed to assertively pursue their agenda of theological and institutional reform in the areas of Christian education, missions, and revivalism.

Singing parts in English was a skill taught in the singing schools, an innovation advocated by the progressives. In fact, Prairie Street Mennonite Church, the congregation of John F. Funk, in Elkhart, Indiana, led the way within the singing schools for Mennonites of northern Indiana.[32]

The Midwestern (Old) Mennonites were linked by belief and history to the Virginia Mennonites, even in the arena of hymnal publication. In 1880, Funk obtained the rights from the successor firm of his distant cousin, Joseph Funk of Singers Glen, Virginia, to publish editions of the 1847 English hymnal *A Collection of Psalms, Hymns, and Spiritual Songs.*[33]

The English hymnal for this time period was *Hymns and Tunes* (HT, 1890), which used all twenty of the most-frequent texts from the ISAE Database. Almost all of these texts are from the eighteenth-century British evangelicals (e.g., Watts, Robinson, Cowper), but a few reflect the nineteenth-century mission thrust—such as "From Greenland's Icy Mountains" by Heber.

The German hymnals of the second time period were *Die Allgemeine Liedersammlung* (AL, 1871) and *Deutsches Lieder und Melodien* (DLM, 1895). For these two hymnals, the order of rubrics was shaped by liturgical themes more than doctrinal ones. For DLM, the highest number were found in discipleship (8.9%) and miscellaneous (8.5%), the first a traditional European Anabaptist theme. However, unlike the earlier German hymnal (UG, 1804), new rubrics reflected a revivalist emphasis: youth hymns (8.9%), eternal life (5.1%), and spread of the gospel (4%). Also, a new flavor was provided by gospel hymn tunes (8%) and some translations of English texts into German.[34]

For the English hymnal (HT, 1890), the order of rubrics was strictly alphabetical, a utilitarian move away from doctrinal and liturgical order. Rubrics with the highest number of hymns include praise (12%), prayer and supplication (10.5%), and trust (6.7%).

The tune style developed by Lowell Mason, Thomas Hastings, and William Bradbury predominates in HT, with only a few gospel hymns. In addition to the classic texts of eighteenth-century British evangelicalism, there also appear twenty-four texts by Thomas MacKellar (b. 1812), a Pennsylvania Presbyterian who published a number of books of hymn texts.[35] This suggests a Calvinist influence. There were only a few (five) German texts translated into English out of 457 total texts—three Wesley translations of Zinzendorf and Gerhardt and two Winkworth translations of Weissel and Krummacher. However, the Winkworth translations (nos. 90, 424) were not set with the German chorale tunes but with tunes ("Migdol" and "Juniata") by North Americans. Of the 216 tunes and 457 texts, only two German tunes were used (eleven).[36]

In a new development, Mennonites composed 34 of the 216 hymn tunes.[37] In a few instances these were tunes set to the classic texts by William Cowper and Isaac Watts. This indicates the next-to-final stage in the homogeneous mixture of the German and English tradition—composing tunes for English texts. (The final stage was reached later in the *Church and Sunday School Hymnal* of 1902 when Mennonite John D. Brunk composed tunes set to English texts, some written by Mennonites.)[38] A comparison of these hymnals suggests that both were moving away from the German-language heritage in an environment characterized by a more homogeneous mixture. Progressive Mennonites now participated in the English-speaking tune and textual traditions in both English and German hymnals.

In 1872 Funk, the publisher, wrote a revealing plea that families not abuse his policy of sending, upon request, both the German and English copies for the price of one subscription. He outlined the various situations in which such an abuse could be avoided: "German families" who "may be enabled to read English better"; "those who have forgotten the German" and could, by reading both papers, "understand the German language"; and families "where the parents are German and the children English."[39] Although many Mennonites in this time period were bilingual, and various translations of theological works written by Mennonites in the 1800s were published, including an English translation of the monumental *Martyrs Mirror*, in 1886, the German hymns were not translated. A small book written by Funk illustrates this pattern. In 1887, he wrote a book that consisted of a biography in English of Lancaster Mennonite Bishop Christian Herr and twenty-five German hymn texts by Herr—with only one text, a funeral hymn ("Nun gute Nacht") translated into English. Funk clearly valued religious expression in the German language but did not undertake any significant effort to transfer German hymnody.[40]

The preface of HT (1890) clearly shows how the introduction of the Sunday school brought new hymns into the church: "One of the principal objects in publishing this book is to bring about a closer union in the singing between the Sunday-school and the church. The hymns and tunes are suitable for Church and Sunday-school services, as well as worship on all occasions: a few are especially adapted to children and the Sunday school."[41] This illustrates clearly how English hymns often became used in Sunday school settings.

Also revealing were the comments of Funk, in 1886, when he noted that the Virginia (Old) Mennonites and the Midwestern (Old) Mennonites both published, without each other's knowledge, new editions of PH—each with a new and different appendix.[42] This disparity illustrates how regional variations arose when musical leaders did not communicate their intentions to each other.

The contrast with Lutheran hymnody in this time period is most striking. The effort to revive and reclaim their German hymns in an English context reached a key point by 1872 when *Church Book with Music* was published.[43] This hymnal was the first in a line of efforts to accomplish this transition with integrity and respect for the beauty of the texts and tunes of the core Lutheran hymns (*Kernlieder*). About seventy-five years had elapsed from the publication of the first Lutheran hymnal in English—a period characterized by the shunning or inept appropriation of Lutheran tradition from the Reformation and Pietist periods. As one authority has noted, "The entire history of English-language Lutheran hymnody in America had [until 1872] shown an aversion to English translations of its German heritage, almost from the first."[44]

Although the Brethren, known in the 1800s as German Baptist Brethren, produced an English hymnal about the same time as the

Lutherans, the Brethren, like the Mennonites, did not translate their German hymns in the 1800s. From the first English hymnal in 1791, which contained no German-origin hymns, to the mid-1900s, the English hymnals did not show any meaningful appropriation of the German hymnic heritage.[45]

(Old) Progressive Mennonites of that time period and region who were undergoing the transition to English did not demonstrate the theological commitment, the linguistic skill, and the musical sensitivity to transfer their German-language hymnic heritage to English. The conservative Amish and Old Order Mennonites, who wanted to retain the German language for their worship services, of course, also did not demonstrate any desire to transfer their hymnic heritage to English.[46] Although Mennonites published and used a variety of biblical, devotional, and journalistic literature, no colleges or seminaries had been formed in this time period where such theological creativity and linguistic skills might have been nurtured to effect a smoother hymnological transition from German to English.

1891–1927: (U.S.) General Conference Mennonites of the Plains

By 1926 the General Conference (GC) Mennonites comprised persons stemming from three major waves of immigration from German-speaking regions in Europe. The Eastern District in Pennsylvania had its origins in the immigration of the 1700–1750 period, the same origins as the (Old) Mennonites noted in the previous two sections. The Middle District of Ohio, Indiana, Illinois, and Iowa had its origins in the Swiss-background Mennonites who emigrated from Switzerland and South Germany in the period from approximately 1820 to 1850, and finally the massive immigration of 1874–84 from Russia to the Plains states and provinces of the United States and Canada of Mennonites with ancestral roots in the Netherlands and northern Germany. In 1926, the GC Mennonites of the Plains comprised about sixty-nine percent of the total Mennonite population, the Middle District about nineteen percent, and the Eastern District about twelve percent.[47] By 1926, the recent bilingual immigrants and their children had become dominant in the General Conference.

Significant numbers of these German speakers left the Russian

Ukraine in the 1870s because their German language and religious identity were threatened by the civil authorities. As immigrants or children of immigrants, their dialect (Low German) helped maintain a linguistic boundary with other Protestant groups for a time.[48] The immigrant generation created a German-speaking "Christendom" of churches, denominational committees, schools, colleges, hospitals, and teacher's assocations.[49] However, what individualism and acculturalization began to erode, the impact of World War I hastened the process. During World War I they experienced a significant degree of anti-German hatred and rapidly abandoned the German language in the 1920s.[50]

The period from 1891 to 1927 for the GC Mennonites was critical in language transition. The Eastern District introduced an English periodical in 1885[51] and made the transition in the 1890s, the Middle District was in transition from 1900 to 1910, and the Western District saw major changes in the 1920s. Because the General Conference during this time period included descendants of German speakers (seven generations distant) and German-speaking immigrants, an opportunity was provided to share their German hymnic tradition with English speakers.

In this time period the German hymn tradition is represented by *Gesangbuch Mit Noten* (GMN, 1890) and the English with the *Mennonite Hymn Book* (MHB, 1927), the first English hymnal of the General Conference compiled and published by that group. MHB used eighteen out of twenty of the most frequent texts from the ISAE Database, incorporating the two strains noted earlier (eighteenth-century British evangelical and nineteenth-century American evangelical) with the nineteenth-century British composers in the Victorian style, such as Arthur Sullivan, Joseph Barnby, and John B. Dykes. The latter three composers had the highest numbers of tunes in MHB.[52]

For GMN the order of rubrics was shaped by doctrinal themes more than liturgical ones. Rubrics with the highest number of hymns include cross and suffering (3.6%), praise (3.5%), and missions (3.1%). For MHB the order of rubrics was also shaped by doctrinal themes more than liturgical ones. Worship was a major heading, but subheadings were sparse: morning, evening, opening, closing. Rubrics with the highest number of hymns include confidence and peace (4.1%), penitence and prayer (3.8%), and call/repentance (3.8%).

The German chorales were not absent in MHB, as in the (Old) Mennonite English hymnals of 1847 and 1890, but were very muted in their impact. Of the forty-six German tunes (13% of the total), only seventeen (4%) were chorales.[53] This reduction of German-origin hymns was by no means an articulated goal of all the committee. In fact, one member expressed regrets about the editorial process that resulted in the 1927 hymnal.[54] That the MHB neglected a felt need for German hymns is shown by the publication in 1937 of *English and German Christmas Songs for Schools and Churches,* a compilation of fifteen English songs and twenty-one German ones.[55]

The MHB was not widely accepted by the GC Mennonites, selling approximately 5,000 copies in three editions, in comparison to the GMN, which had fifteen printings of approximately 50,000 copies.[56] In addition to the small number of German chorales and the format, the constituency was not satisfied by the dearth of gospel hymns,[57] at that time the most prevalent style among evangelical Protestants.

The 1920s witnessed the conflict among GC Mennonites, between those influenced by fundamentalism and those influenced by liberalism.[58] The emergence of this conflict served to increase the contrast between advocates of gospel hymns and advocates of more traditional hymns. Walter Hohmann, the major compiler of MHB, later described gospel hymns in the following negative manner: a "cheap, shallow, sentimental, materialistic, type of hymn has crept into our hymnology and even into our hymnbooks."[59] MHB emerged during this intensely acrimonious conflict, compiled by those GC Mennonite leaders in the liberal wing, whose attitude was reflected in the large percentage of British Victorian hymns and the preface's reference to contemporary worship trends: "In the compilation of this Hymnal the chief aim has been to preserve those hymns that have endeared themselves to the Church through generations of use, and to make available the best of those hymns that have been inspired by changing conditions and the modern demands of worship."[60]

1928–40: (Canada and U.S.) General Conference Mennonites

The major influence on the language situation in this period was the massive influx of Mennonite refugees from Russia in the mid-1920s.[61] Fleeing war, revolution, pestilence, and famine, these German-speaking Mennonites primarily settled in Canada and joined either the

General Conference or the Mennonite Brethren. The General Conference eventually published two hymnals within two years, one in 1940 in English, titled *Mennonite Hymnal* (MH), to correct the shortcomings of the MHB, and one in 1942 in German, titled *Gesangbuch der Mennoniten* (GM), to serve the German-speaking immigrants.

The primary impetus for the 1942 German hymnal was the desire on the part of the Conference of Mennonites in Canada, especially the so-called Russlander Mennonites who emigrated from Russia in the 1920s, for a hymnal with text and tunes together in modern notation. Compiled largely by immigrants for immigrants, this hymnal revealed very little influence from English-origin texts and tunes.[62]

For the German GM, the order of rubrics presents a combination of liturgical and doctrinal themes—with groups of rubrics under the categories of church calendar liturgical, daily/seasonal liturgical, worship liturgical, and Christological doctrinal. Rubrics with the highest number of hymns included praise (4.1%), trust (4.1%), and cross and suffering (3.6%), themes associated with European Pietist and Anabaptist hymnals.

For the English MH, a sophisticated order of rubrics was divided into six books or sections: hymns for children; gospel songs; church year in chorales; metrical psalms; and responses, chants, and amens. One finds a combination of liturgical and doctrinal order of rubrics, even four rubrics for musical genres—gospel hymns, metrical psalms, children's hymns, and responses/chants/doxologies/amens. Rubrics with the highest number of hymns include praise (7.3%), missions (4.5%), and courage and comfort (4.3%).

MH used nineteen out of twenty of the most frequent texts in the ISAE Database. As in all three of the other eras, this shows that Mennonites had identified and accepted the most widespread hymn texts from the Protestant usage of that particular era.

By 1940, the U.S. General Conference Mennonites of the prairies were in the very final stages of the language transition. However, the influx of Mennonite immigrants in the 1920s to Canada helped inspire the editors of MH to emphasize the heritage of German chorales held in common by the U.S. and Canadian Mennonites of the General Conference, which I have described elsewhere in more detail.[63] MH was the first conscious and significant effort for Mennonites to incorporate the German-origin hymns in the English language. In addition to including a separate section of seventy German chorales, this hymnal included German texts (along with English) for thirteen of the seventy chorales.

The editor of MH publicly articulated the difficulty that the language transition had brought to Mennonites: "Many of the good hymns and chorales which our elders absorbed in their religious training are no longer known. When the change in language was made from German to English, the younger generations were cut off from the culture, the songs and books which nurtured their elders. In some cases at least, a light type of song which is musically thin, and poetically inferior, and spiritually shallow was substituted."[64]

Although the compilers had some reservations about the long-term contribution of gospel hymns, as the previous quotation suggests, they included a special section of about seventy—basically the same number in the German chorale section. They realized that these simple hymns of evangelical Protestantism had become indispensable for the constituency, even for progressive Mennonites.

In their successful effort to provide an authentic revitalization of German hymnic traditions in MH, the editors were not able or willing to draw on the final category of the homogeneous mixture—that is, Mennonites from the German-background tradition who composed hymns (texts and/or tunes) in English. The GC Mennonite musical development had not yet progressed to the point where hymn composers created in English. A few minor stirrings were seen in one tune (no. 77), by James W. Bixel and translation by Frieda Kaufmann, of a text (no. 562) by Gerhard Tersteegen.

By this time period the impact of Mennonite colleges and the entrance of Mennonites into universities and theological schools became noticeable as an educated generation assumed positions of leadership. The GC Mennonites had created Bethel College (1887) in North Newton, Kansas, and Bluffton College (1899) in Bluffton, Ohio. The (Old) Mennonite Church had founded Goshen College (1894) in Goshen, Indiana, and Eastern Mennonite College (1917) in Harrisonburg, Virginia. The compilers of MH, Lester Hostetler and Walter Hohmann, received theological education in Mennonite denominational colleges (Goshen and Bethel) and in larger, more specialized, more urban non-Mennonite schools (Chicago Music Conservatory and Union Theological Seminary).[65] This education enabled them to see the language transition in a broader context and shaped their self-consciously ecumenical approach to the hymnal while simultaneously emphasizing the denominational heritage of German hymnody.

Rubrics

An analysis of the order of the rubrics of these nine hymnals over a century (ca. 1840–1940) reveals a shift from liturgical order to doctrinal order, a shift somewhat associated with the move from German to English. This shift is not strictly correlated with the language transition; we can see that the later German hymnals have increased doctrinal order. This most likely reflects the appropriation of patterns of church life and hymns shaped by North American Evangelical Calvinism and Methodism more than the Continental German Pietism that Mennonites and Amish had internalized to a significant degree by the time of their eighteenth-century immigration to North America.

An analysis of the contents of the rubrics is presented in the following chart. The first time period (1804–47) shows signs of revivalism when the English hymnal PH featured the rubric of "Invitation" and reduced "Cross and Suffering" from 6.9 percent to 3.8 percent. The second time period (1848–90) showed the signs of revivalism when the English hymnal HT featured "Prayer," "Praise," and "Refuge" as rubrics. The third time period (1891–1927) was the only one in which the highest five rubrics of the German hymnal GMN did not correspond with any of the highest five of the English hymnal MHB; the rubric of "Confidence" and "Service" in the English hymnal has the flavor of progressive optimism. The fourth time period (1928–42) shows a marked contrast between the German GM and the English MH hymnal; the German one featured classic rubrics of European Pietism such as "Cross and Suffering," "Trust," and "Preparation for Death," whereas the English hymnal featured the progressive themes of "Children," "Courage and Comfort," and "Missions."

Lutheran and Mennonite Hymnic Traditions in Language Transition

North American Lutherans initially stumbled, especially in the early 1800s, in their attempt to recover their German hymnic heritage in the English language.[66] As an advantage in the recovery process, they had closer links to a living body of hymns, which could more readily apply to altered circumstances than could some of the hymns in the Anabaptist-Mennonite tradition, namely the Anabaptist martyr ballads.[67] Also, the Lutheran hymn tradition was much more thoroughly embedded in and distributed throughout the entire liturgical experience than the hymn tradition of Anabaptists. Musical responses of congregation and choir were composed and sung for many parts of the Lutheran worship service, whereas for the Old Order Amish (and presumably for North American Mennonites in the early 1800s) the singing of hymns by the congregation occurs primarily at the beginning of the service—mainly while the ordained men are in another room. The Amish singing stops soon after the ministers enter the room with the congregation, then preaching and praying begin.[68]

Lutherans founded educational institutions of higher learning— seminaries, colleges, and academies—in North America in the early and middle 1800s, which produced skilled musicians and educated leaders who performed the tasks of transferring their liturgy and its hymns to the English language. The most notable early seminaries were founded in Gettysburg, Pennsylvania (1826), various locations in South Carolina (beginning 1830), Springfield, Ohio (1845), and Philadelphia, Pennsylvania (1864).[69] On the other hand, the first Mennonite college wasn't founded until 1887, in Kansas, and the first long-lasting and significant seminaries were founded much later, in the 1940s, by the (Old) Mennonite Church and General Conference Mennonite Church.[70]

The Lutheran hymnic tradition benefited from the strong influx of immigrants in the mid- and late-1800s, who brought a living liturgical tradition of German hymnody plus concerns for confessional orthodoxy and the fruits of scholarly hymnological reform originating in Germany.[71] Like the Lutherans, the German hymn tradition of North American Mennonites was bolstered by nineteenth-century immigration. Unlike the Lutherans, these immigrant Mennonites did not bring any self-conscious hymnological reform and recovery impulse; the sheer presence of these German-speaking immigrants did provide crucial access to a living hymnological tradition. However, the English-speaking Mennonites did not initiate their own translations or draw extensively on other translations until the 1940 hymnal. In

Table 6.1
Chart of Hymn Text Rubrics in Nine Mennonite Hymnals in German and English: Five Largest Rubrics and Percentages in Each Hymnal by David Rempel Smucker

	UG 1804 Ger	PH 1847 Eng	AL 1871 Ger	DLM 1895 Ger	HT 1890 Eng	GMN 1890 Ger	MHB 1927 Eng	GM 1942 Ger	MH 1940 Eng
Children									7.5
Confidence + Peace								4.1	
Courage + Comfort								4.3	
Cross + Suffering	6.9	3.8				3.6	3.4		
Death + Burial	6.2		8.1	4.4	3.0	3.1			
Death, Preparation for							3.2		
Discipleship (*Nachfolge*)			3.9	8.9					
Encouragement (*Aufmunterung*)	9.3								
Eternal Life			3.9	5.1	5.9				
God's Love		4.2							
God the Father							3.6		4.3
Holiness/ Breathing after God		7.6							

Category								
Invitation			5.2			3.8		
Miscellaneous		18.4	8.5					
Missions		7.9		10.5		3.8		4.5
Prayer + Supplication	6.0				3.5			
Praise				12.0			4.7	7.3
Refuge				5.6				
Repentance	7.3					3.1		
Service						3.6		
Trust				6.7	3.1		4.1	
Watchfulness		3.4						
Youth Hymns			8.9					7.3

contrast, the Lutheran *Church Book with Music* (1872) drew on the hymnal of Catherine Winkworth, the skillful British translator of texts and compiler of German-origin tunes of *The Chorale Book for England* (1863).[72]

In its effort to revive English language links to the German-speaking past, editors of MH drew upon the German chorales of the sixteenth and seventeenth centuries composed in Lutheran, Reformed, and Pietist circles, not the Anabaptist martyr ballads found in the *Ausbund* hymnal.[73] The Old Order Amish and Old Order Mennonites adhered to the *Ausbund* hymns, and they confined their worship to the German language, with theology and church life constrained in the boundaries of their discipline.[74] Lutherans also divided into synods based on a variety of factors, including the degree of openness to American Protestant movements such as revivalism. However, even the most theologically conservative synods did not ultimately banish English from the worship service or higher education from the discipline, as did and do the Old Order Amish and some Old Order Mennonites. The progressive Lutherans had the option of benefiting from the English translations of the theologically conservative and confessional Lutherans, whereas progressive Mennonites did not have that option with respect to their Old Order counterparts.

Summary and Conclusion

For most of the century under consideration (ca. 1840–1940) contact between the German and English hymnic traditions exhibited heterogeneous mixtures (protect, use, abandon) and homogeneous mixtures (translate, compose). The Old Order Amish and Old Order Mennonites (the latter emerging between 1870 and 1890) never did make a transition to English hymns in their worship services. Conversely, we have seen that the progressive Mennonites accepted the most popular English hymns of their particular era from the wider Protestant hymn traditions.

The first time period (1737–1847) favored the heterogeneous borrowing from the hymnody of eighteenth-century British evangelicals. The second period (1848–90) favored the nineteenth-century North American evangelical hymn writers, including the activity of one Mennonite group who began to compose tunes to borrowed English texts—a sign of homogeneous mixture. In the third period (1890–1927), one Mennonite group favored the nineteenth-century British Victorians, while another Mennonite group had some leaders who composed both English texts and tunes. The fourth period (1927–40) illustrated an ecumenical embrace of various Protestant traditions and a special recovery of translated German chorales.

In terms of the wider Protestant theological influences mediated by the acceptance of these English hymn traditions, all the influences had taken root among progressive Mennonites before their English hymnals were published. We saw that revivalism was introduced in the first period and foreign missions in the second period. Optimistic liberalism characterized the new aspect of the third period. A broad ecumenical ethos, which included a revitalization of the German hymnic heritage, was the distinctive feature of the fourth period and its English hymnal, MH. This feature illustrated the effort of progressive Mennonites to affirm their denominational identity in a context of openness toward other Christian denominations.

A preparatory phase to the appropriation of the German hymn tradition among English-speaking Mennonites was provided by the historical studies of sixteenth-century Anabaptism. As reflected in the articles in *Mennonite Quarterly Review* in the 1930s and 1940s, and the writings of its editor, Harold S. Bender, the hymns of the Anabaptists were studied for what the texts revealed about the biographical details of the authors and the theological beliefs of the movement.[75] This confessional revival, often described as the "Anabaptist vision," used hymn texts as a fund of theological ideas. However, this perspective did not view the Anabaptist hymns in their worship context or as text-tune resources for contemporary renewal of a living worship tradition.

Until the 1930s and 1940s, very little sustained effort occurred among Mennonites to transfer their German tradition to English. For GC Mennonites in the United States, it was during this time that the first stirrings of a genuine and realistic consciousness arose for recovery of their German-language hymns. Theological and literary education provided the needed skills for certain leaders to emerge, and the denomination provided the institutional will to accomplish it in the English language. More importantly, the major immigrations of German-speaking Mennonites from Russia in the 1870s and the 1920s, many of whom joined the General Conference Mennonite Church group, confronted the English-speaking Mennonites of that conference with a thriving devotional and hymnological tradition that the English-speaking Mennonites could not ignore and that reminded them of the German hymns they were losing in the transition to English.

By the 1950s and 1960s the (Old) Mennonite Church leaders underwent similar developments with respect to assessing their German hymnic heritage.[76] They cooperated with the General Conference Mennonite Church on a hymnal in 1969, *The Mennonite Hymnal*, which continued to feature some German-origin hymns, primarily the classic German chorales of Lutheran and Reformed origins, but also a few hymns from the *Ausbund*, the latter of which reached back to the very beginnings of the Anabaptist movement.[77]

Notes

1. Alvin J. Beachy, *Worship as Celebration of Covenant and Incarnation* (Newton, Kans.: Faith and Life Press, 1968); Walter Klaassen, *Biblical and Theological Bases for Worship in the Believers' Church* (Newton, Kans.: Faith and Life Press, 1978); John D. Rempel, *The Lord's Supper in Anabaptism* (Scottdale, Pa.: Herald Press, 1993); Alvin J. Beachy, "The Theology and Practice of Anabaptist Worship," *Mennonite Quarterly Review* 40 (July 1966): 163–78.

2. *Mennonite Encyclopedia*, s.v. "Hymnology" (Scottdale, Pa.: Herald Press, 1990), 409–11, includes an overview.

3. Rosella Reimer Duerksen, "The Music of the Sixteenth Century Anabaptists," *Proceedings of the Eleventh Conference on Mennonite Educational and Cultural Problems* (Bethel College, North Newton, Kans., June 6–7, 1957), 67–76, which was based on research for her 1965 Ph.D. dissertation, "Anabaptist Hymnody of the Sixteenth Century" (Union Theological Seminary, New York, N.Y).

4. Kenneth Nafziger and Marlene Kropf, *Singing: A Mennonite Voice* (Scottdale, Pa.: Herald Press, 2001), explores these themes in a Mennonite context. In "Tributes to Robert Shaw," *Canadian Mennonite* 3 (February 15, 1999): 9, Shaw is quoted with comments on the style of singing that North American Mennonites have developed.

5. Cornelius J. Dyck, *An Introduction to Mennonite History*, 3d ed. (Scott-

dale, Pa.: Herald Press, 1993) describes these waves of immigration and also the marked increase in the latter 1900s among Mennonites outside Europe and North America without a Swiss, Dutch, or German ethnic origin.

6. The ISAE Database of the American Protestant Hymns Project was developed by Stephen Marini of Wellesley College in Massachusetts. See chapter 1.

7. Walter Jost, "The Hymn Tune Tradition of the General Conference Mennonite Church," *Proceedings of the Sixteenth Conference on Mennonite Educational and Cultural Problems* (Hesston College, Hesston, Kansas, June 8–9, 1967), 123, suggests this sequence. Elma Esau to David Rempel Smucker, December 18, 1998: A member of Emmaus Mennonite Church, Whitewater, Kansas, writes that the first English hymnal of that congregation was *Hymns and Sacred Songs* (1918), acquired between 1918 and 1927 for the Christian Endeavor youth group. Not until 1932 did the pastor preach any sermons in English.

8. Richard B. Rosewall, "Singing Schools of Pennsylvania, 1800–1900" (Ph.D. diss., University of Minnesota, 1969), 23, 188–91, describes the attempt of the early nineteenth-century Pennsylvania German singing schools to maintain the German language. See also Gerald C. Ediger, "Deutsch und Religion: Ethnicity, Religion and Canadian Mennonite Brethren, 1940–1970" (Th.D. diss., Victoria University and University of Toronto, 1993).

9. *Minutes of the Virginia [Mennonite] Conference*, 1939, 32: "The grand and never-to-be-worn-out old harmonies were selected and sung after the following order . . . with the same earnestness and 'joist-lifting' zeal so characteristic of the singers of 40 and 50 years ago."

10. John M. Janzen and Reinhild K. Janzen, *Mennonite Furniture: A Migrant Tradition (1766–1910)* (Intercourse, Pa.: Good Books, 1991), 198.

11. Joshua Fishman, "Demographic and Institutional Indicators of German Language Maintenance in the United States, 1960–1980," in *America and Germans: An Assessment of a Three Hundred Year History,* vol. 1, *Immigration, Language, Ethnicity,* ed. Frank Tremmler and Joseph McVeigh (Philadelphia: University of Pennsylvania Press, 1985), 259, describes what survives in language transition for mainstream German Americans beyond the third generation: "certain ritualized aspects of certain prayers, and particular formulaic acts and expressions."

12. The process of language death was described by a Pennsylvania German Reformed correspondent in 1849 when he reported on the practice of lining out hymns: "Some will say: 'We can sing German, but we cannot read it.' This is to be deplored, for it leads to the ruin of the German congregations." See Don Yoder, *Pennsylvania Spirituals* (Lancaster, Pa.: Pennsylvania Folklife Society, 1961), 127.

13. Bernard Holland, "In Language Sung Best by Its Own," *New York Times,* March 7, 1999, 37.

14. Paul Westermeyer, "Religious Music and Hymnody," *Encyclopedia of the American Religious Experience,* vol. 3, ed. Charles H. Lippy and Peter W. Williams (New York: Charles Scribner's Sons, 1988), 1285–86.

15. A few examples of the very rich literature on Lutheran hymnody are Carl F. Schalk, *God's Song in a New Land: Lutheran Hymnals in America* (St. Louis, Mo.: Concordia Publishing House, 1995); Paul Westermeyer, "What Shall We Sing in a Foreign Land? Theology and Cultic Song in the German Reformed and Lutheran Church of Pennsylvania, 1830–1900" (Ph.D. diss., University of Chicago, 1978), and his article based on this dissertation, "Liturgy and Hymnody in Nineteenth Century Pennsylvania," *Church Music* 80 (1980): 2–22.

16. *Unpartheyisches Gesangbuch* (Lancaster, Pa.: John Baer and Sons, 1804). J. Murray Barbour, "The Unpartheyishes Gesang-buch," in *Cantors at the Crossroads: Essays on Church Music,* ed. Johannes Riedel (St. Louis, Mo.: Concordia Publishing House, 1967), 92; Phillip E. Stoltzfus, "Partheyisches or Unpartheyisches?: Theological Themes in the Hymns of Ein Unpartheyisches Gesangbuch," unpublished MS for History Seminar, Goshen College, Goshen, Ind., 1987; Paul M. Yoder, ed., *Four Hundred Years with the Ausbund* (Scottdale, Pa.: Herald Press, 1964) provides an overview of this ancient hymnal.

17. Irvin B. Horst, "Joseph Funk, Early Mennonite Printer and Publisher," *Mennonite Quarterly Review* 31 (October 1957): 13.

18. Steven Nolt, "Finding a Context for Mennonite History: Pennsylvania German Ethnicity and (Old) Mennonite Experience," *Pennsylvania Mennonite Heritage* 21 (October 1998): 2–14, describes this Pennsylvania German ethnic context. Theron F. Schlabach, *Peace, Faith, Nation: Mennonites and Amish in Nineteenth Century America* (Scottdale, Pa.: Herald Press, 1988), 82, notes that Virginia Mennonites, by the 1830s, had a more tolerant policy toward disciplining members who married non-Mennonites. Virginia Mennonites exhibited a more open religious stance toward other denominations earlier than Mennonites in Pennsylvania.

19. Klaus Wust, *The Virginia Germans* (Charlottesville, N.C.: University Press of Virginia, 1969), 138–41.

20. Paul M. Yoder, "Nineteenth Century Sacred Music of the Mennonite Church in the United States" (Ph.D. diss., Florida State University, 1961), 93.

21. Horst, "Joseph Funk," 13.

22. Ibid., 8. Schalk, *God's Song,* 62–63. However, Henkel clearly desired to express Lutheran catechisms, hymnody, liturgy, and confessions in English and was willing to disseminate those efforts.

23. *A Collection of Psalms, Hymns, and Spiritual Songs* (Mountain Valley, Va.: Joseph Funk and Sons, 1847), 4.

24. *A Collection of Psalms, Hymns, and Spiritual Songs,* 2d ed. (Mountain Valley, Va.: Joseph Funk and Sons, 1851).

25. Harry L. Eskew, "Shape-Note Hymnody in the Shenandoah Valley, 1816–1860" (Ph.D. diss., Tulane University, 1966), 94.

26. *Collection of Psalms, Hymns and Spiritual Songs,* 3.

27. Leonard Gross, "Through the Eyes of Benjamin Hershey and Benjamin Eby: Insights into Lancaster Mennonite History and Theology," *Pennsylvania Mennonite Heritage* 19 (January 1996): 2–8.

28. John Reist, *Collection of Hymns, Designed for the Use of the Church of Christ* (Buffalo, N.Y.: A. W. Wilgus, 1847).

29. Nolt, "Finding a Context," 9–10.

30. Schlabach, *Peace, Faith, Nation,* 295–321.

31. John C. Wenger, *The Mennonites in Indiana and Michigan* (Scottdale, Pa.: Herald Press, 1961), 35.

32. Ibid., 33.

33. Horst, "John Funk," 10. Harold Bender, *Two Centuries of American Mennonite Literature: A Bibliography of Mennonitica Americana, 1727–1928* (Goshen, Ind.: Mennonite Historical Society, 1929), 21–22.

34. Yoder, "Nineteenth-Century Sacred Music," 45.

35. Samuel W. Duffield, *English Hymns: Their Authors and History* (New York and London: Funk and Wagnalls, 1888), 550–52.

36. Paul W. Wohlgemuth, "Mennonite Hymnals Published in the English Language" (D.Mus. diss., University of Southern California, 1956), 88–89, 92.

37. Ibid., 90.

38. Mary Oyer, *Exploring the Mennonite Hymnal: Essays* (Scottdale, Pa., and Newton, Kans.: Herald Press and Faith and Life Press, 1980), 66–68.

39. John F. Funk, *Herald of Truth* (January 1872): 8.

40. John F. Funk, *A Biographical Sketch of Bish.[op] Christian Herr, also a Collection of Hymns, Written by Him in the German Language* (Elkhart, Ind.: John F. Funk, 1887), 16–17.

41. *Hymns and Tunes for Public and Private Worship, and Sunday Schools* (Elkhart, Ind.: Mennonite Publishing House, 1890), iii–iv.

42. Funk, *Herald of Truth* (April 15, 1886): 120–21.

43. Carl F. Schalk, *Source Documents in American Lutheran Hymnody* (St. Louis: Concordia Publishing House, 1996), 92–99, reproduces the preface of *Church Book with Music* (1872) in which the editor, Harriet Porterfield Krauth, discusses some of the considerations used in translating German hymn texts and setting them with tunes.

44. Schalk, *God's Song,* 146.

45. Hedwig T. Durnbaugh, "Music in Worship, 1708–1850," *Brethren Life and Thought* 33 (autumn 1988): 276–77.

46. In John F. Funk, "On the Wissler Schism: A John F. Funk Letter," trans. by Nelson Springer, *Mennonite Historical Bulletin* 32 (January 1971): 7–8, Funk wrote that Wissler "had no objection to English preaching when it is necessary."

47. Leland Harder, "A Century of Statistics," *The Mennonite* 75 (November 15, 1960): 736–37.

48. David A. Haury, *Prairie People: A History of the Western District Conference* (Newton, Kans.: Faith and Life Press, 1981).

49. James C. Juhnke, *Vision, Doctrine, War: Mennonite Identity and Organization in America, 1890–1930* (Scottdale, Pa.: Herald Press, 1990), 313–15.

50. Gerlof Homan, *American Mennonites and the Great War, 1914–1918* (Scottdale, Pa.: Herald Press, 1994), 63–71.

51. David Rempel Smucker, "Understanding the General Conference Mennonite Church and Its Eastern District, 1875 to 1925," *Pennsylvania Mennonite Heritage* 17 (October 1994): 10.

52. Wohlgemuth, "Mennonite Hymnals," 236–37.

53. Ibid., 239.

54. David Rempel Smucker, "Singing God's Praises in Two Nations and Two Tongues," *Mennonite Quarterly Review* 73 (July 1999): 621.

55. *English and German Christmas Songs for Schools and Churches* (Newton, Kans.: Herald Press, 1937).

56. *Mennonite Encyclopedia,* s.v. "Hymnology," 883.

57. Wohlgemuth, "Mennonite Hymnals," 236. Smucker, "Singing God's Praises," 621.

58. Studies that cover this topic include Paul Toews, *Mennonites in American Society, 1930–1970* (Scottdale, Pa.: Herald Press, 1996), 64–83, which has a chapter titled "Mennonite Fundamentalism"; Nathan Yoder, "Mennonite Fundamentalism: Shaping an Identity for an American Context" (Ph.D. diss., University of Notre Dame, 1999); Beulah S. Hostetler, "Eastern Pennsylvania Mennonites and Fundamentalism, 1890–1950," unpublished MS at Lancaster Mennonite Historical Society.

59. Walter Hohmann, "Development of Music in the Mennonite Church," *Proceedings of the Third Annual Conference on Mennonite Cultural Problems* (North Newton, Kansas, August 18–19, 1944), 16.

60. *Mennonite Hymn Book* (Berne, Ind.: Mennonite Book Concern, 1927). The preface is unpaginated.

61. Frank H. Epp, *Mennonites in Canada, 1920–1940: A People's Struggle for Survival* (Scottdale, Pa.: Herald Press, 1982).

62. Wesley Berg, "Gesangbuch, Ziffern, and Deutschtum: A Study of the Life and Work of J. P. Claszen, Mennonite Hymnologist," *Journal of Mennonite Studies* 4 (1986) includes background on the situation that produced the 1942 hymnal. Also see George D. Wiebe, "The Hymnody of the Conference of Mennonites in Canada" (Master of Music thesis, University of Southern California, 1962).

63. Smucker, "Singing God's Praises," 622.

64. Lester Hostetler, "The Future of Our Church Music," *Mennonite Life* 3 (April 1948): 37.

65. A. Warkentin, ed., and Melvin Gingerich, asst. ed., *Who's Who among the Mennonites* (North Newton, Kans.: A. Warkentin, 1943), 115, 119–20. Paul Westermeyer, *Te Deum: The Church and Music* (Minneapolis: Fortress Press, 1998), 311–12, notes the "ecumenical hymnic vision . . . led to the common hymnic and musical quarry from which twentieth-century editors of hymnals have drawn their materials." The theme is developed by David Farr, "Protestant Hymn-Singing in the United States, 1916–1943: Affirming an Ecumenical Heritage," in *The Hymnal 1982 Companion,* ed. by Raymond F. Glover (New York: Church Hymnal Corporation, 1990), 505–26.

66. Schalk, *God's Song,* 51–66. See also Westermeyer, "What Shall We Sing."

67. Duerksen, "The Music of the Sixteenth Century," 74. See also A. J. Ramaker, "Hymns and Hymn Writers among the Anabaptists of the Sixteenth-Century," *Mennonite Quarterly Review* 3 (April 1929): 111.

68. John A. Hostetler, *Amish Society,* 4th ed. (Baltimore: Johns Hopkins University Press, 1993), 213–14.

69. E. Clifford Nelson, ed., *The Lutherans in North America* (Philadelphia: Fortress Press, 1980), 204–5.

70. Toews, *Mennonites in American Society,* 279–81.

71. Carl F. Schalk, *The Roots of Hymnody in the Lutheran Church—Missouri Synod* (St. Louis: Concordia Publishing House, 1965), 39–47. Westermeyer, "Liturgy and Hymnody," 14–16, describes the music in the Lutheran confessional recovery in Pennsylvania.

72. J. R. Watson, *The English Hymn: A Critical and Historical Study* (Oxford: Clarendon Press, 1997), 413–21. An example of the level of linguistic and theological skill needed to produce excellent translation of German hymn texts is Madeleine Forrell Marshall, "Translating 'Jesu Meine Freude,'" *Lutheran Quarterly* 2 (summer 1988): 225–43; T. D. Regehr, *Mennonites in Canada, 1939–1970: A People Transformed* (Toronto: University of Toronto Press, 1996), 281–82.

73. Jost, "Hymn Tune Tradition," 131, where he lists seventeen tunes, all from the sixteenth and seventeenth centuries, found in all five General Conference hymnals, from 1873 to 1965.

74. *Songs of the Ausbund,* vol. 1, *History and Translations of Ausbund Hymns* (Millersburg, Ohio: Ohio Amish Library, 1998), 5.

75. Ernest Correll, "The Value of Hymns for Mennonite History," *Mennonite Quarterly Review* 4 (July 1930): 218–19, illustrates this use of early Anabaptist hymn texts as biographical and theological sources.

76. See *Mennonite Encyclopedia,* s.v. "Hymnology," 882. *The Mennonite Hymnal* (Newton, Kans., and Scottdale, Pa.: Faith and Life Press and Herald Press, 1969) includes generous (thirty) translations by Catherine Winkworth, illustrating the flowering of this recovery of the German hymnic tradition: Oyer, *Exploring the Mennonite Hymnal,* 102–6.

77. *Mennonite Hymnal,* preface (unpaginated) by Mary Oyer points out three texts (nos. 40, 344, 384) translated from the *Ausbund* hymnal.

7

"Wrestling Jacob"

The Central Struggle and Emotional Scripts of Camp-Meeting Holiness Hymnody

Chris Armstrong

That which distinguishes lyric poetry is its subjectivity. If genuine, it must bear the stamp of personal experience; and so it becomes one of the most important records of human life. The history which lies imbedded in the poetry of the world is more comprehensive and more minute than any other written history.

F. D. Hemenway, "The Literature of Sacred Song"

Affection is like bread, unnoticed till we starve, and then we dream of it, and sing of it, and paint it.

Emily Dickinson, *The Letters of Emily Dickinson*

The Holiness Movement

From the early 1830s until the early 1890s and beyond, a renewal movement arose and operated first within American Methodism, then within other Protestant denominations in America.[1] This was the so-called holiness movement. Its proponents sought to function as a prophetic voice within their denominations for reform— particularly reform of the Christian life. The explicitly Wesleyan part of the movement believed it was reclaiming an earlier, purer, more powerful Methodism. From 1867 through the early 1890s (prior to the spread of holiness "come-outism"), the holiness movement enjoyed a phase of growth as it operated from the organizational base of the National Camp Meeting Association for the Promotion of Holiness (NCMAPH) and the denominational base of the Methodist Episcopal Church—North. Although many outside of that denomination sought holiness experience, espoused holiness doctrine, and sang holiness songs, this study will deal with the hymnody and history of the NCMAPH's core group of Northern Methodists, from which its leadership was chosen.

Holiness folk were solidly middle class, with the time and money to attend camp meetings each summer, where they arrayed themselves in neat rows, well-dressed and expectant, ready to enjoy (decently and in order) some of the strong emotions that had characterized the revivalistic rise of Methodism. Most of all, they had the time—as they worshipped at their many camp, midweek, and prayer meetings and read their periodicals, poetry, biography, and other literature—to explore and elaborate their own "inner worlds."

The Holiness Hymnody

Methodist hymns were already more closely instantiated in the experience of their singers than those of other Protestant denominations. Even casual inspection shows a propensity throughout Methodist texts of all sorts—from testimony and autobiography to didactic and theological writings—to quote hymns at key moments. Steven Cooley suggests that this is distinctive to Methodists, finding "nothing like it in the landmark revivalists Charles Finney, D. L. Moody, or Billy Sunday." More than this, "instances of Methodist revivalists urging the seeker to pray the text of a song are commonplace," and deathbed narratives almost always include requests for favorite songs. It is no surprise, then, that singing featured prominently in the camp-meeting holiness movement. In painting a word-picture of the holiness camp meeting, Bishop Matthew Simpson wrote of "the full notes of song that gush out by morning, noon, and night, from thousands of hearts, moved by a spirit of earnest piety."[2] And beyond the camp meeting, the "images, pictures, and narrative rhythms" of the holiness people's hymnody strongly and integrally shaped "their theological reflections, their religious experiences, their ritual, their institutional development, and their use of scripture,"[3] among other areas.

Which Hymns Are "Holiness"?

The answer to the question of which hymns are "holiness" is not as obvious as it may first seem. My answer—certainly not the only one possible—was to focus on seven hymnals either published by the NCMAPH, or in other ways strongly linked to the movement. The seven chosen were *Beulah Songs,* with 120 hymns; *Songs of Triumph,* with 157 hymns; *Songs of Joy and Gladness [word ed.],* with 271 hymns; *Songs of Perfect Love,* with 164 hymns; *Glad Hallelujahs,* with 192 hymns; *The Joyful Sound,* with 230 hymns; and *Radiant Songs,* with 195 hymns.[4]

The body of hymns in these hymnals comprised a smattering of Anglo-Protestant chestnuts; a larger selection of Wesley favorites;[5] plus, most prominently, a large number of hymns penned from within the movement itself. These were almost all evanescent. Authors included a few prolific lyricists and many "fly-by-night" lyricists, with both groups tending to have their words set to music by musicians associated with hymn-publishing outfits—often the editors of the songbooks themselves. A significant percentage of lyricists, in both categories, were women.[6] This raging current of literary aspiration (if not, often, inspiration) poured hundreds and probably thousands of new songs into the movement, which by the end of our period had swept all but the hardiest of the Protestant and Wesleyan classics into the back pages of the hymnals, and thence out of the hymnals altogether.

Fifteen Popular Hymns in Holiness Hymnals

A database containing most of the songs in these hymnals yielded 995 separate songs, of which a good many—perhaps even half—were unique publications (appearing in only one of the seven hymnals). When correlated with data from publications of hymns in selected holiness periodicals,[7] periodical advertisements for hymns sold as single sheets, and reports in various holiness literatures of the use of certain hymns at camp meetings, a holiness "top fifteen" surfaced. These were chosen based on frequency of mention and frequency of publication. They are as follows:

"There Is a Fountain Filled with Blood," William Cowper
"Wrestling Jacob," Charles Wesley
"I Am Trusting, Lord, in Thee" ("Coming to the Cross"), William McDonald
"Entire Consecration," Frances Ridley Havergal
"All for Jesus," Mary D. James

"Companionship with Jesus," Mary D. James
"The Cleansing Wave," Phoebe Palmer
"Are You Washed in the Blood?" Elisha Hoffman
"Must Jesus Bear the Cross Alone," Thomas Shepherd (and others)
"When I Survey the Wondrous Cross," Isaac Watts
"Blessed Assurance," Fanny Crosby
"Jesus, My Joy," Mrs. J. F. Crewdson
"More Like Thee," William J. Kirkpatrick
"I Love to Tell the Story," Miss Katherine Hankey
"Wondrous Love," Mrs. M. Stockton.

Note that more than half are by women—a figure somewhat higher than the gender breakdown of the whole holiness corpus (see note 6). Note further that a number of even the most popular holiness songs were not unique to the movement. Particularly notable are "There Is a Fountain" and "When I Survey."

Characteristics of Holiness Hymnody

What the holiness folk were about was the search for (1) a secure union with God in Christ, ensuring (2) a stable, integrated identity, cemented in (3) a human "community of feeling." They conducted this search in the midst of a society that seemed to threaten all three kinds of integration: spiritual/religious, inner, and communal. The theme of struggle toward a "uniting of divided hearts" appropriately describes all three levels: (1) God and the worshipper united, (2) the worshipper's divided and opaque "heart" both united and revealed as a "romantic self" that has attained stable identity through stable relationship, and (3) Christians united as participants in the same communion with their Lord. The holiness people knew, as did the sentimental novelists, that the key to finding the kinds of integration they sought was "heart knowledge"—the understanding and expressing of appropriate emotions.

The line between holiness and Methodist hymnody might be considered harder to draw. After all, the core constituency of the NCMAPH was solidly Methodist, and as one Methodist commentator wrote, "Our hymns are fairly aglow with the glory of this exalted experience [of sanctification]."[8] Nonetheless, holiness people made a pointed distinction between the Methodist hymnody—what was sung on Sunday morning worship in a Methodist Episcopal church (MEC)—and those songs that might appropriately be sung in their own favored settings of social meetings, Sunday schools, and camp meetings (see the following section "Setting"). In the words of an 1879 "book notice" on the latest MEC hymnal/tune book, printed in the NCMAPH organ *Advocate of Christian Holiness,* "The New Methodist Hymnal is a valuable collection of hymns for the sanctuary. . . . In our judgment, it will never be introduced to any considerable extent into the Sunday-school, nor into social meetings. The music usually sung in the Sabbath service is a little too staid for social service, except in those churches where the people are content to remain 'correctly cool and regularly low.'"[9]

This sort of distinction, made from within the movement, only sharpens the question of what the "crossover" songs are doing in our holiness top fifteen. Probably the foremost zone of permeability (or shared trope) was the graphic, emotional reflection on the passion and the effects (appropriation) of Jesus' atonement, and the holiness favorite "I Am Trusting, Lord, in Thee."

Holiness advocates were quite aware that an applied, bloody atonement was the hymnic common ground between themselves and the wider Protestant church. They cannily chose—not only from their own deep commitment to its imagery, but as a sort of marketing technique—to adopt "When I Survey the Wondrous Cross" and "There Is a Fountain" and to make the latter the early "theme song" or "battle song" of the movement. In other words, holiness advocates no doubt hoped to draw in outsiders (especially Methodists outside the movement) through this common trope.[10] At the same time, NCMAPH leaders gave unique holiness meaning to the "blood applied" trope, and indeed to the image of a "fountain" of benefits from the atonement.[11] Clearly, for holiness believers as for most other Protestants who sang these songs, this image of the powerful, life-giving blood of a crucified savior was anything but a "theory of the atonement." It was an image with deep emotional, visceral effect in the lives of those who meditated upon it. And besides the vividness imparted to it by the recent (and many felt, redemptive) national bloodbath (the Civil War), its sanguinary resonances echoed through the history of evangelicalism—back to the devotional hymns of the Pietists translated by John Wesley, and to Charles's excursions into Pietistic "blood-and-wounds" imagery.

Style

The style of holiness music may tell us much that supplements the meanings found in the texts themselves. Holiness folk equated "artistic" music with lack of the kind of emotional, relational "spiritual power" they valued. For example, when the editors of the *Advocate of Christian Holiness* reported in March 1877 on the Moody/Sankey revival meetings in Boston, they remarked dryly, "That his singing should be criticized is not surprising, especially in Boston, where music, as an *art,* is supposed to be considerably ahead of heaven," and concluded, "What simpletons there are in this world. '*Artistic*' singing by Mr. Sankey would be much like lectures on *oratory* by Mr. Moody to bring the people to Christ. The churches have been nearly killed by this artistic nonsense, and it is to be hoped that this so-called 'inartistic' singing will introduce a new dispensation into Boston."

George Hughes, in *Days of Power in the Forest Temple,* brought the critique home: "Methodism has been greatly extended by [the use of song]. She is in danger, however, of being shorn of much of her musical potency. Ritualistic ideas, where they have sway, demand what is very artistic in this department, but very soul-less, possessing little of the spirit of Christian worship."[12] In music as in oratory, plainer, more direct, and more undisguised transparent communication was simply better. In lieu of "artistic" singing, which drew attention away from the message and the relationship with God and toward the conventions and beauties of the music itself, Hughes and others demanded a warmer style of " 'singing with the spirit and with the understanding,'—the making melody with the heart unto the Lord."[13] This stylistic commitment was consistent not only with evangelical goals of mass communication of the gospel but also with sentimental goals of direct communication of emotion. As a contemporary Methodist put it, a simple, popular hymn when sung can become "a channel through which the full tide of sympathy [note this sentimentalist keyword] is made to flow."[14]

"Artistic" music, on the other hand, represented yet another incursion of cold, rationalistic discourse into the Lord's work, sapping "spiritual power" both from the worshipper's experience and from the communication of the evangelistic message. Here, holiness hymnody, as evangelical hymnody in general, only took a leaf from the original Methodist hymnody, of which it could be said "the heightening of emotion by means of the music was one of the most effective agencies in creating the atmosphere in which conversions [we may add for our subjects "and sanctifications"] were to be expected."[15]

Setting

As we have already seen in the 1879 holiness "book notice" of the MEC hymnal, the Sunday school and social meeting were being marked as the turf of the more raucously evangelical, more stylistically popular holiness hymns. Settings mentioned in holiness hymnals and periodicals include camp and revival meetings (seemingly pre-eminent, at least initially); holiness conferences; "social meetings," "family meetings," or "social circles"—including prayer meetings and the weekday meetings listed by city in *Advocate of Christian Holiness*; and Sunday school classes.

There is another setting that differs not only in locale but in type from any of those previously mentioned. This is not a "performance" setting, but instead the use of hymn fragments in spoken and written narratives. These included (a) accounts of intense moments of private devotion, (b) narratives of experiences of sanctification, and (c) death-bed narratives. Here, narrators tended to repeat in fragmentary lines or stanzas familiar rhetorical expressions evoking the desired emotional experiences of communion with God and community with fellow believers.[16] The ubiquity of quotations from hymns and poems in all kinds of holiness accounts must point to some real practice: some habit of singing, speaking, or just remembering verses from songs and poems in a wide variety of life situations, both public and private. It seems clear that holiness people took seriously the Pauline injunction to "be filled with the Spirit; speaking to yourselves in psalms and hymns and spiritual songs, singing and making melody in your heart to the Lord" (Ephesians 5:18, 19), and that such singing was not limited to public settings, but was often private and directed inwardly.[17] Indeed, this practice points to the private, separated, literary exploration of the inner subjective space opened up by the soaking of holiness culture in print, and beyond this, to a permeability between performed hymns and orally quoted hymns, hymns quoted in print, and poetry printed in books and periodicals. All of these latter uses of hymnody and poetry may be considered as part of "setting"—that is, the attempts to attain both individual, inner knowledge and "literary community" with other readers that were typical of Victorian sentimental literature.[18]

Narrative

Holiness hymnody differed from the older, established Protestant hymnody in four respects: (1) central narrative, (2) subjectivity, (3) emotional expressiveness, and (4) emotional scripts.

Leonard I. Sweet once remarked that evangelicals seem to possess "almost a genetic predisposition to organize experience through stories."[19] Like their evangelical forebears and compatriots, Gilded Age holiness folk soaked themselves in narrative at every turn. Almost every form of writing and oral communication took narrative shape: biography and autobiography, testimony, hymnody, camp-meeting report, deathbed account, and so on.

Narrative was so important to holiness believers because its recital could impart and shape emotions by placing the reader/singer in situations as vicarious participants. As early holiness radical G. W. Henry put it, "When everything in the shape of theology fails, it is often the case that the simple relation of what the soul knows and enjoys will kindle the fire, which, like electricity, will leap from heart to heart."[20] Given their philosophical commitment to "heart knowledge," narrative was naturally the preferred method of moral training for holiness folk as it was for their early revivalist Methodist predecessors. Even the movement's increasingly strident doctrinal/polemical literature broke out at times into story or quoted portions of hymns.

Apart from the undeniable presence in many holiness hymns of narrative form, and of certain characteristic narrative movements, we may catch a glimpse of how hymnody functioned to draw the singer into the actual experience and emotions described in its narrative scenarios. We may do this by attending to the way the functions of holiness song were reported in the genre of camp-meeting reports. There, holiness preachers are shown repeatedly weaving song lyrics into their exhortations—using them at key "altar moments" to bring their audience into various phases of holiness experience. At a camp meeting in 1872, NCMAPH president John Inskip used "Wrestling Jacob" in this manner: "At the close of the sermon, we bowed before the throne, and Brother Inskip repeated the beautiful lines of Charles Wesley: 'Come, O thou traveller unknown!' He repeated it all, while a deep solemnity pervaded the assembly, and many realized the truth of these words: 'Thy nature and thy name is love.'"[21]

This use of hymns could become quite complex in the hands of a skillful preacher, who would use a song not just to bring people to a single experience, but to walk them through a number of emotional scripts from the holiness repertoire. At a holiness meeting held in Union M.E. Church, Philadelphia, Pennsylvania, October 22, 1871, future NCMAPH president William McDonald wove his own "I Am Trusting, Lord, in Thee" into an extended narrative appeal for his audience to come and experience the redeemed emotions of sanctification. (Note that the movement's familiarity with this favorite allowed the reporter to simply insert "etceteras" in place of many lines of the song.)[22]

First, McDonald coaxed his hearers toward consecration (the whole-hearted "laying all on the altar" that holiness believers alleged must precede entire sanctification): "After a season of solemn silence, Brother McDonald sung,—'I am coming to the cross,' & *Chorus.*—'I am trusting, Lord, in thee,' &c. 'How many here can say,' 'Long my heart has sighed for thee,' &c. 'If that has been your feeling, your desire, can you not come to him now singing,'—'Here I give my all to thee,' &c."

Then he exhorted them to stand fast, sustaining and hanging on to their consecration: "If you have made that entire consecration, you are just in a state where you can sing,—'In the promises I trust,' &c." Next, he urged them to rest assured in the communion with God that comes with sanctification: "If we have come to him, if we have given our all to him, if we have believed his promise, we can sing,— 'Jesus comes. He fills my soul; Perfected in love I am; I am every whit made whole: Glory! Glory to the Lamb! Still I'm trusting, Lord, in thee,' &c."

Finally, he drew his hearers into assurance of that communion in face of death and even Armageddon: "If death, on the pale horse, should come to me now, I would sing,—'I am trusting, Lord, in thee,' &c. If the heavens should pass away with a great noise; if there should come the form of the Son of Man, amid 'the wreck of matter, and the crash of worlds,' I would reverently sing,—'Still I'm trusting, Lord, in thee,' &c."

The Central Holiness Narrative: "Divided Hearts United"

A single romantic-sentimental narrative stands at the center of the holiness hymnody—though it rarely appears from beginning to end in one hymn. This narrative portrays (1) the emotional struggle toward, (2) the emotional assurance of, and (3) the emotional results of a relationship with Jesus Christ. It may be divided roughly into four key tropes or scenarios: weariness/battle/storm, consecration/ pledging of affections, sanctification/union with Christ, and rest/ peace/security. Again, it is rare to find all four tropes in one hymn.

So, for instance, the editors of *Penuel; or, Face to Face with God,* a chronicle of the early NCMAPH camp meetings, took its title and the theme of its introductory paragraph from the ever-popular story of Jacob wrestling with the angel. Jacob's contest had the advantages— for those seeking an emotional path from world-weary turmoil and distress to union with God and its concomitant feelings of rest and security—of compactness, vivid personality, high drama, and, best of all, Biblical warrant. Said the editors: "In the midst of seeming dis-couragements and denials, [Jacob] persevered till his victorious faith laid hold of the prize he sought, and the soul-cheering words were uttered, 'As a prince hast thou power with God and with men, and hast prevailed.'" Charles Wesley's famous rendering of Jacob's story became itself the guarantee that modern believers might reenact his struggle and receive the same result: "To *every fully consecrated and believing soul,* shall be found other Penuels than that beside the ford Jabbok." These believers would, in other words, "have 'Holiness to the Lord' written upon their hearts, and be brought to Jacob's inti-mate and blessed communion with the Master, both here and here-after."[23]

Struggle

The theme of struggle was expressed in holiness hymnody through many images: battles, wrestling, storms, foes, and unrest. Where these images occur, they point to the kind of tenacious striving toward communion described in "Wrestling Jacob." In many cases, however, where no "struggle" term is used, the theme is still present. This happens most often as the singer expresses a determination to "give over" certain worldly impediments to a relationship with Christ. These areas of sin—these worldly distractions that threaten to displace the worshipper's affection away from God—constitute the inner "foes" against which the singer struggles.

These impediments or foes may be divided into three categories. The first of these was the consumer goods and pleasures that arrived with the Victorian middle class's new economic success. The second was the self *itself*, now aggrandized by these new material supports of the middle class, which made available a degree of personal independence that ran directly counter to their tradition's historically high valuation on communal and divine dependence. The third included the social, and especially *domestic*, affections that now threatened to swallow up the "way of the cross" (i.e., the way of mortification of affections and their revivification Godward) that they and their forebears had followed. We see the three categories of potential competing affection—thus of consecration—mentioned in a single line from McDonald's "I Am Trusting, Lord, in Thee": "Here, I give my all to thee,—Friends, and time, and earthly store."[24] Two of the three foes appear in the adopted holiness hymn "When I Survey the Wondrous Cross" ("My richest gain I count but loss, / And pour contempt on all my pride"). This hymn was given a new chorus and retitled "Clinging to the Cross" to heighten the sense of struggle.

The language of struggle, consecration, and relational exclusivity owes much to the ideal of the "romantic self," so beloved of sentimentalism. Karen Lystra tells us that couples under the influence of that ideal were "obsessed with eliminating any barriers of communication between themselves"[25] and worked feverishly to dismantle various impediments to self-disclosure in order to achieve both true communion and realization of their own "romantic selves." The Victorian sentimental notion of the romantic self meant a full, integrated, elaborated subjective self, "known beyond social conventions and roles,"[26] could be discovered only in the process of intimate, affective encounter and dialogue. Apart from this process, Victorian romantic lovers (holiness folk included) felt that such a fully realized identity was unavailable to them within the increasingly restricted, conventional, impersonal performance roles of a specializing, professionalizing modern middle-class society. The romantic self, like the Methodist induction into a new and emotionally intense community via conversion (and sustenance in that community via sanctification), offered not only a sense of "separateness transcended," but in the same moment one of "distinctiveness confirmed."[27] Because the struggle toward sanctification was also a struggle toward a romantic self, here too "self-revelation and disclosure held the highest priority."[28] One reason that "Wrestling Jacob" was so popular in holiness circles was no doubt its assurance that Jesus, too, was disclosing himself personally to the worshipper. In any case, there is no question that just as "while in the throes of romantic love couples devoted obsessive attention to the identification of inner states," holiness believers made introspection their primary objective as they sought to achieve, maintain, or renew sanctification.[29]

Similarly, holiness folk battled their own worldly, fleshly, and satanic impediments to romantic communion, as they pushed toward the "perfect love" of entire sanctification. Transparency, self-disclosure, identity, communion, and happiness were all threatened by the various classes of sinful impediment identified, enumerated, and supernaturally overcome in the holiness narrative of "divided hearts united." And when cleansing was achieved, as in Phoebe Palmer's "The Cleansing Wave," it was achieved both as a result of and as a means to deepened divine communion: "With heart made pure, and garments white, And Christ enthroned within," reads one verse. And "Amazing grace! 'tis heaven below, To feel the blood applied; And Jesus, only Jesus know, My Jesus crucified."[30] Similarly, Elisha Hoffman's "Are You Wash'd in the Blood" proceeded immediately from asking the title question to asking: "Are you walking daily by the Saviour's side? . . . Do you rest each moment in the Crucified?"

The holiness people's struggle toward divine union, it should be noted, was itself rarely elaborate or painful. These were, after all, the legatees of Phoebe Palmer's "shorter way" to holiness. The typical emotions alluded to in the movement toward consecration and sanctification were steadfastness, resolve, and tenacity. It was through the "spiritual power of weakness"—the resolve to relinquish struggle and "give all to Christ"—that one found the door opened to a grace-filled relationship with Jesus and the emotion of "victory" that this relationship made available. As William Kirkpatrick put it, "When temptations fiercely lower, / And my shrinking soul would flee, / Change each weakness into power, / Keep me spotless: more like thee."[31] There was little here of the prolonged, agonized struggle characteristic of Puritan diaries.

Nonetheless, this theme of struggle ran as a muted obbligato beneath the texts of many holiness hymns. Apart from its appearance in statements of abnegation and consecration, where it was often followed by expressions of assured "victory," the theme also appeared much more explicitly as a foil for the emotions of rest and security that resulted from the new divine union of "perfect love." Here we find more generalized language of "trials," "battle," "foes," "storms," and so forth, *all now having been overcome,* and having no effect on the sanctified singer, owing to the security of his or her position in Jesus.

The Struggle behind the Struggles: Ordering the Unruly Realm of Emotion

Beneath the more explicit battles of antiself, anticonsumerism, and antidomesticity existed an implicit one—"the central struggle" of the movement: the sentimental struggle to plumb one's own heart, toward the end of achieving romantic communion with the Other.

The Methodist love affair with poetic language owed much to its ability to express the complexities of emotion and relation through the connotative richness and "fuzzy logic" of representational (rather than conceptual) language.[32] But far from seeking to lose themselves in the soup of inner experience, what the holiness folk wished to gain by their poetic explorations of familiar, repeated tropes, metaphors, and images was a measure of expressive and active control over their own emotional lives—and thus their own identities as "romantic selves." Because transparent self-disclosure was the romantic prerequisite to realization of one's identity in communion with the Other, this opened up two further difficulties. The first was the ineffability of persons (and especially of others)—thus the deficiencies of language as vehicles of romantic testimony. Granted, this difficulty was usually expressed by holiness folks as a joyous limitation of the tongue to tell of the wonders of divine communion rather than as an impediment to that communion.

However, the second difficulty really did threaten communion. This was the problem of the ambivalence and elusiveness of the self *itself*—"the difficulty of explaining [or grasping] an amorphous inner life."[33]

For Victorian holiness believers living in a cultural context that made introspection and self-disclosure imperative, the need for emotional scripts was a deep and existential one: "I *must* know how to label what I am feeling, because in order to cement a relationship with my God and others, I must be able to disclose it fully and accurately." It was to gain *this* "victory" that holiness people drew from and modified the elaborate poetic library of symbols, images, metaphors, situations, and tropes available to them in their inherited hymnody and fashioned them into their own emotional language. The narrative experience that they sought to attain, keep, and explore seems from these hymns to have been more limited than that of their forebears—almost everything was encapsulated in a single, standardized experience of entire sanctification. But the emotions that surrounded that experience became more and more elaborate through a shared, communal, literary process of multiplying and ritually learning emotional scripts.[34]

Scripted Emotions

Finally, then, we move to a suggestive consideration of three sets of "emotion scripts" that figured largely in holiness hymnody. These are the scripts of comfort/strength, joy, and rest/security/protection.

Comfort/Strength in Weariness/Weakness

The themes of the singer's weariness or weakness usually appear early in the larger narrative—that is, in connection with the struggle toward consecration. There they form the pattern against which the Lord's comforting strength stands out as the design. This was the theme of Mrs. R. N. Turner's assurance that those who fell

"Low at His Feet" would find there "joy for the comfortless heart," or Fanny Crosby's plea: "Jesus, Saviour, comfort me, / Draw thy weary child to thee; / Thou,—my Rock, my Strength, my All, / —Loving Saviour, hear my call." Often this script of comfort and strength came intermingled with tropes of companionship (e.g., Crosby, in the same song: "Leave me not, my life, my own, In this dreary world alone") and of another pervasive emotional category: security and protection.[35]

This theme of strength in weakness was by no means dominated by women writers. E. H. Stokes asked that the Holy Spirit "Bathe my trembling heart and brow," because "I am weakness, full of weakness." He concluded his plea: "Cleanse and comfort; bless and save me; . . . Thou art comforting and saving, Thou art sweetly filling now."[36] Probably the most famous instance in the holiness hymnody of weakness seeking power and comfort was Charles Wesley's "Wrestling Jacob," which demanded at the critical moment, "Yield to me now, for I am weak, / But confident in self-despair."

In this trope, the weakness of the singer elicited not only a call for comfort and strength, but also for the emotional, relational power that transforms the heart. The "filling" sought by Stokes in the hymn just cited was one of "power." And in the popular "Jesus Paid It All," the singer heard his "Saviour say, Thy strength indeed is small; Child of weakness, watch and pray." Pray for what? The next verse answered, "Thy pow'r, and thine alone, / Can change this heart of mine, / And make it all thine own." In other words, one's affections might be properly oriented, and as the song says, one's "sin-sick soul . . . made whole," only by overmastering grace.[37] Often, the two themes of comfort and power were placed in apposition, as in the song that exulted in its first verse, "Fresh springs so holy, All needed power," and then, in its second verse, enjoyed "Fresh springs of comfort, In deserts dry."[38] Fanny Crosby picked up the theme of refreshment with a song that asked in its first verse, "Come, Lord, and let thy power, On each and all descend," and reiterated in its chorus, "Refresh our waiting souls, Our feeble faith inspire."[39]

Joy

Attached to the central narrative moment of the attainment of divine communion in "perfect love," and to the subsequent reiteration of assurance of its reality, is the emotion-concept of joy. Marie Griffith

has noted of "the Pentecostal vocabulary around the emotional complex of joy" that "metaphors of light and biblically derived images
of sweetness, feasting, singing, shouting, and intimacy with Jesus"
helped shape and define this emotion, which was considered by the
Pentecostals as "the cure for every sorrow, worry, and longing."[40]
The same image-rich vocabulary of joy suffused the hymnody of
Pentecostalism's holiness parent. In one randomly chosen hymnic example, we find light, sweetness, feasting, and intimate rest in Jesus—
all arrayed in describing a joyous holiness life. The song, by William
Kirkpatrick, exulted:

> Sweetly I'm resting in Jesus,
> Glory-light beams on my way,
> Bright'ning my path through the darkness,
> Chasing the clouds away,
> Feeding in pastures green and fair,
> Drinking from fountains flowing there,
> Tenderly guarded by His loving care,
> Sweetly I'm resting in Jesus.[41]

This layering of images and mixture of metaphors is a ubiquitous feature of the holiness hymnody.

The temptation for many scholars is to read this "scripted language
of rapturous joy and encouragement" under the heading of depriva-
tion theory—that is, as relief and release in otherwise dreary lives.
This may perhaps be exacerbated by an academic tendency toward cul-
tured distaste or condescension for the vulnerability and loss of control
entailed in these intense emotions.[42] This value of joy was also deeply
rooted in Methodism, however—where it was lauded not primarily for
its therapeutic qualities, but as an evidential mark of the believer
whose relationship with his Lord is so close as to involve the uninter-
rupted communion of perfect love. John Wesley, when pressed to define "the character of a Methodist," did so in a 1742 tract of that title,
first and foremost under the rubric of a joy-producing love:

> God is the joy of [the Methodist's] heart. . . . He is therefore
> happy in God, yea, always happy, as having in him "a well of
> water springing up into everlasting life," and "overflowing his

soul with peace and joy," "Perfect love" having now "cast out fear," he "rejoices evermore," He "rejoices in the Lord always." . . . [H]e cannot but rejoice whenever he looks back on the horrible pit out of which he is delivered. . . . He cannot but rejoice whenever he looks on the state wherein he now is, "being justified freely," and "having peace with God through our Lord Jesus Christ." . . . He rejoiceth also, whenever he looks forward, "in hope of" "the glory that shall be revealed." Yea, this his joy is full, and all his bones cry out, "Blessed be the God and Father of our Lord Jesus Christ."

It was from this cornerstone, then, that Wesley proceeded, point by point, to build a catalogue of the emotion-involved virtues of the Methodist.[43]

Given this Wesleyan priority of joy or happiness as standing at the fountainhead of those emotional virtues that result from the repaired, purified relationship of the sanctified believer with God, we should be little surprised to see that same emotion taking pride of place in the later American movement. Nor should we be surprised to see it attached to essentially the same script: it appears as the result and proof of communion with God—the romantic/sentimental goal and fulcrum of the whole movement. No wonder, then, that when Mary James turned her thoughts and pen to a song titled "Companionship with Jesus," she began by writing out the script of joy: "Oh, blessed fellowship divine! / Oh, joy supremely sweet! / Companionship with Jesus here Makes life with bliss replete. / In union with the purest one I find my heav'n on earth begun." Not content to stop there, she added the chorus: "Oh, wondrous bliss, oh, joy sublime, / I've Jesus with me all the time, / Oh wondrous bliss, oh, joy sublime, / I've Jesus with me all the time." Mrs. J. F. Crewdon's "Jesus, My Joy" joined James's hymn among the most popular holiness hymns, in hymnals with titles such as *Radiant Songs, Glad Hallelujahs, Songs of Joy and Gladness, The Joyful Sound, Notes of Joy,* and *Songs of Triumph.*

Rest/Security/Protection

Closely related to joy but usually attached more to the final narrative movement in the drama of "divided hearts united" was the emotional state of rest or peace. This script so suffused the discourse of Wesleyan Methodism's close kin, the Keswick and Victorious Life movements, that it led Reformed scholar Douglas W. Frank to claim it arose in response to the intensive pressure of modern middle-class life, which stretched holiness folk nearly to the breaking point by the "severe and moralistic" imperative of Christian perfection, under which their lives became "a matter of intense daily struggle, guilt in the event of failure, and often utter exhaustion."[44] Although I see little evidence in the early postbellum years for applying Frank's second, theological claim to our Wesleyan subjects, his first claim, about the pressures of "modern" life (and especially the lives of the new middle class to which the majority of camp-meeting holiness devotees seem to belong), was well attested at the time—perhaps most famously in George M. Beard's 1881 opus, *American Nervousness, Its Causes and Consequences*. Beard attributed "American nervousness" to a panoply of modern bourgeois factors, including the exhausting pursuit of material wealth and social status and "the conventionalities of society" that "require the emotions to be repressed, while the activity of our civilization gives an unprecedented freedom and opportunity for the expression of the intellect," so that "the more we feel the more we must restrain our feelings."[45]

The hymnals surveyed contained fourteen separate songs with the word *rest* or a derivative in the title, along with eleven more containing it in the first line and not the title. The word *peace* appeared in the title of four hymns, and the first line of four more. However, the typical placement of these terms was in the final verse, along with images of security and protection, and opposed to images of battle, storm, and trial. It is almost as if an extra measure of reassurance was called for when one neared the end of the act of expressive communal singing and faced the silence that might ensue. Looking again at Mary James's popular "Companionship with Jesus," James injected at the end of the second verse an assurance that "his great Almighty hand / Protects me in this hostile land" and ended with a lingering sense of protected, secure rest:

No foes, no woes my heart can fear,
With my almighty Friend so near.
I know His shelt'ring wings of love

Are always o'er me spread,
And tho' the storms may fiercely rage,
All calm and free from dread,
My peaceful spirit ever sings
"I'll trust the covert of Thy wings."[46]

William Kirkpatrick's "Beautiful Day" ended with language of Christ as a "haven of rest," where "naught can dismay." Each chorus ended with "Saviour, I pray, keep me always, Safe in this beautiful day."[47]

When appearing elsewhere in the hymns, or as the ruling theme, these terms seemed to carry a more simply therapeutic meaning. For example, in Fanny Crosby's "Jesus Will Give You Rest," Jesus offered this coveted emotional state in return for the singer's "poor broken heart, Burden'd and sin-oppressed," and as "Balm for your aching breast." In short, "whatever your sin or your sorrow may be," Jesus offered "sweet, happy rest." This He did in response to the bare action of "simple, trusting faith." Notice that even in these cases, however, rest was an answer for sin as much as for any emotional concomitant of sin. This linkage between relief from sin and a change in emotional state appeared most explicitly in "Wondrous Love," which spoke of "the blessed rest from inbred sin." Sin, in other words, was closely identified in holiness experience with psychological trouble or inner turbulence—the "battles" so prominent in the movement's ruling narrative. Quite often, however, the emotional script to which rest was the "answer" was not sin alone but the "world-weariness" of the pilgrimage of walk, work, and trials on earth. So, for example, the first verse of William Johnson's "Hem of His Garment" lamented "Weak and weary, poor and sinful, / Vainly I cry; / Bound and crush'd with years of sorrow, / What help is nigh?" and the third verse answers, in the climactic, performative present tense, "Long my heart has felt its burden, Seeking for peace; Now, at last I find in Jesus My sweet release."[48]

Given this subdued but real sense of struggle that underlay the believer's progress toward communion, it is reasonable to suppose that the ubiquitous holiness term "victory" represented for its users not any *one* particular skirmish won in the struggle, but the winning of the relational and emotional battle that I have suggested underlay and united them all. Thus the promised "rest" and "peace" and feelings of security and protectedness that inevitably followed battle and storm may be interpreted as the secure ordering and tidy expression of one's complex, conflicted emotional life and the emotional assurance of secure, exclusive attachment to God that perpetuates, circularly, its own inner source of strength against pride, greed, and the divinization of human affections.

Conclusion

What can we conclude about the relationship between desired emotions, as they are scripted in these hymns, the divine communion that is the theme of the holiness movement's central narrative, and the singers' motivations and mentality? Do holiness hymns seem most interested in the emotions they script as (1) ends in themselves, (2) results or benefits of relationship with Jesus, (3) tokens of assurance of that relationship, or (4) guarantors of, or steps toward, that relationship? The answer, though not tidy enough to satisfy either partisans or detractors, is no doubt a mixture of the four. The central concern of the movement was always to make personal communion with God possible, available, and assured in the modern world. It is precisely because American holiness folk looked around at aspects of then-current social structures and habits of language, saw threatening impediments to this primary program of apprehending and presenting God, and used their hymnody to structure the movement's emotional culture.

Wrestling Jacob
Come, O thou traveller unknown,
Whom still I hold, but cannot see;
My company before is gone,
And I am left alone with thee;
With thee all night I mean to stay,
And wrestle till the break of day

I need not tell Thee who I am:
My sin and misery declare;
Thyself hast called me by my name;

Look on thy hands, and read it there;
But who, I ask thee, who are thou?
Tell me thy name, and tell me now.

In vain thou strugglest to get free;
I never will unloose my hold:
Art thou the Man that died for me?
The secret of thy love unfold:
Wrestling, I will not let thee go,
Till I thy name, thy nature know.

Wilt thou not yet to me reveal
Thy new, unutterable name?
Tell me, I still beseech thee, tell;
To know it now resolved I am:
Wrestling, I will not let thee go,
Till I thy name, thy nature know.

What tho' my shrinking flesh complain,
And murmur to contend so long?
I rise superior to my pain:
When I am weak, then I am strong;
And when my all of strength shall fail,
I shall with the God-man prevail.

Yield to me now, for I am weak,
But confident in self-despair;
Speak to my heart, in blessing, speak;
Be conquer'd by my instant prayer;
Speak, or thou never hence shalt move,
And tell me if thy name be Love.

'Tis Love! 'tis Love! thou di'dst for me;
I hear thy whisper in my heart;
The morning breaks, the shadows flee;
Pure, universal Love thou art:
To me, to all, thy bowels move,—
Thy nature and thy name is Love.

My prayer has pow'r with God; the grace
Unspeakable I now receive;
Through faith I see thee face to face;
I see thee face to face, and live!
In vain I have not wept and strove;
Thy nature and thy name is Love.

I know thee, Saviour, who thou art—
Jesus, the feeble sinner's friend;
Nor wilt thou with the night depart,
But stay and love me to the end:
Thy mercies never shall remove;
Thy nature and thy name is Love.[49]

Notes

1. The first epigraph comes from F. D. Hemenway, D.D., "The Literature of Sacred Song," in *Methodism and Literature,* ed. by F. A. Archibald (Cincinnati: Walden and Stowe, 1883), 146. The second epigraph is taken from an Emily Dickinson letter to her cousins Fanny and Lou Norcross, late 1872, *The Letters of Emily Dickinson,* ed. Thomas H. Johnson and Theodora Ward, 3 vols. (Cambridge: Harvard University Press, 1958), L379 [Johnson and Ward's numbering]; in Joanne Dobson, "Reclaiming Sentimental Literature," *American Literature* 69 (June 1997): 266.

2. A. McLean and J. W. Eaton, eds., *Penuel; or, Face to Face with God* (New York: W. C. Palmer Jr., 1869), xvii.

3. Steven D. Cooley, *The Possibilities of Grace: Poetic Discourse and Reflection in Methodist/Holiness Revivalism.* (Ph.D. diss., University of Chicago, 1991), 44, 45, 28.

4. W. McDonald and L. Hartsough, eds., *Beulah Songs* (Philadelphia: National Publishing Association for the Promotion of Holiness, 1879); J. S. Inskip [really ed. by John R. Sweney and Wm. J. Kirkpatrick], *Songs of Triumph* (Philadelphia: National Publishing Association for the Promotion of Holiness, 1882); William McDonald, Joshua Gill, and John R. Sweney, eds., *Songs of Joy and Gladness [word ed.]* (Boston: McDonald, Gill, and Co., 1886); R[ussell] Kelso Carter, ed., *Songs of Perfect Love* (Philadelphia: John J. Hood, 1886); John R. Sweney and Wm. J. Kirkpatrick, eds., *Glad Hallelujahs* (Philadelphia: Thos. T. Tasker Sr. [National Publishing Association for the Promotion of Holiness], 1887); John R. Sweney and Wm. J. Kirkpatrick, eds., *The Joyful Sound* (Philadelphia: John J. Hood, 1889); John R. Sweney, Wm. J. Kirkpat-

rick, and H. L. Gilmour, eds., *Radiant Songs* (Philadelphia: John J. Hood, 1891). Three of the hymnals chosen were published by the NCMAPH's Philadelphia press (*Beulah Songs, Songs of Triumph, Glad Hallelujahs*). Several others involved two editors with connections to the movement. William McDonald, editor of *Songs of Faith* and *Songs of Joy and Gladness,* would become the NCMAPH's second president. R. Kelso Carter, editor of *Songs of Perfect Love,* was well-known for his involvement in the movement; the title of his hymnal places it squarely in the holiness camp, and his hymnal shows a high degree of overlap in songs and, even more, lyricists and music-authors, with the others on the list. Finally, I chose two hymnals, *The Joyful Sound* and *Radiant Songs,* both published late in the period by John Sweney and William Kirkpatrick, also from a Philadelphia press. These two men had edited two of the three holiness hymnals published by the NCMAPH's press (including *Songs of Triumph,* as "ghost-editors" under J. S. Inskip's name). *Radiant Songs* also bears an introduction by J. Elwood Stokes, from the holiness Ocean Grove camp meeting, and is advertised as one of a series of hymnals issued "from year to year" from Ocean Grove, where Sweney was the longtime music director: Mel R. Wilhoit, "American Holiness Hymnody—Some Questions: A Methodology," *Wesleyan Theological Journal* 25 (fall 1990): 56–57.

5. The most-published Wesley hymn in the ten hymnals and two periodicals I surveyed, with four separate hymnal publications and two periodical publications, was "Wrestling Jacob." Other popular Wesley hymns included "A Charge to Keep I Have," "Lord, I Believe a Rest Remains," "Love Divine, All Loves Excelling," "O For a Heart to Praise My God," and "O How Happy Are They Who the Saviour Obey." George Hughes, *Days of Power in the Forest Temple; A Review of the Wonderful Work of God at Fourteen National Camp-meetings, from 1867–1872* (Boston: John Bent, 1873), 244; cited in Wilhoit, "American Holiness Hymnody," 39–63; 63 n. 32.

6. Three hymnals were surveyed for gender: In *Beulah Songs,* 12.5 percent of the total 120 hymns, and 24 percent of the newly written, gender-identifiable songs were written by women. In *Songs of Triumph,* 34 percent of the total 157 hymns, and over 56 percent of the newly written, gender-identifiable songs were written by women. In *Radiant Songs,* 42 percent of the total 195 hymns, and 50 percent of the newly written, gender-identifiable songs were written by women. Among the more prolific female songwriters were Fanny Crosby (76 hymns of the 995), Lizzie Edwards (29 hymns), Lidie H. Edmunds (20), Mary Dagworthy Yard James (15), Priscilla J. Owens (13), Sallie Smith (12), Henrietta E. Blair (11), and Mrs. R. N. Turner (9 hymns).

7. I used *Advocate of Christian Holiness* (1870–72 only) and *Guide to Holiness* (1870 only).

8. J. Alabaster, "Literature of the Higher Christian Life," in *Methodism and Literature,* ed. F. A. Archibald (Cincinnati: Walden and Stowe, 1883), 251.

9. "Book Notices," *Advocate of Christian Holiness* (July 1879): 167.

10. Note that this was the very same "trope of entry" that served at the turn of the century to solidify support around the budding Pentecostal movement at Azusa Street, where a high proportion of the songs sung painted images of "the blood." Moreover, the healing movement, which allied itself to both the holiness and the Pentecostal movements, drew on the same image of the "blood applied" in making its claims for "healing provided for in the atonement."

11. See Wilhoit, "American Holiness Hymnody," 39–63, 45–46.

12. Hughes, *Days of Power*, 243.

13. Ibid., 244.

14. Hemenway, "Literature of Sacred Song," 143.

15. Sydney Dimond, *The Psychology of the Methodist Revival* (Nashville: Whitmore and Smith, 1926), 123.

16. See Sandra S. Sizer, "Passion and Order: The Problem of Social Religion," *Gospel Hymns and Social Religion* (Philadelphia: Temple University Press, 1978), 50–82.

17. The holiness folk were predisposed to, if not replace the communal function of singing with the interior, individual function, at least add the latter to the former.

18. John Mullan, *Sentiment and Sociability: The Language of Feeling in the Eighteenth Century* (New York: Clarendon Press, 1988); Ronald Zboray, *A Fictive People: Antebellum Economic Development and the American Reading Public* (New York: Oxford University Press, 1993), esp. 82, 118, 178.

19. Leonard I. Sweet, *Health and Medicine in the Evangelical Tradition: 'Not by Might nor Power'* (Valley Forge, Pa.: Trinity Press International, 1994), 7.

20. G. W. Henry, *Shouting, Genuine and Spurious: In All Ages of the Church* (1859; reprint, Chicago: Metropolitan Church Association, 1903), 18.

21. See *Advocate of Christian Holiness* 3 (September 1872), 56.

22. The following account is quoted from the report by "Juniata," *Advocate of Christian Holiness* (January 1872).

23. McLean and Eaton, *Penuel*, ix–x.

24. William McDonald, "I Am Trusting, Lord, in Thee," *Beulah Songs*, 5.

25. Karen Lystra, *Searching the Heart: Women, Men, and Romantic Love in Nineteenth Century America* (New York: Oxford University Press, 1989), 33.

26. Ibid., 30.

27. A. Gregory Schneider, *The Way of the Cross Leads Home: The Domestication of American Methodism* (Bloomington: Indiana University Press, 1993), 39.

28. Lystra, *Searching the Heart*, 31.

29. For the "sanctified self," as for the "romantic self," subjectivity was almost always explored and expressed in terms of the other.

30. Phoebe Palmer, "The Cleansing Wave," *Beulah Songs*, 6.

31. William Kirkpatrick, "More Like Thee," *Beulah Songs*, 51.

32. Cooley, *Possibilities of Grace*.

33. Lystra, *Searching the Heart*, 35.

34. Cooley asserts that holiness folk applied "the stock of [hymn] quotations to manage a wide range of particular experiences and situations." The same hymn fragment could, because of the connotative nature of poetic language, perform a wide variety of "scripting" work: "Although the words [of the hymn fragments] remained unchanged from one statement [in which the fragment was embedded] to the next, the statements themselves hardly ever did the same work." Cooley, *Possibilities of Grace*, 50.

35. Mrs. R. N. Turner, "Low at His Feet," *Glad Hallelujahs*, 114; Fanny J. Crosby, "Saviour, Hear My Call," in *Joyful Songs*, ed. James R. Murray (Cleveland: S. Brainard's Sons, 1875), 47.

36. E. H. Stokes, "Fill Me Now," *Songs of Triumph*, 48.

37. "Jesus Paid It All," words arr. William McDonald, *Beulah Songs*, 47.

38. E. E. Hewitt, "Fresh Springs," *Joyful Sound*, 59.

39. Fanny J. Crosby, "Refreshing," *Songs of Joy and Gladness*, 77.

40. R. Marie Griffith, "'Joy Unspeakable and Full of Glory': The Vocabulary of Pious Emotion in the Narratives of American Pentecostal Women, 1910–1945," in *An Emotional History of the United States*, ed. Peter N. Stearns and Jan Lewis (New York: New York University Press, 1998), 221, 232.

41. William Kirkpatrick, "Sweetly I'm Resting in Jesus," *Songs of Triumph*, 42–43.

42. Griffith, "Joy Unspeakable," 229.

43. John Wesley, "The Character of a Methodist," *The Works of John Wesley*, vol. 9, *The Methodist Societies*, ed. Rupert E. Davies (Nashville: Abingdon Press, 1989), 31–41.

44. Douglas Frank, *Less Than Conquerors: How Evangelicals Entered the Twentieth Century* (Grand Rapids: Eerdmans, 1986), 146, 158–59; cf. 126–27, 136–38.

45. G. Beard, *American Nervousness, Its Causes and Consequences* (Salem, N.H.: Ayer Co., 1981), esp. 96–133, 292–98.

46. *Songs of Triumph*, 24; and several other hymnals.

47. *Songs of Triumph*, 47.

48. *Songs of Triumph*, 23.

49. *Beulah Songs*, 44.

8

Alabaré a mi Señor

Hymnody as Ideology in Latino Protestantism

Daniel Ramírez

> I stepped over last evening to a chapel opposite my hotel, where
> one of these congregations was holding service. . . . It was after
> nine, and the regular meeting had closed. But there stood a group
> of twenty or so; in the upper corner, "going it," like a corner
> after a revival meeting, in these same songs of Zion. . . . [T]hey
> all put with all their heart and voice, a few sitting about on the
> benches enjoying the exercise. It was so perfectly Methodistic that
> I wished to go forward and tell them it seemed just like home.
>
> Gilbert Haven, *Mexico: Our Next-Door Neighbor*, 1875

Methodist bishop Gilbert Haven's 1875 eyewitness report on
liturgy within the proto-Anglican *Iglesia de Jesús* (Church of Jesus),
founded by liberal, dissident Roman Catholic priests, surely stirred the
hearts and loosened the wallets of potential benefactors in the United
States. The hearty anthems sung "lustily" by a Mexico City congregation heralded the dawn of Christian truth after dark centuries of
"popery." They also evoked, in their primitive power, painful comparisons with the cooled liturgical passions of Haven's home denomination, the Methodist Episcopal Church, in the antebellum period.

The missionary strategist got it half right. Latin American and Latino converts would indeed learn to sing new versions of the Lord's
song in their own and foreign lands. But over time they would also
insist on authoring their own version of that song. Such assertions
inevitably led to (or reflected) contests over aesthetics, autonomy, and
power. In the end, music would prove essential in the shaping of Latino Protestant identities. Both the historian seeking to understand
this process and the musicologist seeking to understand the ethno-
poetics of these songs may benefit from closer study of the life trajectories of the composers and singers.

Early Latino Protestant Hymnody

U.S. Latino Protestantism begins with the half-century of evangelization efforts by mainline U.S. denominations in the southwestern United States, northern Mexico, Florida, and the Caribbean. Also, by the last quarter of the nineteenth century, Protestants in Spain had constituted themselves as the Spanish Reformed and Lutheran Churches. The bulk of hymnody from this period reflected missionaries' preference. The repertoire contained few surprises. The hymns of Martin Luther, Isaac Watts, Charles Wesley,[1] Fanny Crosby, and Ira Sankey proved ubiquitous in early Spanish-language compilations.[2] The period of vigorous missionary expansion coincided with the apex of the last two collaborators' careers. Accordingly, the translated music of Fanny Crosby (1820–1915) and Ira Sankey (1840–1908) occupied a privileged position in the liturgy of the missions.[3]

An important cadre of Protestant leaders from Mexico, Cuba, and Spain proved equally as active in translation work as the missionaries. In Spain these included Anglican bishop Juan Bautista Cabrera (1837–1916), translator of Martin Luther's "A Mighty Fortress Is Our God," and Pedro Castro (d. 1887), who collaborated in translation/compilation, under the auspices of New York's Tract Society, with Henry Riley (1835–1904). Among the Mexicans and Mexican Americans, Methodists Vincente Mendoza (1875–1955), Pedro Grado (1862–1923), Juan N. de los Santos (1876–1944), and Nazarene Honorato Reza (1913–2001) proved prolific translators as well. One result of the combined efforts was the *Himnario Evangélico,* published in 1893 by the American Tract Society, and thoroughly revised as the *Nuevo Himnario Evangélico* in 1914 for use in Methodist, Baptist, Congregational, and Presbyterian churches. In 1905, Mendoza and Grado each published modest hymnals, *Himnos Selectos* and *La Pequeña Colección de Himnos,* respectively, for use in the Methodist Mexican and Mexican American churches.[4]

Original compositions also began to appear—albeit rarely—alongside translations. Mendoza's original composition "*Jesús es mi rey soberano*" ("Jesus Is My Sovereign King"), composed during a long sojourn in California, ranks as Latino and Latin American Protestantism's most widely sung hymn.

Harvard-trained and Nashville-based Episcopalian Primitivo Rodríguez (from Mexico's Church of Jesus) undertook a significant
compilation/redaction project at the behest of Cuban Methodists.[5]
The official editor and translator of Spanish-language material for the
Methodist Episcopal Church South's (MECS) Board of Missions and
Methodist Publishing House,[6] Rodríguez sifted through twenty-seven
preexisting Spanish-language hymnals, published from 1869 to 1907,
to compile his authoritative *Himnario Cristiano* in 1908, one that
would "be for the good of Spain and Latin America" and one that
contained more of Charles Wesley's hymns than any other extant
hymnal. Rodríguez limited his redaction of Iberian hymnody to the
previous forty years, because the earlier hymnody of the peninsula,
although attractive in some aspects, was hopelessly mixed with "the
leaven of Romanist teachings."[7]

The new compilations did not meet with universal acclaim. Spanish
classicist Marcelino Menéndez y Pelayo relegated the heretics' latest
poetic attempts to a disdainful footnote at the end of his volumi-
nous survey *Historia de los Heterodoxos Expañoles.* "In general," he
sniffed, "the Spanish Protestant muse is one of deplorable and drowsy
monotony and insipidity."[8]

Perhaps Menéndez y Pelayo, defender of Spanish Catholic orthodox
identity and arbiter of taste in turn-of-the-century Madrid, doubted
the muse's authenticity. He may have been on to something. Although
the revised *Nuevo Himnario Evangélico* contained an impressive 348
hymns, only about 4 percent (13–15) were original Spanish-language
compositions. The situation was not improved in the more evangelical sectors of the church. As late as 1955, the fourth edition of *Cantos
de Alabanza, Pureza y Poder* (Songs of Praise, Purity and Power), published by the Free Tract Society in Los Angeles, maintained a similar proportion of 4 percent original Latino composition among its
234 hymns. The least inclusive hymnal was produced under the aegis
of the emerging Assemblies of God (the flagship denomination in
American Pentecostalism), the *Himnos de Gloria* (Hymns of Glory),
compiled in 1916 by H. C. Ball, the Texas-based longtime superintendent of the Assemblies' Spanish-speaking work and an MECS-trained
preacher. Less than 2 percent of *Gloria's* 339 hymns were of original Latino composition. That the most widely disseminated Spanish-
language hymnal of the twentieth century bore faint Latino imprint

says as much about Anglo-American paternalism as it does about Latino and Latin American dependency.[9] Only J. Paul Cragin's *Melodías Evangélicas,* first compiled in 1928 and circulated widely up through the 1960s, contained a significant representation of original Latino composition, 25 out of 165, or 15 percent. (Of these, about one-third were borrowed from the Apostolic hymnals discussed in the following section.)

The role assumed by Anglo-American missionaries in hymnal redaction helps to explain the suppression of indigenous musical culture. Recent critiques of U.S. Latino and Latin American Protestant music have argued that mainline Protestant church music facilitated subordination of popular liturgical development through the introduction of Euro-American ethnocentrism, Greek body-soul dualism, concepts of private faith and practice, devaluation of folk culture, and the exclusion of indigenous (Latino) musical styles.[10]

Missionaries insisted on strict musical and liturgical boundaries. In a 1928 address to the Baptist State Association of Chihuahua (reprinted in full in the Methodist *Evangelista Mexicano*), a speaker rhapsodized about the centrality of one privileged instrument:

> Music should never be absent from the church. As far as the instruments to be used, in my thinking, it is the organ that should never be absent from the church. Although it may not lend itself to the adornment of music, it is the most appropriate to accompany religious songs. It is not only songs that the organ can accompany; it can also be used to play preludes for the services, which is of utmost importance, as this prepares us better to receive the message. During the offering time something can be played. If not a classical piece, since the organ or organist may not be up to it, then something slow and sweet.[11]

The speaker proceeded to call for a removal of all melancholy and languidness from hymnody. A missionary need not have been present at the conclave to affirm the concern for liturgical propriety. Indeed, after a half-century of tutelage, Latino converts seemed to have thoroughly endorsed the value of a liturgy bleached of folk elements.

Small wonder, then, that in his landmark study of Mexican immigrants in the late 1920s, Manuel Gamio downplayed the possibility of any significant inroads among this population, due to the "cold, intellectual, moralistic quality of Protestantism, and lack of color and artistic impression."[12] Clearly, Gamio had mainline Protestantism in mind. A survey of the more emotive, folkloric "*aleluya*" barrio and rural churches then springing up throughout the Southwest and Mexico might have led Mexico's foremost anthropologist to other conclusions.

Historian Russell Richey has characterized early American Methodism as a "movement of the voice—a preaching, singing, testifying, praying, shouting, crying, arguing movement,"[13] a description that carries important explanatory value. However, not all these voices carried over into adolescent Methodism, the Methodism encountered by Mexicans and Chicanos, nor were they all within the hearing range of Latino would-be converts. It was when their voice was stifled that Latino Methodists and other Protestants sought out other vocal and aural spaces, spaces many found in Pentecostalism. The religious musical culture forged in these alternative sonic spaces would crescendo and later find echo in the experience of both popular Catholic and mainline Protestant believers in Mexico and in the United States.

Early Latino Pentecostal Hymnody

In contrast to mainline Protestantism's retreat from folk culture, Pentecostal hymnody recaptured the fiesta of Mexican and Latino culture, liberating it from seemingly intractable pathologies of alcoholism and double-standard sexism, and returning it to the sacred place of ritual, performance, and spectacle. Pentecostals forged a new aural universe that incorporated as much sensory corporeality as the earlier popular Catholic visual one of saints, candles, gilded altars, and paintings (which had been erased by earlier Latino Protestantism).[14]

Musical Cultural Practice among
Early Latino Pentecostals

In 1925, one of the fledgling Chicano Pentecostal movements (hereafter referred to interchangeably as Apostolic) had gathered in its inaugural convention as the *Iglesia de la Fé Apostólica Pentecostés*. Its leading ministers, Francisco Llorente and Antonio Nava (the latter a refugee from Mexico's revolutionary upheaval), carried credentials issued by Garfield T. Haywood, the African American leader of the Indianapolis-based Pentecostal Assemblies of the World (PAW), at that time the biracial (black and white) flagship denomination for the Oneness (non-Trinitarian) wing of American Pentecostalism. Bernardo Hernández, the convention secretary (and a former Baptist elder from Yuma, Arizona), recorded in his minutes that the first ministers' meetings were opened with the hymns "*Ama el Pastor Sus Ovejas*" ("As the Shepherd Loves His Sheep," a translation of "Dear to the Heart of the Shepherd"), "*Cerca, Mas Cerca, Oh Dios de Tí*" ("Near, Nearer, Oh God, to Thee," translation of "Nearer, Still Nearer"), and "*Jesus, Yo He Provmetido*" (translation of "Oh, Jesus, I Have Promised" ["Angel's Song"]). Hernández listed sixteen of the hymns sung by the conventioneers—all but four taken from Spanish-language Protestant hymnals. He also highlighted the debut of several compositions by Marcial de la Cruz, early Apostolicism's most prolific composer (seventy-plus compositions by the time of his death in 1935), and his daughter, Beatriz.[15]

During this time the movement also appropriated African American musical forms (e.g., call and response), theology (e.g., radical monotheistic doctrine), and ecclesiology (e.g., episcopal polity). Although he remained monolingual in Spanish, de la Cruz proved an avid student of the music he encountered in his fellowship with black congregations and with African American members of Latino Apostolic churches. Antonio Nava, who took up the mandolin to form a duet with guitarist de la Cruz, noted his colleague's immediate recall of rhythms and chords he heard in such services.[16]

For at least the first decade and a half of growth, Latino Apostolics, while negotiating their place as newcomers on the half-century-old Latino Protestant block, forged alliances with other groups on the religious and social periphery, groups similarly cut off from the ecclesiastical structures and institutions at the center. Latino Apostolics found in African American heterodox hymnody a ready-made "defensive, counter-ideological, symbolic expression"[17] to employ on behalf of their community's identity, continuity, and autonomy.[18] And when strengthened, this autonomy bred creativity.

Such creative agency presents itself in the case of Elvira Herrera, a member of one of the few Mexican Methodist families in the

California-Mexico border town of Calexico in the early twentieth century. The immigrant family settled in Calexico in the latter part of the 1910s after three years in the Central Valley town of Fresno. Elvira and her younger brother, Luis, finished high school in the United States. Both were bilingual.[19] Vernon McCombs, Superintendent of the MEC's Spanish and Portuguese District and a returned missionary from the Andes region, saw Calexico as a "center from which to work godless Lower California," especially Mexicali, "where they assemble in troops in the harlots' houses" and where "the devil has certainly sported undisturbed these decades past."[20]

Despite the zone's bleak morality, religious musical culture flourished there, at least for the young Herreras and other borderlanders. With Luis as her accompanist, Elvira translated or adapted several English-language hymns into Spanish. Her most popular one was disseminated widely throughout the hemisphere in Spanish-language Protestant hymnals during the twentieth and twenty-first centuries.[21] "*Es la Oración*" ("It Is Prayer") represented an extremely loose adaptation of F. M. Lehman's 1909 composition "The Royal Telephone," or "Central's Never Busy," which was published in more than eighteen Evangelical, Holiness, and Pentecostal hymnals from 1914 to 1949.[22]

What is most striking in this example is Herrera's decision to excise completely any mention of the still-novel appliance, the very title of Lehman's song. Although this omission may disappoint scholars of material religious culture,[23] Herrera seems to have been purposeful in moving from the material to the symbolic. In an era of economic scarcity and limited communication technology, her coreligionists could scarcely identify a luxury appliance that only gringos and wealthy Mexicans owned. So rather than get lost in the metaphors of American consumerism, better just to have an intimate talk with Jesus instead: Jesus the shepherd, Jesus the Word-giver, Jesus who sits on the Throne, all metaphors readily understandable in popular religious idioms. The spirit of the message, the direct line to the heart of Jesus, remained intact, helped along by Herrera's aggressive translation/ adaptation.

We can surmise that Herrera adapted the hymn early in her shift from Methodism to Apostolicism. The Herrera home, which invited Bible studies from Baptist and Salvation Army evangelists, was the site of the first Apostolic congregation in the Calexico-Mexicali area.

Elvira and Luis's prior musical training in the Methodist church equipped them for the tasks of hymn translation and performance—gifts they generously shared with the Apostolic and broader Pentecostal movement.

Clearly, the Herreras were more than restive Methodists or prodigal Catholics. Rather Elvira was a creative agent, busily fashioning an identity in the margins between two societies: Protestant United States and Catholic Mexico. For her, that periphery was a center, a zone in which she moved comfortably, usually oblivious to the hegemonic centers. In the case of such borderlanders, robust agency is especially evident when they are left to their own devices, either by design or neglect from their would-be sponsors. Eventually, for Herrera, Methodism's tentative support system in the Imperial Valley (the MEC reported that the Mexican mission in Calexico and surrounding towns were without supply in 1918 and 1919), like the telephone metaphor, proved inadequate to her community's needs. She and her family embraced a heterodox Pentecostal movement represented in the charismatic ministry of a young immigrant evangelist, Antonio Nava, who established his transborder base in Calexico in 1921 (the same year that the MEC began building a parsonage for the Mexican pastor).

The case of Elvira Herrera and her religious community challenges us to reconsider a seemingly inconsequential border region as a central site for popular religious imagination, for contest over religious identity, and for production of religious musical culture. It invites us to recognize the ability of the subjects of our study to assume agency, forge identities, and sing songs of their own making.

The onset of the Great Depression wreaked havoc upon young Latino Pentecostal churches. Political scapegoating compounded already dire economic straits. Federal, state, and local authorities combined to push nearly a million Mexicans and Chicanos south of the border.[24] This persecution tore at the fabric of barrio life. Ultimately, however, that fabric proved resilient, and in the case of Pentecostal communities, stretched to encompass a broad swath of territory far beyond the movement's origin in southern California. Solidarity amidst scarcity bred fecundity. Also, the retreat of sponsor denominations under financial duress left wider margins for innovation.

Set against the grim backdrop of economic recession and political persecution, Apostolic hymnody (to take just one Pentecostal variant)

Figure 8.1

"The Royal Telephone"	"Es la Oración"	("Prayer Is")
author: F.M. Lehman (1909)	tr./author: Elvira Herrera (c. 1921)	(translation of Herrera lyrics--mine)
I Central's never busy, always on the line You may hear from heaven almost any time 'Tis a royal service free for one and all When you get in trouble give this royal line a call	Es la oración un medio que el Señor le dejó a su grey, que anda con temor Viendo Su Palabra, en ella tu verás que la oración te acerca a Cristo más y más	Prayer is a medium that the Lord left his flock that walks in the fear (of God) Looking at His Word you will see that prayer brings you close to Jesus more and more
C Telephone to glory, O what joy divine! I can feel the current moving on the line Built by God the Father for his loved and own We may talk to Jesus thro' this royal telephone	¡Oh! Hablar con Cristo, qué felicidad! Y contarle todo, todo en verdad Expondiendole tu necesidad El te escuchará desde su Trono Celestial	Oh, to speak with Jesus, what happiness! And to tell him everything, everything in truth Laying bare all your need He will hear you from his celestial throne
II There will be no charges, telephone is free It was built for service, just for you and me There will be no waiting on this royal line Telephone to glory always answers just in time	Si estás tú triste, ponte en oración Habla hacia la gloria con el corazón Es un mandamiento que el Señor dejó Y tendrás respuesta porque así lo prometió	If you are sad, put yourself in prayer Pray toward Glory with your heart This is a commandment that the Lord left (us) And you'll receive an answer for so he has promised

III

Fail to get the answer, Satan's crossed
your wire
By some strong delusion or some base
desire
Take away obstructions, God is on the
throne
And you'll get the answer thro' this
royal telephone

IV

If your line is "grounded," and
connection true
has been lost with Jesus, tell you what to
do
Pray'r and faith and promise mend the
broken wire
till your soul is burning with the
Pentecostal fire

V

Carnal combinations cannot get control
of this line to glory, anchored in the soul
Storm and trial cannot disconnect the
line
held in constant keeping by the Father's
hand divine

¿Estás en espera del Consolador?
Ten fe y paciencia, constancia y amor
Y el Señor al ver tu ferviente prez
Cumplirá tu gozo dándote un
Pentecostés

Si no hay respuesta, ora más y más
No te desamines, Cristo no es falaz
Siempre a sus promesas, fiel responderá
Lo que necesites, ésto El te lo dará

Are you tarrying for the Comforter?
Have faith and patience, constancy and
love
and the Lord, upon seeing your fervent
press(ing)
Will fulfill your joy giving you a
Pentecost

If there is no answer keep praying on
and on
Do not be disheartened, Jesus never fails
To his promises he will always hold
Whatever you may need this he will give
you

expanded into such a large corpus that the first compilation effort in the early 1930s, *Himnos de Consolación*,[25] contained more that 200 hymns, the large majority of them original compositions. A concurrent compilation in Mexico, *Himnos de Suprema Alabanza*,[26] gathered more than 160 hymns; again the majority were organic to the movement. Even after accounting for a significant number of simultaneously published hymns, by the late 1930s, the overall number of published original Apostolic hymns can be conservatively estimated at 300. Apostolic hymn writers matched perennial Mexican poetic themes (e.g., pilgrimage) with popular musical genres (e.g., polka) to produce a sensory and physical experience that resonated in the community's ears, hearts, and bodies. They composed songs for every ritual occasion—births/child dedications, water and Spirit baptisms, initiations, birthdays, communion services, marriages, partings, welcomings, offerings, and death—thereby reuniting popular music and religious ritual in a stronger bond than even Mexican/Chicano Catholicism enjoyed at the time and in a vein similar to that of Nahuatl and other ancient Mesoamerican cultures. Beginning in the late nineteenth century, Mexican Catholicism had experienced a revival of high art and cathedral choral music that had once again pushed folk music and instruments out of that country's principal sanctuaries and relegated them to village churches and the external performance spaces of pilgrimages and fiestas.[27] The situation for Mexican American Catholics under the tutelage of a Baltimore-based hierarchy bent on Americanizing the culturally and theologically recalcitrant flock seemed even bleaker.[28]

Form mattered as much as content in Apostolic and Pentecostal hymnody. Composers appropriated most of the current popular Mexican musical idioms and instruments from polka to *ranchera* to *corrido* to *vals* to *huapango* to *marcial* to *canción romántica* to bolero—all, apparently, except *cha-cha-cha* and *danzón*, which were probably considered too irredeemably wedded to the carnal dance floor. Yet even the latter's exclusion cannot be maintained strictly, given the bolero's derivation from the *danzón*, *conga*, and *contradanza*, the former two demonstrating clear Afro-Cuban roots and the third Afro-Cuban adaptations.[29] Although introduced into Mexico (Yucatán) and Central America through marimba bands in the nineteenth century, bolero's wider dissemination awaited transmission in the 1930s through Mexico

City's powerful XEW radio station and the virtuoso interpretation of the genre by guitar *tríos* such as *Los Panchos, Las Calaveras,* and *Los Diamantes.*[30] Almost simultaneously, *bolero's* slightly syncopated 2/4 rhythm (eight beats with the third left out), crowded out its Andalusian cousin-progenitor and was applied to Mexican regional repertoires and to Pentecostal hymnody.

Apostolic musical poetics, emanating from the fields and orchards where many of the songwriters labored, could not help but reflect the contours of the borderlands. Indeed music captured something of the experience of exhausted bodies dragged in from a day's work, quickly splashed with water and nourished with beans and tortillas before dashing off to the campsite or tent to embrace other bodies in fervent and ecstatic worship.

The process of inspiration/composition itself often occurred in the workplace, as in the case of Filenón Zaragoza, author of the tender *vals* hymn *"Mi Plegaria"* ("My Plea"). The melancholy melody and lyrics came to him as he toiled in the cotton fields outside of El Paso in 1940. Zaragoza understood the epiphany as an answer to a long-standing prayer he had often breathed in envy of other church members' ease in hymn composition. The Ciudad Juárez resident stooped to trace the lyrics in the dirt and returned to the spot throughout the day to commit the words to memory. Upon returning across the border to Juarez after the day's work, and before going home to wash the dirt off his weary body, he dashed to the church to find paper and pencil.[31] The song proved an instant hit in Pentecostal churches in Juarez, El Paso, Chihuahua City, Las Cruces, New Mexico, and beyond.

Borderlands Pentecostal composers drew liberally from mundane agricultural metaphors, such as "Vamos Todos a la Siembra" ("Let's All Go to the Sowing") and "El Sembrador" ("The Sower"); bakeries, barren and flowery landscapes, such as "Rosa de Saron" ("Rose of Sharon") and "Como La Primavera" ("As the Springtime"); and even railroads and trains, such as "El Tren del Evangelio" ("The Gospel Train"). The sweet emotive wells of matriarchy and maternity inspired numerous elegies, such as "Mi Madre Oraba por Mí" ("My Mother Prayed for Me"). The bitter fruit of poverty, in hymns such as "Tu Eres Refugio Del Pobre" ("You Are the Refuge of the Poor"), fed scathing prophetic and social commentary, in hymns such as "Profecia de Habacuc" ("Prophecy of Habakuk"). Composers wrapped entire biblical passages in *corrido* and *décima* forms, a practice essential for the improved general and biblical literacy of a community long denied the scriptures by a gate-keeping clergy. Traditional Christian hagiography received similar treatment. For example, a ten-stanza-long *corrido* about Christian martyrs in the Roman Coliseum opens with the troubadour's obligatory announcement—"Hermanos, voy a contarles—allá en el siglo primero" ("Brethren, I am going to tell you . . . way back in the first century")—and respects metric (e.g., octosyllabic lines), lyric, and other conventions of the corridor genre.

During the same period in other locales, similar liturgical reforms were afoot. Juan Lugo, the "Apostle of Pentecost to Puerto Rico" and founder of the *Iglesia de Dios Pentecostal* (now the commonwealth's largest denomination), found a ready musical collaborator in Juan Concepción.[32] Francisco Olazabal's independent Concilio Lantinoamericano de Iglesias Christianas spawned an indigenous hymnody as well.[33] Like Nava, both leaders had led breakaway movements spurred by a disenchantment with gringo (Assemblies of God) sponsorship, Lugo after a long period of alternating eager and ambivalent collaboration and Olazabal more purposefully and earlier on.[34] Also, the financial straits of white sponsors hampered attempts to contain newly assertive cultural nationalisms. In the case of the Disciples of Christ, the recall of missionaries from Puerto Rico coincided with a successful move for independence by islanders. The ensuing revival and emergence of an indigenous, proto-Pentecostal hymnody so transformed the *Discípulos's* religious culture that longtime Mexico-based Disciples missionary Frederic Huegel, on a trip to the island in 1951, complained that his hosts had carried their liturgy beyond the point of recognition.[35] In these cases, the guitar and kindred instruments emerged as markers of a new liturgical practice and space, a zone replete, as one observer remarked, with transgressive significance: "The (Disciples) revival of '33 redeemed the guitar. This was not well received in devotional circles. Folks thought it too romantic, forgetting that the Gospel itself is a romance."[36]

The contested marker of the guitar and other signifiers prompts an interrogation of traditional historiography, one that will consider insights from ethnomusicology and other disciplines that employ the ethnographic method. Early photos of Apostolic musicians display the ubiquitous guitar (previously disdained as profane—and erotic—by mainline missionaries and their converts), which according to pioneer Antonio Nava was often the only instrument available to a working-class church: *"La guitarra . . . p'al pobre . . . la guitarra"* ("The guitar, for the poor, the guitar").[37] The guitar and banjo could combine in ensembles of wind, string, and percussion instruments, such as the *bajo sexto* and the *tololoche*—two favorites in *tejano conjunto* style. The Latino mainline–Pentecostal contrast seems similar to the tensions between *tejano orquestra* (the middle class Chicano preference exemplified by Little Joe y la Familia) and *conjunto* (the working class preference exemplified by the Conjunto Bernal). As noted by ethnomusicologist Manuel Peña in his study of the two genres, these boil down to a class-informed preference: *"música pa' high society"* versus *"música pa' los pobres"* ("music for high society" versus "music for the poor").[38] The Pentecostal proletariat also democratized liturgy, creating a communitarian performance space for any lay member, singly or in groups, to express or declaim musical and poetic creations.

The methodology used and questions raised by cultural anthropology and its allied fields is a way to expand the historiographical tool kit and to examine the use of religious music as a tool for cultural maintenance, ideological conflict, theological pedagogy, and sociocultural solidarity. Interviews with composers and consideration of such factors as musicality, performance, and social context suggest directions toward understanding how music in its social context has helped to forge popular religious identities in the American religious contact zones.

In a sense, Pentecostals led the way toward a Protestant reencounter with culture. The emergence of a majority Pentecostal movement within Latino and Latin American Protestantism provides an interesting case of the Pentecostalization of the mainstream, especially in terms of liturgy and music. The marginal social position of Pentecostals also led to assertions of social solidarity with fellow sojourners. Pilgrims sang Zion's song to other wanderers. The study of Borderlands religious musical culture thus reveals interesting continuities between the region's two most popular religiosities: Pentecostal and Catholic. The agents of this transformation remain generally anonymous; such is the nature of social movements. However, several interesting case studies present themselves. Among these, the family biography and musical career of the *Hermanos Alvarado,* a guitar-strumming trio whose musical career spanned three decades (1950s through 1970s), could serve as a template for the broader story under discussion as well as for twentieth-century Mexican American history.

Pascual and Dolores Alvarado emigrated from northern Mexico early in that country's decade-long revolution. Pascual had fought on the side of Francisco Villa and then Venustiano Carranza. The couple's seven children were born in Texas, Arizona, and California. The parents and maternal grandparents were among the first generation of Apostolic converts in Bakersfield, California (baptized in 1916). Thus a tight-knit, sectarian Pentecostal community provided the religious formation for the Alvarado children.[39]

In 1932, in spite of her children's U.S. citizenship, Dolores was ordered repatriated to Mexico. In order to keep the family intact, the parents decided to return there with their children. After arriving by train in Torreón, Coahuila, they slowly made their way, following the railway northward, back to the border. Pascual took welding jobs and Dolores sold tortillas to finance the seven-month trek. An infant son, Juan, was kept alive by the milk of a donated goat. Adolescent daughters Luz and Guadalupe died from malnourishment soon after their arrival in Ciudad Juárez, a stone's throw away from the country of their birth. Upon arrival in Juárez, the Alvarado parents set about two tasks: securing housing and a livelihood, and reconnecting with the Apostolic church. A small ranch outside the city limits met the first need; an Apostolic congregation pastored by Juan Ramírez met the second. Apparently, the transborder networks set in place through the preceding decade by Apostolic leaders and laity served to keep the Alvarados and many other families connected during a period of persecution and dislocation (the family dedicated the infant Juan in Torreón's Iglesia Apostólica). Such solidarity was lacking in other Protestant church movements, even Pentecostal ones, especially those led by gringos, as was the case with Aimee Semple McPherson's International Church of the Foursquare Gospel, whose Latino ministerial ranks were decimated by repatriation. That denomination's roster of Mexican American pastors and congregations completely disappeared in the wake of the political persecution. Repatriated Apostolics, on the other hand, could seek out sister congregations in Mexico, or establish new ones.

As they entered their teen years, the Alvarado sons took up guitar playing, soon becoming proficient. As has been the case with African American gospel and blues musicians, the venue for performance and the choice of musical genre became sites of struggle for the artists' souls. Elder brother Román decided early on to dedicate his talents "to the Lord," whereas Rosario and Juan opted to play in cantinas. When pressed by Román, the two prodigals would agree to accompany him in performance in religious services. The trio's virtuosity soon won them a following in the Apostolic churches of Juárez. The brothers experienced a hint of things to come when they were invited to perform on a local radio station. Within a few years, Rosario unequivocally joined Román and the church, leaving behind, in classic conversion mode, a womanizing and drinking past. (Juan would wait two decades to convert.)

After Rosario's conversion, he and Román exchanged the former's smaller *requinto* guitar for the latter's larger, standard one, reasoning that the move to the simpler strumming instrument would help Rosario resist the tempting cantina memories evoked by the *requinto's* fancy riffs. The Alvarados' repertoire consisted chiefly of music composed by Román and other Apostolic songwriters in the United States and Mexico. They adapted and sacralized popular Mexican musical genres. Their thematic emphases on pilgrimage and endurance were as much a defiance against majority religious intolerance as a reworking of ancient Mesoamerican and medieval Catholic motifs. The singers intertwined sweet melancholy with joyful encounter and sheer doggedness in order to express poetic visions similar to medieval Iberian Catholic pilgrim hymns.

After nearly two decades in Juárez, the Alvarado family made their way back to Los Angeles. Their travels exposed them to a widening circle of Latino Protestant churches, a development that discomfited the Apostolic leadership. A fortuitous encounter with Dale Evans and Laura Harper, wives of famous Hollywood musical cowboys, broadened the Alavardos' artistry in ways the singers had never imagined. A 1959 episode bears recounting here.

After assisting two Anglo matrons (Harper and Evans) with their shopping bags at a downtown market, Pascual Alavarado agreed to accompany them to Hollywood Hills to repeat the favor. While standing in their driveway, he heard music drifting from a rear window (probably the Sons of the Pioneers). Pascual boasted to Harper that his progeny could sing much better. Intrigued, she took him up on his claim. After an audition the trio was invited in to record in a state-of-the-art studio. The resulting five-volume LP project, managed by Harper, ushered in a long period of expanding fame as the hemisphere's mostly widely heard *evangélico* musical group, a period that lasted until their disbanding in 1973.

Although outsider savvy and capital may have provided important impetus to the Alvarados' career, Harper's imagination and gaze also crippled them at home. Her decision to photograph the *tejano* singers in *jarocho* costume (from Veracruz) confirmed Apostolic suspicions that the group had become "*mundano*" (worldly). Yet, as doors to Apostolic churches in Los Angeles closed, others opened in the wider Latino *evangélico* community.

The appeal of the Alvarados' music in that era seems to have been matched only by that of Guatemala's Alfredo Colom (1904–71), whose compositions were broadcast through HBJC, the Voice of the Andes, a powerful missionary radio station in Quito, Ecuador.[40] The broad dissemination of the Alvarados' music occurred by means of the LP project, several tours sponsored by Harper and the Christian Faith organization, and widespread pirating (which persists to this day). The extent of the musical influence of these Texas- and California-born troubadours has been shown by recent research in Oaxaca. A veteran Nazarene pastor in that state credits three factors with keeping the first generation of *evangélicos* in southern Mexico "faithful" in the face of great intolerance in the 1950s and 1960s: 1) *la Biblia* (the Bible), 2) *la oración* (prayer), and 3) "*la música de los Hnos. Alvarado*" (the music of the Alvarado Brothers).[41]

The Hermanos Alvarado never visited Oaxaca, but their music arrived early on, possibly in the luggage of the first returning *braceros,* or of immigrants caught up in the *migra* raids, or of converts returning from domestic service jobs in Mexico City. As early converts to Protestantism in southern Mexico set about constructing an alternative aural universe out of new and old cultural elements, they brought home (from Mexico City or the United States or elsewhere) religious remittances of great symbolic value including, especially, music.

The contemporary religious musical culture of Latino Catholics provides intriguing clues about the wandering nature of music. Catholics, too, perform their own type of *briccolage,* combining readily recognizable Marian prayers with musical borrowings from their *aleluya* (this common epithet for Protestants in general hints at the predominance of Pentecostal practice) cousins' musical culture. Clearly, someone is not minding orthodoxy's store. The sound of Pentecostal *coritos* now reverberates in rural mountain pilgrimages, as well as in urban spaces such as Mexico City's Basilica of the Virgin of Guadalupe. By the time Vatican II opened the doors and windows of the mass to vernacular languages and sounds, the *aleluya* siblings and cousins of Catholics had prepared an engaging repertoire for ready borrowing, probably via the Charismatic Renewal. Once again, folks inhabiting borderlands of religious belief and practice proved themselves adept and creative agents. The difficulty in tracing precisely the origin and dissemination of most Latino Pentecostal hymns and choruses suggests that these ride in the luggage and in the hearts of a very mobile religious proletariat that often does not bother to check in with civic, ecclesiastical, and academic authorities. How, for example, did *"Alabaré a mi Señor"* ("I Will Praise My Lord"), *"No hay Dios tan grande como Tú"* ("There Is No God Greater Than You"), and *"Mas allá del Sol"* ("Beyond the Sun") travel from Pentecostal to mainline Protestant and popular Catholic hymnody?[42] In the end, in the U.S.-Mexico Borderlands, popular Pentecostalism and popular Catholicism may have more in common than commonly assumed. The continuities seem as important as the discontinuities.

A dialectical approach to Latino Protestant (mainline vs. Pentecostal) hymnody may hold interpretive value, but it also may obscure important features. Examination of Pentecostal musical practice invites a reexamination of its mainline precursors for similar assertions of agency. Assuming the agency of early Latino Protestants, the work of such prolific translators as Mendoza, Grado, and Reza deserve deeper study. Did they view themselves solely as translators of an imported musical liturgy, as facilitators in an enterprise that would replace features of Mexican and Chicano musical culture with Anglo-American ones? How faithful were their translations? What can we glean from their deviations from the English-language originals and from their editorial decisions? What can we learn from the corpus of their *original* compositions?

Given the ample documentation for both mainline and Pentecostal transborder movement and networks, the study of American Protestantism must transcend geographical boundaries to include influences *from* regions south of the border and at the periphery. Reluctance to undertake such study contrasts with readiness to include non-U.S. sites, especially England and Canada, in approaching modern American Protestantism. A metaphor of concentric or overlapping circles of religious history and experience may prove useful for new mappings of the religious landscape of North America. Such an enterprise should reflect more hemispheric contours and interdisciplinary methods. The new mappings will require careful soundings as much as careful sightings.

Notes

1. Epigraph from Gilbert Haven, *Our Next-Door Neighbor* New York: Harper and Bros., 1875), 95–96. The Wesleyan revival in England and First and Second Great Awakenings in the United States had wrested Reform Protestant liturgy loose from the strictures of lined Psalms, the only acceptable form of congregational song in Puritan New England. See Edward Dickinson, *Music in the History of the Western Church* (New York: Charles Scribner's Sons, 1902; reprint, New York: Greenwood Press, 1969).

2. Translations of the top five hymns ("All Hail the Power of Jesus' Name," "Jesus, Lover of My Soul," "Am I a Soldier of the Cross," "Alas! And Did My Savior Bleed," and "Rock of Ages, Cleft for Me") ranked by frequency of publication in 225 historic (English-language) U.S. hymnals are ubiquitous in Spanish-language hymnals. See chapter 1.

3. For Sankey's collaboration with evangelist Dwight L. Moody and composer Fanny Crosby and his significance as "gospel song's" chief composer/compiler/publisher/promoter/popularizer, see Mel R. Wilhoit, "'Sing Me a Sankey': Ira D. Sankey and Congregational Song," *The Hymn* 24 (January 1991): 13–18.

4. Vicente Mendoza, ed., *Himnos Selectos* (Mexico, D.F.: Vicente Mendoza, 1905); Pedro Grado, ed., *Pequeña Colección de Himnos* (Laredo, Tex.: n.p., 1905).

5. "Cuba Mission," *Annual Report of the Board of Foreign Missions* (Nashville: Methodist Episcopal Church South, 1907), 193.

6. Rodríguez's official collaboration began in 1888. His translations of a significant part of the John Wesley theological corpus were used extensively in Methodist Spanish-language ministerial training curricula. He also created/redacted the MECS's Sunday school Spanish-language curriculum. Upon his

death in 1909, the denominational eulogy boasted that "two-thirds of the Protestant Sunday School children in Mexico are using our literature; in fact, through Mr. Rodríguez's skill and industry our Church has been brought to the front rank in the matter of Spanish literature, and in that respect is steadily widening its influence." "Rev. P. A. Rodríguez," *Annual Report of the Board of Foreign Missions* (Nashville: Methodist Episcopal Church South, 1909), 122–23. See also Alfredo Náñez, *History of the Rio Grande Conference of the United Methodist Church* (Dallas: Southern Methodist University, 1980), 56–57.

7. Primitivo A. Rodríguez, *Himnario cristiano para uso de las iglesias evangélicas* (Nashville: Smith and Lamar, 1908), iv–vii. Of the twenty-seven hymnals, sixteen had been compiled/published in Spain, three in Mexico, three in New York, and one each in Nashville, Philadelphia, Buenos Aires, London, and Laredo (Texas). The MECS Board of Missions posthumously characterized Rodríguez's opus as "his last and in his own estimation, his greatest work . . . perhaps the very best hymnal in the Spanish language [which] has met with a most favorable reception among Protestants in all Spanish-speaking countries. . . . [It] is being used by other denominations . . . and was exhausted in a short time after its appearance." "Rev. P. A. Rodríguez," 122.

8. Marcelino Menéndez y Pelayo, *Historia de los heterodoxos españoles,* vol. 3, 2da Edición Refundida (Madrid: Librería General de Victoriano Suárez, 1911–33), 455.

9. At least 115,000 copies of *Himnos de Gloria* were reported to have been sold in the first decade of publication. See Alice E. Luce, "The Latin-American Pentecostal Work," *The Pentecostal Evangelical,* June 25, 1927, 6. For a critical assessment of the "pious paternalism" of H. C. Ball and Luce, his Los Angeles-based collaborator, see Gaston Espinosa, "Borderlands Religion: Los Angeles and the Origins of the Latino Pentecostal Movement in the U.S., Mexico, and Puerto Rico, 1900–1945" (unpublished Ph.D. dissertation, University of California, Santa Barbara, 1999). For an uncritical chronicle of the tutelage, see Victor de Leon, *The Silent Pentecostals: A Biographical History of the Pentecostal Movement among the Hispanics in the Twentieth Century* (Taylors, S.C.: Faith Printing Company, 1979).

10. Manuel Lockwood, "Recent Developments in U.S. Hispanic and Latin American Protestant Church Music" (unpublished D. Minn. project, Claremont School of Theology, 1981), 16. United Methodism's 1996 *Mil Voces para Celebrar* appears to squarely face the Lockwood critique. See Raquel Mora Martínez, "Mil Voces para Celebrar—Himnario Metodista," *The Hymn* 49 (April 1998): 25–29. An equally remarkable ecumenical compilation project, with significantly greater Pentecostal content than *Mil Voces,* appeared three years earlier under Mennonite auspices. *Alabanzas Favoritas, No. 2,* with 232 hymns, represented a scoring and expansion of the original *Alabanzas Favoritas,* compiled in 1954 by Mennonites in Chihuahua, Mexico. See Iglesia

de Dios en Cristo, Menonita, *Alabanzas Favoritas, No. 2* (Moundridge, Kans.: Gospel Publishers, 1993). For a discussion of hymnody contestation between Brazilian Baptists and missionaries, see E. Edward Spann, "A Tale of Two Hymnals: The Brazilian Baptist *Cantor Cristao* (1891) and *Hinário Para o Culto Cristao* (1991)," *The Hymn* 43 (April 1992): 15-21.

11. *El Evangelista Mexicano,* Chihuahua, Mexico, época 2, año 10, nro. 17 (May 1, 1928): 36-137.

12. Manuel Gamio, *Mexican Immigration to the United States: A Study of Human Migration and Adjustment* (Chicago: University of Chicago Press, 1930; reprint, Dover Publications, New York, 1971), 117. For concern over proselytizing by *aleluyas* (the popular epithet for Apostolics and other Pentecostals) among gullible immigrants, see Manuel Gamio, "The Leader and the Intellectual," in Manuel Gamio, *The Mexican Immigrant: His Life Story* (Chicago: University of Chicago Press, 1930: reprinted as *The Life Story of the Mexican Immigrant: Autobiographical Documents Collected by Manuel Gamio,* Dover Publications, New York, 1971), 223. The study, commissioned by the Social Science Research Council, excerpted interviews conducted during 1926–27 with seventy-six Mexican immigrants (including two Baptist and one Methodist minister) by Mexico's foremost anthropologist. *Life Story* is the companion book to the more analytical *Mexican Immigration to the United States: A Study of Human Migration and Adjustment,* also by Gamio.

13. Russell E. Richey, *Early American Methodism* (Bloomington: Indiana University Press, 1991), 82.

14. Mikhail Bakhtin argues that the medieval festivals and carnivals in the works of Rabelais "always represent[ed] an essential, meaningful content" in uneasy tension with official church-sanctioned feasts. Similarly, over and against missionary censure, Borderlands Pentecostals reintroduced a measure of the carnivalesque (laughter, weeping, body movement, profane instruments, feasts, etc.) into liturgical space and time. Mikhail Bakhtin, *Rabelais and His World* (Bloomington: Indiana University Press, 1984), 8-9.

15. Bernardo Hernández, *Estatutos acordados en la 1.a convención mexicana de la Iglesia de la Fé Apostólica Pentecostés* (Los Angeles: Bernardo Hernández, 1926). Marcial de la Cruz also served as an evangelist in Southern California, Arizona, and New Mexico. He was said to introduce hymns into his services that he had composed on the spot after fasting in a pup tent carried with him for that purpose. Jose A. Ortega, *Mis memorias en la Iglesia y la Asamblea Apostólica de la Fé en Cristo Jesús* (Indio, Calif.: Jose A. Ortega, 1998), 279-80.

16. Antonio C. Nava interview, September 13, 1994.

17. For a discussion of these strategies in another context, see Manuel Peña, *The Texas-Mexican Conjunto: History of a Working—Class Music* (Austin: University of Texas Press, 1985).

18. The reciprocity of black-Latino contacts is indicated by reports in the 1920s and 1930s of African American enthusiasm for Mexican worship in South Texas: "The brethren worship in a large room in a private house, perhaps some thirty gathering there, and in the back part the colored people gather. These colored people are anxious to hear Pentecost preached in their own language, but a white man could hardly preach to them in this part of the country. Yet, these colored people have learned to sing the Spanish songs with the Mexicans, even though they know very little Spanish." H. C. Ball, "The Work Prospers on the Mexican Border," *The Pentecostal Evangel*, July 8, 1922: 13.

19. Interview with Luis Herrera, September 16, 1994.

20. Vernon McCombs, "Spanish and Portuguese District," *Journal of the Southern California Annual Conference, Methodist Episcopal Church, Forty-Second Annual Session*, 1917. Information on the MEC Latino work in southern California is taken from annual *Journal* reports of the conference from 1901–27.

21. Luis F. del Pilar, *Himnos de "El Avivamiento,"* 2d ed. (Bayamón, Puerto Rico: Impresos Quintana, 1983). J. Paul Cragin, an independent Holiness missionary, correctly attributed the hymn to Herrera in his *Melodías Evangélicas*. The hymn continues to circulate throughout the continent, appearing in the latest edition of the hymnal of Mexico's *Iglesia Evangélica Independiente*. See Santos Parra Herrera, Josefina Huerta de Parra, and Cesar Rodríguez Camara, eds., *Himnos de Victoria* (Mexico, D.F.: Iglesia Evangélica Independiente, 2000), n. 338.

22. Letter from Mary L. Van Dyke, The Hymn Society, to Daniel Ramírez, October 28, 1998.

23. See Colleen McDannell, *Material Christianity, Religion and Popular Culture in America* (New Haven, Conn.: Yale University Press, 1995).

24. Francisco E. Balderrama and Raymond Rodríguez, *Decade of Betrayal: Mexican Repatriation in the 1930s* (Albuquerque: University of New Mexico Press, 1995).

25. Letter from Mary L. VanDyke, The Hymn Society, to Daniel Ramírez, October 28, 1998.

26. Macolvio Gaxiola, ed., *Himnos de Suprema Alabanza a Jesús,* 2da ed. (Hermosillo: Sonora, 1942).

27. Rubén Campos, *El folklore y la música mexicana: Investigación acerca de la cultura musical en Mexico, 1525–1925* (Mexico, D.F.: Secretaría de Educación Pública, 1928) 191–96.

28. See Jay P. Dolan and Allen Figueroa Deck, eds., *Hispanic Catholic Culture in the U.S.: Issues and Concerns* (Notre Dame, Ind.: University of Notre Dame Press, 1994), and Jay P. Dolan and Gilberto M. Hinojosa, eds. *Mexican*

Americans and the Catholic Church, 1900–1965 (Notre Dame, Ind.: University of Notre Dame Press, 1994).

29. Willi Kahl, "Bolero," in *The New Grove Dictionary of Music and Musicians,* ed. Sir George Grove and Stanley Sadie (London: Macmillan, 1980), 870–71.

30. Claes af Geijerstam, *Popular Music in Mexico* (Albuquerque: University of New Mexico Press, 1976), 77.

31. Interview with Filemón Zaragoza, September 17, 1994.

32. Juan Concepción, ed., *Eco de vida: Selección especial de himnos y canciones espirituales por compositors hispanos* (Brooklyn: Editorial Ebenezer, n.d.).

33. Felipe Gutiérrez, ed., *Nuevo himnario de melodies evangélicas selectas* (Brownsville, Tex.: Latin American Council of Christian Churches, 1944).

34. See Espinosa, "Borderlands Religion."

35. Juan E. Huegel, *Apostol de la cruz: La vida y labor misionera de Federico J. Huegel* (Mexico, D.F.: Ediciones Transformación, 1995), 273–74.

36. Florentino Santana, "Address to the Annual Assembly of the Iglesia Discipulos de Cristo en Puerto Rico," February 19, 1983. Quoted in Del Pilar, *Himnos de "El Avivamiento."*

37. Antonio C. Nava interview, September 13, 1994.

38. Peña, *Texas-Mexican Conjunto,* 139. See also Manuel Peña, *The Mexican American Orquesta: Music, Culture, and the Dialectic of Conflict* (Austin: University of Texas Press, 1999).

39. Interviews with Rosario, Juan, and Román Alvarado in San Jose and Whittier, California, from August 5, 1999, to December 29, 2000.

40. Alfredo Colom M., *Música en su alma: Autobiografía de Alfredo Colom M.* (Guatemala: Ediciones SABER, 1985).

41. Interview with José Hernández, May 20, 2002, Oaxaca de Juárez, Oaxaca.

42. The 1989 Spanish-language Catholic hymnal includes Pentecostal standards such as "Una Mirada de Fe" ("A Glimpse of Faith"), "Alabaré" ("I Will Praise"), and "La Mañana Gloriosa ("Glorious Morning"). Owen Alstott, ed., *Flor y Canto* (Portland: Oregon Catholic Press, 1989).

9

"Sing Thy Power to Save"

Music on the "Old Fashioned Revival Hour" Radio Broadcast

Daniel Fuller, Philip Goff, and Katherine McGinn

We have heard the joyful sound, Jesus saves, Jesus saves;
Spread the tidings all around, Jesus saves, Jesus saves;
Bear the news to ev'ry land, Climb the steeps and cross the waves,
Onward!
—'tis our Lord's command, Jesus saves, Jesus saves.
    Priscilla J. Owens and William J. Kirkpartrick, "Jesus Saves"

So began every broadcast of the "Old Fashioned Revival Hour," from its first coast-to-coast connection in 1937 to its final program in 1969. Over fifteen hundred weekly programs beamed the music and the message of revival throughout the world in a story that remains unequaled in religious radio broadcasting. By the end of each show, listeners had heard not only the preaching of Charles E. Fuller, but also ten to twelve musical numbers—by a famed quartet, a military-precise chorus, and a congregation of thousands—that helped define evangelical Christianity in the twentieth century. From the first strains of "Jesus Saves," to the last notes of the invitation hymn, music held a central place in the most popular religious program of radio's golden age and in turn drew thousands into the fold of conservative Protestantism.

From its international debut in 1940 to 1958, when the format was changed from a live one-hour program to a half-hour taped version, this show ruled the religious airwaves. Indeed, its ratings were not only the envy of secular programs during its era, they would even outshine many of today's popular television shows. By tracing the rise of the "Old Fashioned Revival Hour" to prominence and studying its music, we can piece together the beginning of a larger story of religious entertainment in modern America, where faiths still compete for attention.[1]

The Rise of the "Old Fashioned Revival Hour"

Unlike the more colorful Los Angeles–based radio preachers, particularly the flashy Aimee Semple McPherson and the irrepressible Robert "Fightin' Bob" Shuler, Charles Fuller (1887–1968) was born in the city and never lived outside Southern California. His father, Henry Fuller, an active member of the Methodist Church, was an enthusiastic participant in the Holiness Movement that swept through mainline denominations in the late nineteenth century. A strong supporter of A. B. Simpson (founder of the Christian and Missionary Alliance), he twice circumnavigated the globe, visiting missionaries and reporting his findings in the local newspaper. Henry Fuller instilled in his four sons a respect for the Pietist tradition of music by leading the family's morning devotions and hymn singing around the organ, played by his wife Helen. Charles Fuller's notions of conversion and sanctification experiences, their expression in song, and the central role of the gathered family were formed around the parlor organ.

Still, little about Charles Fuller's first thirty years gave any indication of his future. Although he grew up in a religious setting, he exhibited little interest in spiritual matters. After graduating from Pomona College in 1910 and marrying Grace Payton in 1911, he moved south to Orange County to manage a fruit-packing house. He joined the Placentia Presbyterian Church in 1913 and was elected a ruling elder the following year—precisely the course one would expect of a young man hoping to advance in the community. Things changed significantly in 1916. Reading in the *Los Angeles Times* that a famous boxer-turned-preacher was to speak at the Church of the Open Door, Fuller attended the evangelistic service alone. Deeply moved by Paul Rader's message, he was converted to fundamental Christianity.

Feeling called to the ministry and suddenly flush with cash through leasing a small orange grove for oil drilling, Fuller enrolled at the Bible Institute of Los Angeles in the fall of 1919. The curriculum had been refined to a two-year program leading to a diploma. The training was practical as well as academic, requiring courses in music and ministry alongside those in Bible doctrines. Upon graduation, Fuller became disenchanted with his Presbyterian church and began to teach one of its Sunday school classes at the Placentia Women's Club across the street. By 1924 Fuller's attendants outdrew the church's eleven o'clock service by a three-to-one margin, causing the church's new pastor to cut ties with the class in hopes of drawing good Presbyterians back to the fold. Fuller and many in the class broke from the congregation to form an independent, interdenominational, premillennial church. He sought and received ordination in the Baptist Bible Union, a fundamentalist wing of the Northern Baptist Convention.

Fuller put his entire Bible Institute training into action at the new Calvary Church: from his sermons that incorporated dispensationalist doctrine to read the "signs of the times" in current events to his use of entertainment, most especially music, to draw crowds. From the very beginning, Fuller advertised in the *Placentia Courier* that services would have "special music from local favorites, known in the area for musical talent." Not only did he often call on the Bible Institute's quartet and orchestra; he also developed his own "Calvary Church Quartet" and orchestra, replete with a saxophone in that flapper age. For Easter 1929, he publicized a prelude of marimba and piano as well as a marimba solo offertory. Indeed, Fuller understood well the power of religious entertainment to attract audiences who could be made receptive to the gospel. "'A Musical Saw' will be one of the features," proclaimed the *Courier* in 1926. "If you have never heard a musical saw you've missed something. Come and hear it." Nor would Fuller shy away from the strange or unordinary to draw crowds. "LITTLE BETTY CLARK, BLIND GIRL WILL SING," read the newspaper in 1929. Earlier that year, Fuller advertised that the Utica Colored Jubilee Singers from the Utica Normal and Industrial Institute in Mississippi would perform a program of "spirituals, plantation melodies, folk songs and dialect readings." As pastor, it appears, Fuller learned the art of piecing together song and sermon to create both an entertaining and evangelistic service. "Those who enjoy old fashioned revival services should come and share these Sunday evening evangelistic services. Whole hearted congregational singing and Question Box Night," he publicized fully a decade before the nation heard his voice over radio.[2]

Looking back at Fuller's days as a pastor, it is clear that Paul Rader's ministry influenced him in more ways than converting Fuller to fundamentalism. During the 1920s, Rader created the nation's most extensive radio ministry in Chicago. Leaving the Moody Memorial Church—which he felt confined his ministry—he started the Chicago Gospel Tabernacle, which became the center of a maelstrom of activities. Rader had long believed that music drew crowds that could then be made receptive to the gospel message and had perfected the skills of playing lively tunes and preaching on Chicago's streets. In turn, he transferred these skills to radio, broadcasting several hours daily and nearly all day on Sundays over the city's most powerful stations. Fuller, too, felt that the revival style of music and preaching were the most effective ways to win souls. Like Rader, he eventually took it to radio.[3]

By 1924, Fuller was on the air. On occasion the Bible Institute invited him to teach morning lessons over its 750-watt station. Off and on he continued to fill spots on the Institute's thirty-seven hour broadcasting week. It was not until 1929, when on an evangelistic tour in the Midwest (preaching with Paul Rader), however, that Fuller fully understood radio's potential. Substituting for a regular speaker on a gospel program in Indianapolis, he afterward received many letters and calls from people who had been particularly touched by his message. On his return home, Fuller felt called by God to begin a radio ministry.

In early 1930 he contracted with 100-watt KREG of Santa Ana to hook a telephone line into Calvary Church and begin broadcasting his Sunday evening services. He encouraged listeners to write in, and even offered prizes for the one farthest away. (The Bible Institute's low-frequency, 750-watt KTBI could be heard as far away as Vermont and Hawaii.) Fuller expanded his radio ministry over the next two years. Moving outside his congregation, and barely within his means, Fuller began to broadcast "The Pilgrim's Hour" over seven stations of the Columbia Broadcast System. In early 1933, feeling the financial strain of the Depression and the emotional strain of dealing with a pastor whose concerns stretched far beyond the church's stain-glassed windows, Calvary Church requested that Fuller take an undetermined extended leave and hired his assistant pastor to replace him. Charles

Fuller, in his midforties and suffering financial ruin himself, was now forced to seek a living in radio.

As the airwaves were increasingly filled with gospel preachers, more than a few of whom were not above suspicion, Fuller realized the need to create a base of support that lifted him above the religious shills. So, in May 1933, he formed the Gospel Broadcasting Association, calling on the most respected (and financially stable) fundamentalists in the Los Angeles area to serve on the board. He experimented with a number of programs, including "The Voice of Hollywood," "The Prophetic Lamp Hour," "Heart to Heart Hour," "Sunday School Hour," "Radio Bible Class," and "Radio Revival Hour," signing on with the powerful KFI (the key southwest station for National Broadcasting) and KHJ (the Pacific Coast station for Columbia Broadcasting) as money allowed. KHJ gave him the exposure he most desired, transmitting his programs as far east as Pennsylvania and New York, but this was expensive and time consuming. By 1935, an overworked Fuller hosted five programs each week that totaled three and a half hours of broadcasting.

The following three years brought unprecedented growth. In January 1937, Fuller linked up with the fledgling Mutual Broadcasting System on fourteen stations. Unable to solicit funds on the air, he simply reminded listeners, "Your prayers and help are greatly needed," followed by his easy-to-remember address of Box 123, Los Angeles, California. People who wrote in were placed on a mailing list to receive the monthly newsletter titled *Heart to Heart Talk*. Edited by Grace Fuller, these newsletters became the means by which the Fullers requested funds to keep the program on the air.[4] This became increasingly important, as Mutual required the show to expand with the network or risk losing its much-coveted Sunday evening slot, the period with greatest listenership. With Mutual the Fullers made the jump to a skeleton coast-to-coast network of thirty stations in October 1937. By the next month, the show ran on eighty-six stations, with a weekly budget financed entirely by listeners, which had tripled in only six weeks from $1,500 to $4,500. Much like musicians today who tour to increase album sales, Charles Fuller took his show and its quartet on the road in early 1938 to generate interest. A choir, comprised of those from local churches, also shared the stage. Fuller's success culminated that year at an Easter service in Chicago, where he spoke to more than forty thousand people at Soldier Field, one of the largest evangelistic meetings in North America to that point.

No other religious radio program can rival the story of the "Old Fashioned Revival Hour." Stations playing the program leapt from 256 in 1940 to 575 in 1944. By that time, the Gospel Broadcasting Association employed more than thirty secretaries to handle the bags of mail that arrived daily. In fact, the show had outgrown the network that had pushed it to such heights: Mutual Broadcasting accounted for only half the stations on which Fuller's broadcast ran. Fuller's Gospel Broadcasting Association, meanwhile, generated one-eighth of Mutual's income. As World War II drew to a close, the broadcast boasted twenty million listeners, worldwide coverage, and an annual budget of nearly two million dollars.[5]

We can trace several reasons for the meteoric rise of the program. The style of the show resonated with a nation at war and became one of the most important parts of the story of American religion during that time. "People are going to be at home more in the evenings now," wrote Fuller, as the nation faced rubber and gas rations, "and the listening audience will be greatly increased. We shall do our prayerful best to make the most of this opportunity by making each broadcast just as spiritual and 'homey,' as comforting and cheery as possible." Fuller understood that wartime America had specific needs, and he hoped to meet them. By providing worldwide coverage of his program, he received mail from soldiers around the globe, who wrote in to praise the singing and sermons that reminded them so of home. Meanwhile, knowing that their "soldier boys" and "sailor lads" were overseas listening to the show and writing in about their spiritual experiences, Americans tuned in by the millions.[6]

Extant letters—the Fullers probably received close to ten million of them during the 1940s and 1950s—suggest that the music, first and foremost, brought listeners to the program. At some levels this is no surprise. It certainly was no shock to Fuller, who utilized music over the radio in much the same fashion as he had in his church years before. Music caught the attention of those who would not usually stop to listen. Music touched people profoundly, opening them to the gospel message. Music likewise pushed believers to the deeper life, ever seeking a closer relationship with God. And music could create a sense of community among the saints, even among those who only met around the radio on Sundays.

Hitting the Right Notes

When Charles Fuller took his program coast-to-coast on the Mutual Broadcasting System in 1937, he realized that the musical portion needed improvement. Up to that point, he had relied on local church talent to provide music on his programs—a hit-or-miss plan that, at times, missed badly. Los Angeles, transforming into the entertainment capital of the nation before Fuller's eyes, offered a solution. By landing a young and talented pianist, one of the city's top two quartets, and a perfectionist choir leader, Fuller created a professional sound that rivaled any radio show—sacred or secular. It proved an investment that paid huge dividends. To this day, those who remember the program remark most immediately and consistently about its music.

Only four months into his nationwide programming, Fuller approached pianist Rudy Atwood and the Goose Creek Quartet of the "Little Country Church of Hollywood" program to join his staff permanently. A unique daily show, the "Little Country Church" began under the ministry of William Hogg, a former Rader associate in Chicago and Los Angeles. Set in a rural Tennessee village, the show centered on the Sunday experiences of the Parson Josiah Hopkins, his wife Sarah, their horse Dan, and various villagers, as they made their way to church. Usually a minor crisis occurred among the villagers—played by the quartet members, who also created sound effects, including those of farm animals—which the Parson Hopkins addressed in his message. In 1934, CBS moved Hogg's surprisingly popular program to its national programming after only one year on the air.

Atwood quickly became a fixture on Fuller's program, thrilling audiences with his trills and harmonies. Listeners responded to Atwood's personality, which expressed itself in his piano playing. "The church was a happy place for me, and I wanted its music to be happy music," he later recalled. "I wanted to create the joyful sound of notes, doing what I wanted them to do, and adding majesty to the song service from the praise in my own heart."[7] Known for an improvisational style that combined classical and revivalist techniques, Atwood developed the sound that defined evangelistic music by midcentury. "I believe when you improvise, what you are producing is the sum total of what you have learned," he concluded.[8] He was right. Well-versed in Bach ("the musician's musician," according to Atwood), Beethoven, Chopin, and Mozart by his teacher, Edith Knox—herself a concert pianist and the musical grandchild of Franz Liszt[9]—Atwood practiced the classics almost exclusively. At the same time, he had gained considerable experience on the sawdust trail of tent revivals during his teenaged years, traveling throughout the Midwest every summer. Familiar with both the technicalities of Bach and the experiences of playing a damp piano during a driving rainstorm in an Ohio revival, Atwood married the two into a remarkable style that attracted millions of listeners each week. Placards advertising the show and his concerts referred to him as "the most imitated pianist in the world."

The Goose Creek Quartet also had considerable experience to draw upon. Its early top tenor, Bill Days, was a longtime member of the famous Sportsmen Quartet, featured on the Jack Benny radio and television shows. The bass, Thurl Ravenscroft, had perhaps the deepest and most resonant voice in Hollywood. Many took advantage of it. Today he is best recognized as the voice of the Jolly Green Giant and Kellogg's Tony the Tiger. Atwood and the quartet proved popular throughout the area and even sang, at the request of the mayor, at Amelia Earhart's farewell breakfast at the airport. They performed together on secular radio programs, too, including the popular "Happy Hollow"—an unfortunate moniker, as it was sponsored by a dentist.

Together, Atwood and the Goose Creek Quartet comprised an attractive set for Fuller. Because the "Old Fashioned Revival Hour" schedule did not conflict with their other duties, they accepted Fuller's offer and joined the program just as it began its drive to the top of the charts. Capitalizing on the music, Fuller brought his new crew along with him on a number of evangelistic campaigns throughout the country. By uniting the radio program with rallies, and those revival services back to the program, Fuller accomplished the unthinkable: he kept his national radio program on year-round, something no one else dared attempt.

Shortly after signing Atwood and the quartet, Fuller approached his old friend Leland Green about taking over the choir. Green had been converted under Fuller's early ministry in Placentia and had played a large part in the musical program in Fuller's church. Like Fuller, he cut his teeth on Biola's radio station, singing and playing the trumpet. Green had worked as a janitor by day in order to complete his college education as a music major. In time, he would go on to earn a doctorate in musicology at the University of Southern California; but for now, he taught in local schools. Fuller recognized in him a disciplined musical mind who could take control of the chorus and create a more professional sound each week. In fact, under Green's leadership, the choir attracted top-notch voices who demanded to be paid scale—something to which Fuller acquiesced reluctantly.

With his musical team in place, Charles Fuller could now put forward the program he had long imagined—a professional show with a revivalist sound. He chose songs that harkened back to an American heritage, as imagined as it was real, that virtually all conservative Protestants held in reverence. Thousands of letters poured in weekly, extolling the music's traditional sound and values, an effect Fuller cultivated. For instance, in 1940, a wealthy businessman offered to purchase an organ for the program, thereby giving it the "churchly" sound other religious shows had. Fuller refused. "We do not use an organ on our broadcasts for the simple reason that we have found that an organ does not hook in well with a revival ministry," he wrote the benefactor. "Nearly all revival meetings make a feature of the piano and we have found that the piano accompaniment is the best for the revival services."[10] Indeed, Fuller required the choir and quartet to each prepare ten musical numbers a week. Sitting in his specially designed director's chair, Fuller pushed a button lighting up the number of the song he wished sung next, thereby following his instinct for creating a "revival sound" that would stir listeners. Some of these songs had the substance and texture of old revival songs but were actually of recent origin, thus corresponding to Fuller's own desire to produce a familiar, if fabricated, sound.[11] In this sense, then, the program helped to propagate the romantic revivalist tradition that characterized evangelicalism during this period.[12]

Listeners were fully aware that the program offered the best religious music on radio. "I would forfeit all earthly possessions if I could Play like Rudy, sing like Don [?], McDougal [sic] or the bass singer in your quartet." Nor were they shy in giving Fuller advice about his musicians. "We all believe if the piano were moved closer to the mike so as to give the piano a chance to be heard it will be a great help to make the music pleasurable," wrote one new fan. "We realize that the piano should not drown out the other parts, but the way it has been, the piano is definitely cheated, and that man's (or woman's) playing is unusually attractive, and should at least be given a chance." Others, more familiar with the performers, spoke of their attachment to them alongside their love for the Fullers. "We just felt like you and your dear wife were here in our room, together with Rudy at piano and all the chorus." Another fan placed the anniversary booklet, which included photographs, on her mantle next to the family pictures. Every few days she changed the page, alternating among pictures of the Fullers and the quartet.[13]

When he took the broadcast on the road, Fuller invited choirs from nearby churches to share the stage with him. In Boston, in 1940, he had more than a thousand voices on stage. When the choirs were not large, he called on the audience. A woman converted at a Good Friday service Fuller held in Detroit, in 1938, chronicled the event ten years later. "I never shall forget that great crowd standing and singing 'Wave the Answer Back to Heaven, by Thy Grace We Will,' and they waved their handkerchiefs."[14] And, when he presented the "Old Fashioned Revival Hour" to a packed house at Carnegie Hall in 1939, Fuller began the meeting with a song. Employing music to emphasize the hominess that attracted new listeners and kept old ones, he surprised everyone when he got up to speak. "When a singer gets to sing in Carnegie Hall, he feels that he has arrived. Now here I am in Carnegie Hall, and I don't want to lose my opportunity." He blasted out an off-key solo of "What Can Wash Away My Sins, Nothing but the Blood of Jesus" to a receptive radio audience that continued to increase weekly, rivaling "Amos 'n' Andy" and "The Bob Hope Show."

Although Fuller consciously promoted the old revival sound, his signature song "Heavenly Sunshine" was, interestingly, a recreation of a Sunday school ditty, "Heavenly Sunlight." In Boston for a meeting, Cutler Whitwell, then in the employ of the New England Fellowship and a friend of the Fullers from their Bible Institute days, approached Fuller with a tune he thought the radio preacher might enjoy. Fuller liked "Heavenly Sunlight," and in trying to recall it back home in California, unwittingly changed it. The words he fashioned were simple—"Heavenly Sunshine, Heavenly Sunshine, Filling My

Soul with Glory Divine / Heavenly Sunshine, Heavenly Sunshine, Alleluia, Jesus is Mine"—but their effect was profound.

Fuller first sang "Heavenly Sunshine" sometime in late 1940 or early 1941. Within a year it had become a regular feature of the broadcast and its most frequently requested song. That Fuller sang quite poorly, in sonorous but out of key tones, with the congregation humming in the background to soften his sharp and flat notes, seemed only to increase the song's popularity. In time, he incorporated "Heavenly Sunshine" into the show's weekly ritual, requesting that the congregation stand to sing it as they turned to greet one another.

Letters recount scores of stories about the song. Folks sang "Heavenly Sunshine" to start the day in a home for the elderly. A mother who lost four in her family to fire requested that the song be sung at the funeral. Parrots sang along in one house. Listeners entreated Fuller to sing it, even if Grace occasionally gently made fun of his bad voice. Sometimes she would note that they received so many letters by folks saying they sang along with Mr. Fuller that she imagined quite a chorus across the nation during that part of the program.[15]

Singing along with the congregation heartened and inspired listeners everywhere. In 1962, Billy Graham reported to Fuller that children in Africa sang the song, and a faithful listener shared with Fuller that someone at his Gideons meeting told of the blessing they got from singing "Heavenly Sunshine all over Europe, especially in Wales."[16] One family even credited the song with bringing their mother out of a coma. When the doctor suggested that something pleasant might influence her recovery, "Daddy happened to think of the Old Fashioned Revival Hour, he slipped down to the living room and turned on the radio just as 'We have heard the joyful sound,' rang through our house. All at once a different look came over mother's face and she said, 'Oh, the Old Fashioned Revival Hour. My, I hope they sing Heavenly Sunshine.'" And from that time on she started to get better.[17] Eventually, the song tied generations to one another. "I enjoy the songs especially 'Heavenly Sunshine,'" wrote one young mother whose nine-year-old enjoyed singing it, "as I can remember when just a small girl my mother sang it."[18]

Other listeners complained that they found the song too simple or Fuller's rendition of it too painful. "It I think is too much like a child's song to be chosen as a theme. I would certainly prefer to hear your quartett [*sic*] sing one of those Good Old Fashioned Hymns," wrote one listener.[19] Nonetheless, the majority loved it. And, fortunately for Fuller, the popular tune coincided with a time when his broadcast could benefit from a song that was catchy, simple, and utterly lacking in theology. Largely because it was innocuous, "Heavenly Sunshine" appealed to Fuller and his diverse audience. In the mid-1940s, with a nation at war and the transformation of large numbers of fundamentalists into "new evangelicals" underway, a song about Jesus' light and love seemed appropriate.

Singing Along

The music performed on the "Old Fashioned Revival Hour" appealed to listeners from a variety of backgrounds—many of whom shared with the Fullers, in writing, their own memories and responses to the choir, the quartet, the pianist, and individual songs. A survey of extant letters and scripts compiled by Grace Fuller from letters now lost, however, does more than recount personal stories. Such a survey illumines the vitality and power of the music as well as documents radio's appeal and the complex relationships that it forged.

Through the music performed on the broadcast, listeners seemed able to gather about them the strings that had been severed by time, distance, and death. For some it was the tone of the music that carried them back to their childhood days. "You get me in a corner," wrote one listener, "when I listen to you sing those old gospel songs that my dear old mother used to sing us to sleep to, and which I had not heard for many, many years, because of being in show business and having shows on Sunday night. You may preach to a man until you are black in the face, but when you get him singing those old hymns that his mother rocked him to sleep with, well you put him in a vulnerable spot." Another described the childish joy she felt when listening. "I am a Papago Indian woman with five [children]. . . . The only bright spot, in all the week, is Sunday afternoon when I listen to you, and it just lifts the worry off my mind and the load of life is lighter. It just lifts me near God, and I raise my voice and sing along with you. The singing takes me back to my childhood days." For others it was a particular hymn sung at a particular time that enabled them to endure: "A husband who drinks will do many other things to break a wife's heart, but thank God for His power to care for us just when we need him most. I suppose that is why the song 'No One Ever Cared For Me Like Jesus,' means so much to me."[20]

The music bolstered individuals involved in Christian endeavors as well. Missionaries and pastors frequently described the encouragement they received from "singing the old hymns and choruses, [from] when the old old story was faithfully preached." Numerous pastors wrote of setting up a radio in front of church on Sunday evenings so their congregations could join the one in Long Beach, California—in a sense, to create electronically the doctrinal truth of one church, broken into many church bodies, worshipping together. Meanwhile, a missionary in Hong Kong thanked God "for this grand privilege of hearing the good old Gospel music in our own tongue and from our own beloved country." Another in Siam wrote movingly of listening to the program from a bomb shelter during air raids. "We enjoy the gospel message and the singing of the old hymns which make us feel as though we were fellowshipping in one of our American churches." Of course, missionaries could always use the American sound to evangelize. As one Alaskan missionary put it, "They say, we like to hear so many white people sing."[21]

Others used the broadcast in evangelistic pursuits. One woman described how she and her husband would listen to the broadcast in their parked car with the windows open, in front of a liquor store. "Once in front of a liquor store the proprietor opened the door and conversation stopped and a good many gathered as the music came floating over the air," she explained. "In some places people will listen most intently." A blind and bedridden man's son publicly sang " 'Heavenly Sunshine' wherever he goes, and is a good advertiser for this program." Across the ocean, a confectioner in Northern Ireland posted a notice in his shop's window, asking folks "to tune on Thursday nights to Luxembourg, and the response has been great. We are asked daily what the program is, but we don't tell them—just advise them to listen, and a great number of listeners have been added." A traveling salesman explained how he had been inexplicably drawn to the program on Sunday evenings. He would listen in his hotel room, where he would ask other traveling salesmen to join him. "After your address tonight my friend turned to me and asked if I would pray for him. This I feel unworthy to do, so I am writing on his behalf, and also for myself, to ask you and your wife to pray for us both."[22]

Community building was an important component of the broadcast. In the early days of the program, the Fullers hosted an annual picnic for listeners in Long Beach, an event at which they always featured music, frequently church choirs, including those from black churches. In their Hollywood studio, and later out of Long Beach Municipal Auditorium, crowds gathered to participate in the broadcast as it was relayed around the world. Over the air, Grace read letters from listeners who comprised the "broadcast family," and Fuller beseeched listeners in the audience and at home to sing, to pray, and to be saved. To those without a conservative Protestant church nearby, Fuller's broadcast gave them a sense of community—in some cases quite literally. For example, one woman in Montana wrote that she gathered to listen each Sunday with neighbors who longed for a good "gospel church" service, as they were surrounded with only more liberal, mainline Protestant denominations. "We all have a common meeting ground that the name of Chas. E. Fuller opens up to all of us. . . . Church people need Chas. E. Fuller just as well as the unsaved."[23]

People often listened to the program in groups—as a family getting ready for church, in the barn milking the cows, or with neighbors. "Last evening there were four of us," wrote workers in a North Carolina orphanage, "all hungry for the beautiful songs and the Word of Life." A listener from Denver wrote with enthusiasm, "The other night we walked into a drive in restaurant and found eight of our young people sitting around a table and they were listening to the O.F.R.H. on the juke box radio attachment. We hurriedly found our place and listened with them, as we had missed the program that morning, and we always received a blessing from it." Numerous letters arrived from prisoners, thanking the Fullers and the musical staff for providing such an uplifting program. "Recently we sent the Warden over three hundred (300) signatures representing a cross section of the men listening to the OLD FASHION REVIVAL HOUR," wrote one inmate in Fulsom Prison. He quoted several of the unsolicited remarks included in the letter to the warden, including one prisoner's thought that "I wouldn't miss the singing for anything, Praise God for such singing." In fact, the warden also wrote Fuller on an earlier occasion, explaining that he broadcast the program "to the inmate body every Sunday night, between the hours of six and seven," and even placed a copy of a new book about the program in the institutional library. One listener linked the richness of heaven particularly to the songs. "The music is beyond compare," he concluded. "When we get to heaven the angels' music may be sweeter, but not so very much."[24]

Yet the community that the Fullers so successfully fostered over radio was not without its ironical components. It was an isolated kind of fellowship communicated once a week by radio. While it ameliorated rather than cured loneliness, the community knit over the broadcast did have certain advantages. Listeners could participate on their own terms, with no eyes (other than God's) on them. Letters do not explain whether or not listeners sensed this irony, but they do supply descriptions of it. "I live alone in a little 7×14 shack," wrote a female listener. "Sometimes I get very lonely. But every Sunday evening I turn out the lights—turn on the radio—and listen to your gospel message and the songs, and my little shack seems transformed into a real House of God. The walls seem higher and wider. I can join with the hundreds of thousands in worship, and can say amen and praise God when I want to and thank Him for the radio." Another wrote, "Last Sunday when the chorus sang Rock of Ages with the old organ I went over to my mother's organ and played along with you. They were exactly in tune, and sounded just like one instrument playing. On the last verse I just listened, and it did sound so good." One man even found a way to incorporate himself into the music. "My wife and I have found a way to sing in your choir, although we may be thousands of miles away from you. When your program comes on the air," he explained, "I record it on my wire recorder, and we sing along with you as it is recorded." Throughout, perceptions of the radio community limned nostalgic memories. Early fans of the broadcast filled their letters with references to the "old log churches, to the revivals of the old days," and their childhood "when we had cottage meeting and Sunday school in our home."[25]

Letters from servicemen during the war associated the broadcast with family seated around the radio, or Sunday afternoons with a girlfriend. "Especially do we enjoy the old hymns," wrote one soldier.

"They are a very close link between us and home. . . . I have found more than one buddie [*sic*] of mine weeping as you all sing those blessed hymns & truly it means much to us to hear you & know that some one is praying." Another admitted, "When I hear all the old hymns I love so well I forget I am in a strange country, thousands of miles from home. I imagine I am back in my own little church in Providence, and all my family sitting together." One army air force trainee listened atop his bunk each Sunday evening, remembering better times and reliving them through the broadcast. "My girlfriend and I promised each other that we would listen to the live broadcast together, and that would be like old times, when we sat on the same couch after church and listened to your program."[26]

But revival music did more than rekindle memories of camp meetings and sing-alongs, or place people who could not travel in a Sunday service. The "Old Fashioned Revival Hour" music revealed the future to listeners along with the past and present. Fuller favorites such as "This World Is Not My Home" reiterated the message he drove home every Sunday. In his sermons he beseeched listeners to accept Christ's promise of salvation. With his music, he encouraged them. The combination could be very successful. After describing "one of those days which unless you saw it you would think existed only in the imagination of a poet," a pilot recounted an incident that occurred on a familiarization flight over Guam during the Second World War. "Hearing the chorus singing 'I Would Love to Tell You What I Think of Jesus,' was almost too much. As I remember it now, Bill MacDougal was singing a solo part, with the chorus in the background. When they all opened up on that chorus of the song, it seemed as if the sky had rolled back, and we were standing at the very gates of Heaven. Never in my life have I known the very nearness and presence of the Lord as I did at that moment. In fact to this day the music on the Old Fashioned Revival Hour has, in a very special way, been able to draw out my heart to a precious awareness of the Lord's presence within me." Or, in more prosaic language, as a miner noted, "I love the Old Fashioned Revival Hour and while listening to the songs of Zion my mind flashes ahead to the time when we shall sing redemption songs."[27]

The music lifted, comforted, sustained, and confirmed the promises of salvation. It was a conduit to a fluid world, where past, present, and, most importantly, future merged in the mere singing of a song. In song the elderly were reminded that they would, one day soon, be reunited with deceased loved ones in the sweet by and by, where they gathered at the river. The isolated, shut-in, and infirm found solace in song titles that assured them that the harsh lonely world they inhabited was not their home and that Jesus was their friend, leading the way to happiness with lantern and marking the trail with footprints. Day-laborers, who listened while they changed linens in Boston and Chicago hotels, could take heart as they imagined the ivory palaces and shady green pastures in store for them.

It was a message with transcendent appeal, sung and preached in the universal language of hope. Surviving pictures of Fuller's national campaigns show a number of African Americans in attendance. White listeners' letters tell of settling down in public places to listen with their black brothers and sisters in Christ. Although the Fullers rarely addressed the issue of race in a black-white context, they clearly intended with their broadcast to bridge the gap that segregated Sunday mornings. One listener wrote in to ask whether the Fullers were black or white, for she and her friends could not tell. Grace answered the query. "I will say that Mr. Fuller is not a colored man, he is white, and I am, and all the singers are white folks. Maybe some people think the singers sing as well as the colored folk—but they are not colored." Meanwhile, she encouraged a despondent African American boy who wrote in, worried that God failed to hear him because of his race. "I hope he is listening and will understand that color makes no difference to God. He loves his children and will answer prayer—maybe not always just in their way but he does answer."[28]

Having grown up near Native Americans, the Fullers dedicated airtime to race issues through their plight. Again, song was often the medium. "I am a young Pima Indian woman and my husband is in the Navy, and I know God will watch over him," read Grace Fuller in 1944. "Every Sunday I sit here by the radio when your program comes on and I try to sing along with you, and it is such a comfort and blessing to me." Grace Fuller often used these letters to demonstrate that God loved all people equally, even though society often treated people unequally. "Now an Indian man in Kentucky writes a very good letter. Though he has had few advantages, yet he has made the most of what he has, and his letter rings true," she began. "Hello

Mr. Fuller. . . . I am glad that you explain your sermon so a man can understand it. . . . As a Indian, I may not understand just like a white man, but I know how to trust in God, and to believe in Jesus Christ our Lord and Saviour. And that makes me happy."[29]

Fuller's message, given in song and scripture, cut across national lines too. Differences in letters from Americans and those of other nationalities are sometimes difficult to discern. In October 1936, a Californian, recently removed from the east, thanked the Fullers for the program. "And how we enjoy the singing of the old gospel songs. We can close our eyes and imagine ourselves back in the old church with all of the loved ones. . . . A good full choir of singers singing the familiar songs, is so much more satisfying to us than a very talented soloist singing the most perfect solo which is unfamiliar to us."[30] Comments from a fan in Yorkshire, England, penned fifteen years later echo the same sentiments. "Although thousands of miles across the ocean, we feel very close to you. We have a great thrill as we hear the wonderful music and singing, that just sets a melody ringing in our hearts."[31]

On the other hand, many around the world appreciated the particularly American sound of the program, notably the music. One English merchant seaman wrote how he was too lazy to put down his book and turn off the radio once the popular music went off. "Then your religious hour came on. I was disappointed," he explained, "for you see I like records very much. . . . After awhile I lost interest in my book. I found myself listening very intently to melodious hymns, and the way you preached was enthralling. . . . [I]t's such a change from our religious programs, which seem to be so dismal with the same monotonous tone of a parson, and the near tuneless hymns." An "Okinawa girl" described how lonely she was, living with only seven families on her side of the island. But the broadcast's music brought her joy—especially the song "He Lives." "We Okinawa people love to sing Heavenly Sunshine. Even in the darkest place in this world we can get the light of the gospel by hearing your program." An American naval chaplain described how, walking through the streets of Colon in the Canal Zone, he overheard the "Old Fashioned Revival Hour" coming over many radios. "Walking six blocks I heard your program from over about thirty radios from the saloons, no attempt seemed to be made to turn them off. . . . It was the background that made it so impressive." Scores of letters recount how thirty minutes of American music, some of it toe-tapping quartet renditions, attracted listeners from every continent—sometimes through calculated means. One missionary wrote, "Your program has provided the bait that we so often need."[32]

Though she had little to do with the musical or preaching portions of the program, Grace Fuller did play a part in striking the correct balance. Her selection of letters sometimes emphasized preaching and sometimes music. With occasional staged spontaneity Grace would finish a particularly arresting letter, such as one by a woman who had sent Fuller the money from her dead son's piggy bank, and ask Rudy to play "In the Sweet By and By." On a lighter note, she would tell a mother whose son fighting overseas had requested that the quartet sing "On the Jericho Road," that although they could not take requests, she did think it had been a while since they'd heard that song, and it was due. Her use of songs, as poetry, each month in the *Heart To Heart Talk* newsletters, speaks to her own commitment to music in the ministry. She frequently dedicated the newsletter to the elderly, "countless numbers of whom gather by their radios each week to listen with shining eyes—often misty with tears—to the old songs which they loved and sang in their youth."[33]

It was, however, Charles Fuller who best understood how music and scripture worked together to convey the power of Jesus' message. He sometimes appropriated from songs sermon titles, such as "White as Snow," "The Footprints to Jesus," and "The Walls of Jericho." In his sermons he interspersed lyrics with Biblical passages—at times moving back and forth so quickly between them that scripture and song blurred together to reveal one truth. In fact, many gospel songs were so familiar, their cadence as common as scripture, that many listeners no doubt had trouble distinguishing between the two. Likewise, the audience employed lyrics to articulate or emphasize a point. "I would like to meet you sometime," wrote one fan. "If I never have the opportunity here, I will see you over there, 'Where the Roses Never Fade.'"[34]

Listening Closely

With such a large audience and purposefully broad appeal, when it came to music, the "Old Fashioned Revival Hour" paradoxically fell outside the historic Protestant fold. Literally millions of letters arrived, authored by individuals who loved the show because of the "old songs," yet the most popular traditional hymns were, generally speaking, rarely performed on the program. How could Fuller and the musicians, hoping to draw as large an audience as possible, ignore the most popular Protestant hymns? And, in doing so, how could they draw the ratings they did? Like many aspects of this remarkable show, the answer exists on several levels.

One must look closely into the manner in which songs were used by the quartet, the choir, and the congregation. Fuller apparently employed the choir and congregation to attract the more mainstream listener. The choir covered more of the traditional hymns, and the congregation provided more coverage of generally popular Protestant songs. By relegating to the choir and congregation what traditional music the program used, Fuller released the quartet to sing fewer conventional hymns, and to do so in a low-church fashion.

Musical style enters most clearly into the picture here. An examination of how Fuller divided music among the various musical elements clarifies his attitudes toward style and whom he sought to attract through different sounds. After he moved the program to the Long Beach Municipal Auditorium in 1943, where he had previously broadcast a more "churchly" Bible study on Mutual Broadcasting under the title of "The Pilgrims Hour," Fuller began to take advantage of the organ—the instrument he had previously ignored. George Broadbent was hired to accompany the congregation and choir, both of whom made greater use of the top traditional hymns. Between Broadbent's playing and Leland Green's disciplined direction, the choir, especially, took on an air of conventionality that sounded more like that on the mainstream "National Radio Pulpit," sponsored by the Federal Council of Churches. Meanwhile, Rudy Atwood and the quartet embraced the revivalist style, singing enjoyable ditties alongside serious songs about conversion set to a more rural sound. In fact, one study of religious television and radio completed in the early 1950s claimed that the program was "almost purely an adventure in nostalgia for the audience, a religious version of the old WLS Saturday Night Barn Dance."[35]

While that classification no doubt misses the reason why many listeners tuned in, it highlights the importance of the sound the "Old Fashioned Revival Hour" sought to re-create, specifically in regard to the quartet. Millions of conservative Protestants found comfort in the familiar tunes. Although mainstream Protestant programs lacked the evangelical music that had defined the childhoods of so many, the "Old Fashioned Revival Hour" quartet numbers clearly invoked the revivalist heritage. One look at the most popular songs used by Billy Sunday bears out this fact. An early recording of his campaign music includes "Brighten the Corner Where You Are," "I Walk with the King," and "In the Garden," which resonated deeply with those revivalist Protestants who supported his ministry, but those songs did not find their way into mainstream hymnbooks. It is doubtful that many mainline Protestants ever sang some of the revivalist standards— "The Church in the Wildwood," "Saved by Grace," or "Sweeter as the Years Go By." Indeed, there remained a virtual cottage industry of revivalist song publishers who ignored many Protestant standards in favor of evangelical songs that emphasized conversion and sanctification. Homer Rodeheaver, who wrote and led music in later Billy Sunday revivals, published dozens of hymnbooks, including some dedicated to quartets and particular styles, as well as a how-to songbook for singing in the African American tradition. It proves no wonder, then, that Rodeheaver (also a close friend of Paul Rader) published Fuller's *Old Fashioned Revival Hour Songs*. Fuller sought out and won the former–Billy Sunday supporters through song, especially the quartet's singing.

But this decision to pursue various audiences through different styles was not without its difficulties. Some people—both listeners and performers—complained. "Perhaps a little slowdown in the music would help," one woman advised, as she told how an unsaved friend remarked to her, "That's pretty fast music. Sounds to me more like music for a dance." If the unregenerate thought Fuller's music too close to the entertainment world, how could it convert people? Another stated that many felt Atwood should stop trilling on serious songs, but were afraid to tell him, as musicians are so sensitive. Still others, attracted by the quartet's style, complained that the songs had gotten "a bit 'fancy,'" longing instead to hear more of "Heavenly Sunshine" and "The Lord Knows the Way through the Wilderness." "How great they used to be to me," wrote a listener after Fuller released the quartet when the show went to a half-hour format in 1958. That sentiment was not shared by Leland Green, who had for years wanted the quartet off the set. On several occasions he approached Fuller about ridding the program of Atwood and the quartet, once even sobbing that he could not continue to direct the choir if they stayed.[36] But Fuller knew his old friend too well. He refused to dismiss the exceedingly popular quartet until the format changed. And even then, he kept Atwood as the pianist on the new half-hour version.

The dynamic of low-church and high-church Protestant music, while it created rifts behind the scenes among temperamental musicians, produced precisely the results Fuller anticipated. Though not a theologian, Fuller did understand the currents that separated the various Protestant traditions. He stood squarely in the evangelistic heritage and sought to recall the sounds of the old revivals through music. But the complexities of mid-century Protestantism required that he do so while incorporating more traditional music into the program. He achieved this by having the choir cover some popular songs and by having the congregation directly sing the most popular Protestant songs alongside the "Rodeheaver style" revivalist songs. The quartet, meanwhile, bounced between revivalist standards and some of the new evangelical numbers that had appeared in postwar America. Grace Fuller attempted at various times to explain what they hoped to accomplish. "A few of you have felt that some of the musical numbers were too lively," she reported. "[But] it depends on what your religious background has been. We are trying to give some of the old songs, like 'In the Cross of Christ I Glory,' and 'Son of My Soul,' but we [are] also going to have many of the more popular choruses, and a good many of the lively gospel songs, too, for the young folks and those who enjoy them."[37]

Conclusion

There's lots o' music in 'em, the hymns of long ago,
An' when some gray-haired brother sings the ones I know
I sorter want to take a hand—I think o' days gone by.
"On Jordan's stormy banks I stand and cast a wistful eye."

They seem to sing forever of holier, sweeter days,
When the lilies of the love of God bloomed white in all the
ways;

And I want to hear their music from the old time meetin's rise
Till "I can read my title clear to mansions in the skies."

We never needed singin' books in them old days, we knew
The words—the tunes of every one the dear old hymn book
through!
We didn't have no trumpets then—no organs built for show;
We only sang to praise the Lord "from whom all blessings
flow."

An' so I love the old hymns, and when my time shall come—
Before the light has left me, and my singing lips are dumb—
If I can only hear 'em then, I'll pass without a sigh
"To Canaan's fair and happy land, where my possessions lie!"[38]

This poem, which Grace Fuller included in the February 1944 issue of *Heart to Heart Talk,* illustrates the "old fashioned" aspect of the Revival Hour—nostalgic memories of songs that expressed eternal truths. Those with a revivalist background would have recognized the lyrics quoted at the end of each verse. Those outside that tradition might have missed the specific allusions, but would still have understood the sentiment. Like other programs during the golden age of radio, the "Old Fashioned Revival Hour" purposefully sought to bridge traditions through music. Whether the choir and congregation sang a popular Protestant hymn or the quartet sang a subcultural revivalist tune, conservatives across the board felt at home with the program. In drawing such a large audience for so many years, the "Old Fashioned Revival Hour" profoundly influenced the shape of modern evangelicalism.

As evidenced through letters, entertainment—more than ideological distinctions—drew listeners to the broadcast. One listener caught the irony behind the show: "We shall never cease to marvel at the power of God, and how He has chosen the very place (Hollywood) which is the center of so much worldliness, to be also the place from which originates, 'in our estimation' the greatest ministry in the world to-day."[39] While always looking to God for salvation and support, Fuller still kept one eye on audience ratings as he pursued many avenues to garner more listeners. In this, his show borrowed secular radio formulas. Meanwhile, Fuller helped teach Hollywood the successful art of syndication. The wall that separates the sacred from the secular is a low one and at times is less important than the one that fences the two in the same media yard together.

Although he receded from the limelight, those Charles Fuller mentored have continued to adhere closely to his script. Billy Graham, an early Fuller protégé, tapped southern California talent to produce several influential films. In 1979, Bill Bright, charter student of Fuller Theological Seminary and founder of Campus Crusade for Christ, hired Hollywood filmmakers to create a film about the life of Jesus for missionaries. Thus far the film has been translated into 520 languages, with 200 more on the way, and viewed by nearly 2.1 billion people—making it the most-watched film in history. Numerous local ministries walk in Charles Fuller's steps in taking advantage of mass media opportunities available in southern California, utilizing satellite technology and cable television. Trinity Broadcasting Network (based in Santa Ana) has grown in its thirty years to worldwide coverage and weekly audiences estimated at 50 million viewers. Likewise, Robert Schuller of the Crystal Cathedral (Garden Grove), who grew up listening to the "Old Fashioned Revival Hour" and credits it with inspiring the best aspects of his own program, now draws more American viewers than any other television preacher. The recent advent of religious music videos shown on cable television most clearly exhibits the give-and-take relationship between religion and culture in the twentieth century that Fuller helped to generate. Even other faith groups have used their proximity to Los Angeles to set aside the doctrinal debates that often divide their religious communities in order to buy television time. By underscoring shared principles and practices, groups as varied as the Baptist Men's Association and American Muslims have unified their constituencies across the country. They often employ "entertainment," that is, common ritual practices their groups shared and enjoyed hearing or watching together, thereby more easily sidestepping controversial dogma—exactly as Fuller did. This shows no signs of slowing down. Los Angeles is today the most ethnically and religiously diverse city in the world, and its media role has not abated. As future ethnic religions arrive here and grow accustomed to American religious pluralism, they will doubtless find the "entertainment over doctrine" road an easy one to follow. Pan-Hindu and pan-

Islamic, as well as East Asian television religious broadcasts already serve both to consolidate diasporic communities and to improve public relations with the larger American public. By placing themselves in the living rooms of traditional Americans, these groups make themselves less exotic to occasional viewers.

It is, in the end, difficult to assess the contribution of the music of the "Old Fashioned Revival Hour" to contemporary currents in American religion. The influence of the Fullers and their broadcast on such individuals as Cameron Townsend, Dawson Trottman, Bill Bright, Billy Graham, Merv Rosell, and Jerry Falwell is well known. The clout wielded by Fuller to aid fledgling institutions such as the National Association of Evangelicals and Fuller Theological Seminary is coming into full view. But how much Fuller owed his place atop the pyramid of midcentury fundamentalism to the music on his broadcast cannot be ascertained. The music and its meaning were, in the end, as personal, as vital, and as immeasurable as the conversions wrought by the broadcast. Both Fuller and his musicians understood this.

Beyond the artifice of creating a "revival sound," those involved with the music of the "Old Fashioned Revival Hour" took seriously the spiritual effects of song. The musicians, to be sure, made their living off their talents. But they chose to do so, not because they could get rich (they didn't), but because they believed God had given them the opportunity to minister to others. Music was a profound part of their personal faith and work. Rudy Atwood explained, "Many times when I play in public, I am playing to myself, too. There are times when I personally need the encouragement and comfort that only the old songs can bring." One particular occasion stood out. "I remember after Dr. Fuller's funeral, I came home, sat at the piano, and played 'He the Pearly Gates Will Open.' As I thought of the loss of that great Christian warrior, and his abundant entrance into Our Lord's presence, I felt the need of the comfort and inspiration of that old hymn."[40] Not surprisingly, old friends for decades, Atwood knew that Fuller would understand the need for music.

Finally, it seems fitting that when Fuller contemplated what nearly three decades of radio had meant to him, he chose a song to voice his emotions. "As I come up to my 28th anniversary and look back over all the years of preaching the glorious gospel by radio, the one thing that stands out, overshadowing all, is God's faithfulness. As in

the song, I can say 'Great is Thy faithfulness, Lord, Unto Me.' . . .
Yes, as I look back, it has been glorious, and I praise Him for every
step of the way—for every trial, every heartache, every buffeting of
Satan, and for every triumph. From my heart I can say, 'Great is Thy
faithfulness, Lord, unto me.'"[41]

Notes

1. Many thanks to Read Burgen for creating an unparalleled data bank
of "Old Fashioned Revival Hour" programs, most dating from 1946 to 1958.
Although the data are incomplete, they are nonetheless representative of the
period, as programs from every year are included.

2. *Placentia Courier,* January 1, 1925; April 19, 1929; October 25, 1929;
March 29, 1929; October 21, 1926; October 4, 1929; June 21, 1929; September 13, 1928, the Charles E. Fuller and Grace Fuller Collection, and the David
DuPlessis Center Archive, Fuller Theological Seminary, Pasadena, California
(henceforth referred to as FC).

3. Larry K. Eskridge, "Only Believe: Paul Rader and the Chicago Gospel
Tabernacle, 1922–1933" (M.A. thesis, University of Maryland, 1985).

4. Grace Payton Fuller came from a prestigious family in Redlands, California, where her father served as a physician for many years. Intelligent and
well-spoken, her education at Western College (Oxford, Ohio) and the University of Chicago exhibited itself on the radio as she read listeners' letters.
The amount of her airtime did not reveal her importance behind the scenes,
where she advised Charles and edited the *Heart to Heart Talks* newsletter.
Circulation of the *Heart to Heart Talks* reached more than two hundred thousand prior to the divisions within fundamentalism in the late-1940s.

5. Daniel Fuller, *Give the Winds a Mighty Voice: The Charles E. Fuller
Story* (Waco, Tex.: Word Books, 1972), 125–29. It is notoriously difficult to
ascertain with any certitude audience ratings during this period, particularly
for programs that ran on stations outside the NBC/CBS aggregation, as those
networks usually generated ratings only for their programs. The method used
to produce Fuller's ratings was a formulation based on the number of letters
received each month. On that basis, Fuller had the most-listened to radio program in America.

6. *Heart to Heart Talk,* February 1942, FC. For a study of the program
during World War II, see Philip Goff, "'We Have Heard the Joyful Sound':
Charles E. Fuller's Radio Broadcast and the Rise of Modern Evangelicalism,"
Religion and American Culture: A Journal of Interpretation 9 (January 1999):
67–95.

7. Rudy Atwood, *The Rudy Atwood Story* (Old Tappan, N.J.: Revell, 1970), 19.

8. Atwood, *Rudy Atwood Story,* 23.

9. While at New York's Julliard School of Music, Edith Knox was a student of Siloti, who trained under Liszt.

10. Herbert J. Taylor to Charles E. Fuller, February 23, 1940; Fuller to Taylor, March 8, 1940. Billy Graham Center Archives, Wheaton, Illinois.

11. Umberto Eco referred to this phenomenon as "hyperreality," that is, part of the American imagination that seeks the real, but to attain it must fabricate the fake—witness wax museums of the Last Supper, replete with hymns in the background. Yet the false is experienced as if it were real, resulting in dedication to it as the ideal. See Umberto Eco, *Travels in Hyperreality* (New York: Harcourt, Brace and Company, 1986).

12. As Eric Hobsbawm points out, such created traditions hold "a set of practices, normally governed by overtly or tacitly accepted rules of a ritual or symbolic nature, which seek to inculcate certain values and norms of behavior by repetition, which automatically implies continuity with the past." See Eric Hobsbawm, "Introduction: Inventing Traditions," in *The Invention of Tradition,* ed. by Eric Hobsbawm and Terence Ranger (Cambridge: Cambridge University Press, 1983), 1.

13. Everet Schiebant to Charles E. Fuller, January 18, 1950; H. E. Hartman to Fuller, January 24, 1950; Mrs. Ralph Yarliak to Fuller, n.d.; Sarah Veach to Fuller, January 29, 1950, FC.

14. April 18, 1948, FC.

15. Script, n.d., World War II years. Comments on Fuller's Twenty-Eighth Anniversary Show, 1953. Script, n.d., World War II years, FC.

16. June 6, 1948, FC.

17. April 30, 1944, FC.

18. Mrs. Harry Cartwell to Charles E. Fuller, January 9, 1950, FC.

19. Everet Schiebant to Charles E. Fuller, January 18, 1950, FC.

20. Script, n.d.; Script, August 26, 1951; Danville, Virginia, June 13, 1950, FC.

21. Script, March 30, 1952; Script, February 23, 1941, 2; Script, March 2, 1941, 1–2; Script, n.d., file marked "1942? After February," 4, FC.

22. Script, n.d.; Script, August 8, 1948; Script, February 11, 1951; Script, n.d., FC.

23. Helen Schroeder to Charles E. Fuller, January 11, 1950, FC.

24. Script, June 6, 1948, 2; Script, January 16, 1949; Script, n.d.; Script, October 23, 1949. Arthur Edward Higgins to Charles E. Fuller, March 7, 1943; Clinton T. Duffy to Fuller, December 14, 1941; Script, June 4, 1950, FC.

25. Script, n.d.; October 3, 1948; October 25, 1948; December 31, 1939; Alberta, Canada, November 12, 1939, FC.

26. "David" to "Sis Fuller," n.d.; Script, November 2, 1941, 1; Script, January 2, 1944, 2, FC.

27. Letter to Mrs. Fuller, September 29, 1948; January 5 script, n.d., FC.

28. "A Christian" to Charles E. Fuller, Philadelphia, Pennsylvania, n.d.; see Grace Fuller's response written at bottom of letter; Script, August 22, 1948, FC.

29. Script, April 30, 1944; Script, April 8, 1951, FC.

30. Script, October 18, 1936, FC.

31. February 11, 1951, FC.

32. Script, November 26, 1950; Script, May 29, 1950; Script, March 26, 1944, 2–3; Script, n.d., placed in file marked 1941, March 2, 23, 30, p. 3, FC. Grace Fuller changed the word "bait" to "lift"—"your program has provided the lift we so often need."

33. February 20, 1944. *Heart To Heart Talk,* July 1941, Dedicated "For Our Aged Friends," FC. The quotation given is signed by Charles Fuller, but the style of writing is clearly Grace Fuller's. She often wrote, or rewrote, his most public and important statements, as her writing and editing skills far exceeded his.

34. January 14, 1954, FC.

35. Everett C. Parker, David W. Barry, and Dallas W. Smythe, *The Television-Radio Audience and Religion* (New York: Harper & Brothers, 1955), 391. This book, part of "Studies in the Mass Media of Communications," was a joint project conducted by the Communications Research Project, supervised by the Yale University Divinity School and the National Council of Churches in Christ in the U.S.A.

36. Mrs. E. F. House to Charles E. Fuller, January 24, 1950; Mary Rowley to Fuller, February 10, 1942; Ethel Grace Stamper to Fuller, December 9, 1964, FC. Interview with Sue McGill.

37. Script, n.d., FC.

38. Quoted from the *Atlanta Constitution, Heart to Heart Talk,* February 1944, p. 1, FC.

39. Wm. J. DeVey to Charles E. Fuller, June 26, 1942. FC. "(Hollywood)" is in original text.

40. Atwood, *Rudy Atwood Story,* 67–68.

41. Anniversary message from Charles E. Fuller, "Old Fashioned Revival Hour," January 18, 1953.

Contributors

Chris Armstrong is managing editor of *Christian History* magazine.

Edith Blumhofer is director of the Institute for the Study of American Evangelicals and professor of history at Wheaton College.

Scott E. Erickson is chair of the humanities division and Episcopal chaplain at St. Paul's School, Concord, New Hampshire.

Daniel Fuller is senior professor of hermeneutics at Fuller Theological Seminary.

Philip Goff is director of the Center for the Study of Religion and American Culture and associate professor of religious studies at Indiana University-Purdue University, Indianapolis, Indiana.

Darryl G. Hart is the director of academic projects and faculty development at the Intercollegiate Studies Institute, Wilmington, Delaware.

Katherine McGinn is archivist for the Free Methodist Church, World Ministries Center, Indianapolis, Indiana.

Stephen Marini is Elisabeth Luce Moore Professor of Christian Studies at Wellesley College, Wellesley, Massachusetts.

Barbara Murison is assistant professor of history at the University of Western Ontario.

Mark Noll is McManis Professor of Christian Thought at Wheaton College and senior advisor to the ISAE.

Kay Norton is an assistant professor of music history at Arizona State University, Tempe, Arizona.

Daniel Ramírez is a doctoral candidate in the religion department at Duke University, Durham, North Carolina.

David Rempel Smucker is an independent scholar and was editor of *Pennsylvania Mennonite Heritage* (1987–2003), Lancaster Mennonite Historical Society, Lancaster, Pennsylvania.

Index of First Lines, Titles, and Tunes

Main Index